Handbook to
Life in America

Volume IV
The Gilded Age
1870 to 1900

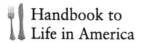

Handbook to
Life in America

Volume IV

The Gilded Age
1870 to 1900

Rodney P. Carlisle
GENERAL EDITOR

Facts On File
An imprint of Infobase Publishing

Handbook to Life in America: The Gilded Age, 1870 to 1900

Copyright © 2009 by Infobase Publishing

Facts On File, Inc.
An Imprint of Infobase Publishing
132 West 31st Street
New York, NY 10001

Library of Congress Cataloging-in-Publication Data

Handbooks to life in America / Rodney P. Carlisle, general editor.
    v. cm.
  Includes bibliographical references and index.
  Contents: v. 1. The colonial and revolutionary era, beginnings to 1783—v. 2. The early national period and expansion, 1783 to 1859—v. 3. The Civil War and Reconstruction, 1860 to 1876—v. 4. The Gilded Age, 1870 to 1900—v. 5. Age of reform, 1890 to 1920—v. 6. The roaring twenties, 1920 to 1929—v. 7. The Great Depression and World War II, 1929 to 1949—v. 8. Postwar America, 1950 to 1969—v. 9. Contemporary America, 1970 to present.
  ISBN 978-0-8160-7785-4 (set : hc : alk. paper)—ISBN 978-0-8160-7174-6 (v. 1 : hc : alk. paper)—ISBN 978-0-8160-7175-3 (v. 2 : hc : alk. paper)—ISBN 978-0-8160-7176-0 (v. 3 : hc : alk. paper)—ISBN 978-0-8160-7177-7 (v. 4 : hc : alk. paper)—ISBN 978-0-8160-7178-4 (v. 5 : hc : alk. paper)—ISBN 978-0-8160-7179-1 (v. 6 : hc : alk. paper)—ISBN 978-0-8160-7180-7 (v. 7 : hc : alk. paper)—ISBN 978-0-8160-7181-4 (v. 8 : hc : alk. paper)—ISBN 978-0-8160-7182-1 (v. 9 : hc : alk. paper) 1. United States—Civilization—Juvenile literature. 2. United States—History—Juvenile literature. 3. National characteristics, American—Juvenile literature. I. Carlisle, Rodney P.
  E169.1.H2644 2008
  973—dc22
                                       2008012630

Cover printed by Yurchak Printing, Landisville, Pa.
Book printed and bound by Yurchak Printing, Landisville, Pa.
Printed in the United States of America

This book is printed on acid-free paper.

Contents

Volume IV

The Gilded Age
1870 to 1900

Preface

*"The problem of our age is the
proper administration of wealth . . ."*
— Andrew Carnegie's "Wealth" essay, 1889

THE FLAVOR OF daily life in previous eras is usually only vaguely conveyed by examining the documents of state and the politics of the era. What people ate, how they spent their time, what entertainment they enjoyed, and how they related to one another in family, church, and employment, constituted the actual life of people, rather than the distant affairs of state. While governance, diplomacy, war, and to an extent, the intellectual life of every era tends to be well-documented, the way people lived is sometimes difficult to tease out from the surviving paper records and literary productions of the past.

For this reason in recent decades, cultural and social historians have turned to other types of physical documentation, such as illustrations, surviving artifacts, tools, furnishings, utensils, and structures. Statistical information can shed light on other aspects of life. Through examination of these and other kinds of evidence, a wholly different set of questions can be asked and tentatively answered.

This series of handbooks looks at the questions of daily life from the perspective of social and cultural history, going well beyond the affairs of government to examine the fabric and texture of what people in the American past experienced in their homes and their families, in their workplaces and schools. Their places of worship, the ways they moved from place to place, the nature of law and order and military service all varied from period to period. As science and technology advanced, the American contributions to those fields became greater and contributed to a different feel of life. Some of this story may be familiar, as historians have for generations commented on the disparity between rural and city life, on the impact of technologies such as the cotton gin, the railroad and the steamboat, and on life on the advancing frontier. However in recent decades, historians have turned to different sources. In an approach called Nearby History, academic historians have increasingly worked with the hosts of professionals who operate local historical societies, keepers of historic homes, and custodians of local records to pull together a deeper understanding of local life. Housed in thousands of small and large museums and preserved homes across America, rich collections of furniture, utensils, farm implements, tools, and other artifacts tell a very different story than that found in the letters and journals of legislators, governors, presidents, and statesmen.

FRESH DISCOVERIES

Another approach to the fabric of daily life first flourished in Europe, through which historians plowed through local customs and tax records, birth and death records, marriage records, and other numerical data, learning a great deal about the actual fabric of daily life through a statistical approach. Aided by computer methods of storing and studying such data, historians have developed fresh discoveries about such basic questions as health, diet, life-expectancy, family patterns, and gender values in past eras. Combined with a fresh look at the relationship between men and women, and at the values of masculinity and femininity in past eras, recent social history has provided a whole new window on the past.

By dividing American history into nine periods, we have sought to provide views of this newly enriched understanding of the actual daily life of ordinary people. Some of the patterns developed in early eras persisted into later eras. And of course, many physical traces of the past remain, in the form of buildings, seaports, roads and canals, artifacts, divisions of real estate, and later structures such as railroads, airports, dams, and superhighways. For these reasons, our own physical environment is made up of overlapping layers inherited from the past, sometimes deeply buried, and at other times lightly papered over with the trappings of the present. Knowing more about the many layers from different periods of American history makes every trip through an American city or suburb or rural place a much richer experience, as the visitor sees not only the present, but the accumulated heritage of the past, silently providing echoes of history.

Thus in our modern era, as we move among the shadowy remnants of a distant past, we may be unconsciously receiving silent messages that tell us: this building is what a home should look like; this stone wall constitutes the definition of a piece of farmland; this street is where a town begins and ends. The sources of our present lie not only in the actions of politicians, generals, princes, and potentates, but also in the patterns of life, child-rearing, education, religion, work, and play lived out by ordinary people.

VOLUME IV: THE GILDED AGE

Although the period from the 1870s through the 1890s became known as the Gilded Age, for the opulence and conspicuous consumption of the wealthy and some sectors of the middle classes in the United States, it was also a period of severe economic crisis and social upheaval. By the mid 1890s the protests of poor farmers, sharecroppers, and industrial workers had mounted into national political movements, including the emergence of a third political party, the Populists. The Populists, or People's Party, succeeded in winning some governorships, control of some state legislatures, and sizeable representation in Congress.

Thus the image of the era as one of growing prosperity and wealth should be tempered by an understanding of the deep social divisions that would continue to affect American political life well into the first decades of the 20th century. Some of those social divisions had been exacerbated by the very technological end economic changes that brought prosperity to some. With the completion of the transcontinental railroad in 1869, the way was paved for the development of national price and market systems. Over the last three decades of the 19th century, the efficiencies of rail transportation allowed each region to specialize—with grain, hog, and cattle production in the midwest, fruit and vegetable production in Florida and California, iron and steel production in Pennsylvania and a few other centers, lumber production in the upper midwest and far west, and so forth. As businessmen with access to capital organized these industries on ever larger scales, the prices of basic commodities continued to fall.

One consequence of the burgeoning national market and brands and the general fall in commodity prices was the economic difficulty faced by those with fixed debts and taxes, particularly small-scale farmers. With investments in land and machinery requiring loans, farm families were faced with the prospect of constantly declining prices for their products while many of their annual expenses remained fixed. Out of the economic hardship faced by farmers came several movements to address their concern, including the formation of the Grangers. Plans to create monetary inflation, advanced by the Greenback Party, also attracted support among farmers, who hoped that rising prices would improve their position. As the Populists organized in the late 1880s and early 1890s, they also advocated monetary inflation through increased coinage of silver.

The impact of all of these and other developments on the lifestyle and daily life of Americans was profound. Technology brought striking changes to the home itself, with middle-class homes in urban areas by the mid 1890s equipped with electric lights and telephones. Horse-drawn vehicles brought ice for iceboxes and daily deliveries of pasteurized bottled milk. Increasingly in urban areas, outdoor toilets, known as privies, gave way to indoor bathrooms with flush toilets, bathtubs, and hot and cold running water. By the end of the decade, daily life for the middle and upper classes would set patterns very familiar in the 20th century.

Homelife for the middle classes included visual and musical entertainment. Three-dimensional slides viewed on hand-held stereopticons, graphophones with cylindrical recordings, and player pianos that automatically played popular and traditional music from rolls of punched paper served as forerunners of the radio, stereo players, and television of later eras. Cheap and easily used cameras spread photography from a form of studio art to a popular pastime. Canned food, branded soap products, hand-cranked clothes washing machines, illustrated daily newspapers, factory-made furniture and kitchen ware, all began to give a shape and feel to middle-class life that would refine over the next decades.

The distinction between urban life and rural life grew ever sharper, as did the gulf between wealth and poverty. As cities expanded, urban transportation continued to depend on horse-drawn vehicles, with the manure from thousands of horses presenting a daily threat to sanitation and health. While the automobile, in its infancy during the 1890s, would soon relieve that condition, it would bring air pollution with exhaust fumes.

The poor in cities lived in increasing squalor, as immigrants from Europe continued to flock to the major seaport cities of the east. Seeking to escape the crowded conditions, more affluent families moved out to suburbs, with the family breadwinners commuting to jobs in the cities by rail and streetcar. These streetcar suburbs of the 1880s and 1890s foreshadowed the more prevalent automobile suburbs of the mid and late 20th century, setting some of the patterns of style, with separate homes surrounded by lawns, whose neatness attested to the prosperity of the owners. With improved millwork, characteristic "gingerbread" trim on Victorian style homes demonstrated prosperity, as did shingled Mansard roofs and turreted Queen-Anne style dwellings.

Rural life saw fewer of the technical improvements, as telephone and electric power lines rarely spread to isolated farms and villages. Nevertheless technical changes affected farm life, with the introduction of stationary gas engines to power water pumps, and with belt-driven connections, to drive shop equipment. Tractors, powered by steam, could be found on larger farms, used to draw reapers, plows, and harrows.

In the field of religion, numerous leaders adopted the social gospel, urging attention to the growing issues of poverty and public morality. Although still barred from many professional fields, increasing numbers of women received higher education and moved into the workforce, not only in industrial jobs, but also as teachers, clerical workers, nurses, and saleswomen. Mass-produced typewriters profoundly altered the nature of the workforce, as women were regarded as more capable of operating the machines than men.

In the field of sports, city-based teams emerged in baseball, forerunners of the teams of later decades. Entertainment, particularly in the form of vaudeville, reflected the increasingly multi-cultural and multi-ethnic nature of the audiences, with Jewish, Irish, and German stereotyped characters vying for stage time with the earlier Jim Crow acts of white actors made up in black-face. As religious and moral reformers came to define some forms of entertainment as sinful, and to pass legislation to enforce their views, blue laws prevented the sale of alcohol on Sundays or eliminated its sale altogether in some local jurisdictions. Likewise reformers focused on eliminating and criminalizing boxing matches, animal-baiting and animal-fighting, gambling, prostitution, opium consumption, brothels, and other activities that the prior generation had defined as part of the sporting life.

ORGANIZATION
Each chapter of this handbook provides a focus on a different aspect of life. The first chapter provides an overview of politics and the economy. Subsequent chapters detail how people lived: centering on family and daily life, the changes to material culture, the changing social values of the period, and specifics of city and rural life. Further chapters explore developments in religion, education, science and technology, entertainment and sports, crime and violence, and the nature of the workplace and the efforts of the working class to organize to improve their status. In 1898 the United States went to war with Spain, and in a brief campaign, liberated Cuba from the Spanish, and took possession of Puerto Rico and the Philippines, as well as Guam. Legacies of that brief war persist, with a U.S. base at Guantanamo in Cuba, and continued American jurisdiction over Puerto Rico and Guam.

At the heart of some of the transitions of the period were the developments in transportation, detailed in a separate chapter. Medicine and public health saw some improvements derived from new technologies and heightened awareness of the effects of crowded living conditions and poor sanitation. The diverse topics covered in this volume are intended to convey a sense and feel for the period. While the political and international developments of the era are the surface history, it is our effort to provide a view and a sense the underlying life of everyday people.

RODNEY CARLISLE
GENERAL EDITOR

Chapter 1

Introduction

*"Who shall say that this is not the golden age of mutual trust,
of unlimited reliance upon human promises?"*
— Mark Twain, co-author of *The Gilded Age*

THE GILDED AGE is the period of American history stretching from the end of Reconstruction to the presidency of William McKinley. It was a time of change and contrast as America rapidly transformed from a provincial and largely agrarian country to a modern nation with a continental reach and awe-inspiring potential.

After 1865 Americans moved westward in large numbers, opening new lands and building permanent settlements west of the Mississippi River, eventually adding over 430 million more acres to the United States. This opening of the grasslands of North America also brought settlers onto the lands of the Plains Indians. Such encroachment ignited a series of Indian Wars that lasted throughout the period. These struggles eventually led to the defeat of the native way of life, and the beginning of the reservation system that endures today, leaving a lasting impression on America's historic record.

The modern American industrial society was also born within these years. Early reliance on the heavy industries permitted a vast manufacturing base to grow. With this came the need for a national infrastructure of roads, railroads, and communication systems, which could link the immense hinterland with the distant Atlantic and Pacific coasts.

Industrialization brought enormous and unrivalled wealth for some, but also created social problems and dangerous working conditions for those

1

who toiled in these new industrial environments. Per capita income steadily rose, as did production to the point that by the 1890s, America had become an industrial giant pressing to overtake the British Empire as the leading economic power in the world. This rapid growth demanded workers, who came by the millions, principally from Europe, to fill the labor demands of an emerging economy.

Politically America saw the much resented Reconstruction of the south end in 1877 and an accompanying resurgence of the Democratic Party as a national force. Yet the overall era was dominated by Republicans, although shifts in congressional majorities to Democrats did occur from time to time. The presidency, with rare exception, was a Republican affair during the Gilded Age.

The rapid industrialization and accumulation of wealth stimulated an environment in which political influence was sought and often paid for by special interests seeking government assistance to become even wealthier. This background set the stage for much scandal and corruption, which at times threatened the civic life of the nation. It would also lead to laws to curb the worst excesses. Civil Service reform, the Interstate Commerce Act, and the Sherman Antitrust Act were primary examples of these legislative changes. The latter act supposedly restored an element of competition and fairness to the economy. A level playing field was needed because large corporations were exerting monopoly control over segments of the market, harming society. The accumulation of vast fortunes increased the influence of individual tycoons, who became known as robber barons. Their wealth elevated their positions in society to the point that they behaved like the medieval barons of old.

POLITICAL OBJECTIVES

Western settlement brought a dramatic expansion of the agricultural sector. However with increased farming production there were also greater agricultural debts. Declining farm prices during these decades brought suffering and subsistence existences for many farmers. This situation bred resentment that increased from the 1870s onward as farmers, once seen as the backbone of the nation, turned to a variety of farming organizations to achieve their political objectives.

By the 1890s the situation had become so pressing that a third party was created to meet the demands of agricultural interests and to challenge the Democratic and Republican parties. The Populist Party that emerged in the 1890s wanted an inflationary money supply, tariff reductions, government loans for farmers, and restrictions on eastern banking interests. Populist influence would in 1896 play a role in changing the direction of the Democratic Party when many Populist desires were incorporated into the William Jennings Bryan presidential campaign.

This 1873 print symbolizes some of the anxieties of the Gilded Age: Wealthy people with a carriage approach a sign reading "cheap farms," and a mansion and smokestacks loom beyond.

The era gained its distinctive name in 1873 when Mark Twain and his Connecticut neighbor, Charles Dudley Warner, co-wrote a novel, *The Gilded Age*. The title was specifically taken from Shakespeare's *King John*, Act Four, Scene Two: "To gild refined gold, to paint the lily . . . is wasteful and ridiculous excess." Their work satirized Washington politics and the get-rich-quick schemes and general corruption of the times. The authors argued that underneath the pleasant appearances and economic successes was a cesspool of corruption, scandal, and intrigue that threatened the democratic spirit of America.

As the rich grew richer they showered themselves with increasing opulence and garish vulgarity, the excess of which shocked many. By 1890, as the rich exhibited their diamonds and splendid country homes, 11 million of the country's 12 million families lived on less than $1,200 per year, or an annual per capita income of only $380, which meant poverty for many. The poor were often crowded into crime-ridden urban tenements and faced lives of disease and despair.

Some saw economic inequality as one of the essentials that oiled the wheels of progress, producing the amazing contrasts that transformed America from an agrarian backwater to a leading industrial nation, where wealth brought power and prestige. Even with its excesses and teeming urban slums, there were also more and more consumer products and new technical innovations such as electric lights, phonographs, sewing machines, and skyscrapers during the Gilded Age.

Crowds gather at Wall Street during a run on banks and subsequent closing of the stock market in the Panic of 1873, one of a series of financial crises in the Gilded Age.

There are competing interpretations of the end of the Gilded Age and the beginning of the early 20th century's Progressive Era. Some would argue that the economic collapse of 1893–97, which was up to then the most severe economic crisis in American history, sealed the end of the Gilded Age. The Agrarian Revolt and the emergence of the Populist Party during the 1890s also revealed a political realignment as seen in the 1896 Democratic Party platform that took on many Populist ideas of reform and reflected a changing political mood. The plight of agriculture did not stop the expansion of farming. For as the nation opened its frontiers westward, the number of people living on farms tripled. Between 1860 and 1905 the rural population grew to over 30 million nationally (out of a total population of 62.6 million). Many European immigrants were attracted by the cheap homestead and railroad lands, and the railroads saw the business sense in building routes into the hinterlands to take produce to the eastern markets.

Other historians feel that the 1898 Spanish-American War marked the fundamental end of Gilded Age America. The war transformed America into a world power that could exert its authority and newly found imperial might to the far reaches of the world. In any case the era was packed with change as well as much directional confusion, and for these reasons the period remains an intriguing age to study.

INDUSTRIALIZATION

One of the key areas in America's Gilded Age transformation was the growth in its industrial capacity. Some historians have described the era as a second industrial revolution, which was dominated by the expansion and development of heavy industries such as mining, railroads, steel production, and capital machine construction. America's manufacturing production grew so rapidly that it soon far exceeded the combined totals of European states such as Great Britain that had pioneered the first industrial revolution.

Northern interests, whose positions were strengthened after the Civil War, were at the heart of this expansion, which was best reflected in the amazing growth of railroad mileage from 35,000 miles of track in 1860 to over 200,000 miles in 1900. This mileage would triple by 1920. The railroads drove growth and tied the nation together. The railroads also carried raw materials and mass produced goods to many national markets. Travel became easier and all quarters of the country could be reached. Trains also provided the means for people to move to the newly created city jobs. In addition the railroads transported increasing numbers of immigrants to the interior cities where industrial growth demanded more and more workers. By 1900 almost 40 percent of Americans lived in cities.

Technological change supported increased mechanization of the economy with new processes making for greater efficiencies and better products. This was most clearly seen in steel production where the Bessemer and Siemens refinements increased both the quality and profitability. It was steel that created tycoon Andrew Carnegie's fortune, and he, in conjunction with financier J.P. Morgan, brought about the creation of the first billion-dollar corporation, U.S. Steel, in 1901.

With mechanization came increased demands in heavy industry for unskilled workers who were required to labor in new ways and face new demands, performing repetitive and often mindless tasks. Along with steel production came a wide scale application

A class H3 steam locomotive built in 1888 for the Pennsylvania Railroad.

A wooden wall telephone from around 1900. The engraving shows Alexander Graham Bell in 1892 opening the New York–Chicago telephone line.

of other technologies, particularly in the use of emerging power sources such as electricity. The period became a boom time for applied engineering and invention, with hundreds of thousands of patents filed. It was also a time of cutthroat competition. Industries consolidated and wealth in the form of capital was concentrated in monolithic corporations or trusts.

These applications transformed the country, creating the basis for new industries and new wealth. George Westinghouse's air brakes improved train travel. Thomas Edison applied his considerable talents to numerous products that brought innovation to American life, and his power plants later became the basis for the General Electric Corporation. Oil production significantly increased and formed the fuel for running the industries and homes of America, making John D. Rockefeller and his Standard Oil Company a dominant economic force. Alexander Bell's telephone furthered the communications revolution and became the backbone of new corporations such as Theodore Vail's American Telephone and Telegraph Company.

As corporate wealth increased, both skilled and unskilled workers looked for better conditions and higher rates of pay. Pay rates did increase during this period, but not as fast as was required for a more comfortable standard of living. Workers began to organize to gain advantages against the concentrated power of the large corporations. This gave birth to America's union movement, which was seen as a threat by the industrial capitalists. Conditions created confrontation, and disruptions came through strikes and violence. Permanent social discord seemed a real possibility that frightened some in America, as did the tides of immigration, particularly as the new immigrants competed for jobs with older workers. This discord also applied to African-American workers migrating from the south, and women who were in growing numbers seeking jobs away from the farms and small towns.

The industrial expansion benefited a small number of capitalists and employed millions of the unskilled laboring masses. It also created an array of skilled jobs that required education and in particular, management and engineering skills. The effect produced an enormous growth in the urban middle class who filled slots in the new corporate bureaucracies. They earned better wages and became salary men. Women also were better educated, but were still excluded from certain career paths. With increased responsibilities and wages, there was increased social standing for the middle class, as well as a growing sense of professionalism in American life.

THE UNION MOVEMENT

The rapid industrialization of the Gilded Age and the concentration of capital and power with corporations caused the workers in these new and expanding industries to look for the protection that could come in numbers. The National Labor Union, founded after the Civil War by Philadelphia garment workers, met little success. The Depression of 1873 brought about its collapse. The Knights of Labor followed and expanded rapidly in the late 1870s under the leadership of Terence V. Powderly. The Knights was a union for both skilled and unskilled workers. It maintained an inclusive policy welcoming all regardless of race or gender. The Knights argued that a large broad-based union would be able to extend workers rights and attain better conditions. However its size did not help it win strikes.

Eventually autocratic leadership and divides between skilled and unskilled members, as well as unsuccessful strike action, lost it support. Its association in the popular imagination with the 1886 Haymarket Square bombing in Chicago, and competition from the emerging American Federation of Labor, caused the union's demise as a serious organization by the end of the 1880s.

The engraving shows Frank J. Farrell, an African-American delegate, introducing Terence Powderly to an 1886 Knights of Labor convention.

In the eyes of much of the American public the threat of labor anarchy stemming from the particularly violent strikes of the era, such as the Great Railroad Strike (1877), Homestead Strike (1892), and the Pullman Strike (1894), undercut enthusiasm for unions.

The gaps left in the movement were partially filled by the American Federation of Labor (AFL), founded in 1886 and led by Samuel Gompers. The union was committed to improving working conditions, which included health and safety, child labor prohibition, and wages and hours protection. It drew its strength from a selective membership based upon the skilled crafts.

In addition the union focused on ways to pressure employers besides strikes, and it remained detached from socialist political goals that challenged capitalism. The AFL believed that too much politics would alienate both its members and the nation. Ultimately the union was not as inclusive as the Knights, or as egalitarian in its membership. The AFL also, by the early 1900s, had to struggle against company unions, the demand for open shops, and the frequent use of court injunctions by employers. The courts argued that the unions often acted in restraint of trade.

ROBBER BARONS, CAPTAINS OF INDUSTRY

The great fortunes that were made in this era through the rapid industrialization of the country came by controlling the driving forces of expansion. In practice this meant domination of steel, oil, finance, and most importantly, the railroads. Domineering and cutthroat activities were associated with those individuals who built great fortunes in a relatively short time, making themselves and their heirs scions of high society, as well as major philanthropists.

In 1934 Matthew Josephson, in the midst of the Great Depression, coined the pejorative term "robber baron" to describe successful Gilded Age industrialists who he viewed as little more than brigands. For him they were capitalist brutes whose wealth was built on the backs of their workers. They squeezed the workers dry and played immigrant against immigrant as they bought favors from corrupt politicians. Other historians have seen these industrialists in less menacing terms. Instead an alternative view emerged that looked upon these individuals as captains of industry who raised America to a position of industrial supremacy.

Many amassed significant wealth in the Gilded Age, including Andrew Carnegie (1835–1919), steel; J.P. Morgan (1837–1913), banking and steel (U.S. Steel); John D. Rockefeller (1839–1937), Standard Oil; Henry C. Frick (1849–1919), steel; Cornelius Vanderbilt (1794–1877), transport and railroads; Jay Gould (1836–92), railroads and financial speculation; Edward H. Harriman (1848–1909), Union Pacific Railroad; Leland Stanford (1824–93), Southern Pacific Railroad; and James J. Hill (1838–1916), Great Northern and Northern Pacific railroads.

Titled "The Great Race for the Western Stakes 1870," this cartoon shows Cornelius Vanderbilt and James Fisk straddling the railroads in their race for control of New York's rails.

Although these names represent some of the most prominent business-men of the era, other names tied to newer industries also had roots in the Gilded Age. They too accumulated great wealth and influence. The electrical inventions of Thomas Edison (1847–1931) and the automobiles of Henry Ford (1883–1947) produced lasting impact upon the 20th century American landscape. Likewise electricity generation and the electrical products of George Westinghouse (1846–1914), and the railroad car of George Pullman (1831–97) allowed these individuals to amass fantastic wealth.

What is important to note about these individuals, besides their great wealth, was the fact that their actions, behavior, and morality varied greatly from the crude and swashbuckling to the clever and industrious. All of them possessed the insights, persistence, and business acumen to take advantage of opportunities that later brought them wealth. There are even some who saw the accumulation of individual wealth as a worldly reward that reflected personal virtue.

Many of these tycoons came from humble backgrounds and had to struggle and apply themselves to succeed. Although tough competitors and often ruthless and insensitive employers who relentlessly opposed unionization of their industries, they in many cases became great benefactors to society, giving fortunes that promoted education, museums, and other charitable good works. Andrew Carnegie, John D. Rockefeller, J.P. Morgan, Leland Stanford, and Henry Ford all left behind positive legacies, as well as reputations as tough and uncompromising businessmen.

All were entrepreneurs whose organizational talents strengthened their industries as they sought market advantages, and in some cases monopoly control. Other barons exploited personal greed, as well as corrupt politicians, to seek advantage. They were also helped by federal subsidies that they manipulated to their own benefit. This use of government support clearly undercut their claims to be pure *laissez-faire* capitalists. In some cases their ruthless speculations on Wall Street contributed to the cycle of panics that occurred during the Gilded Age. However the end result was that by 1900 the American economy had grown enormously and this benefited the country at large. The vertical integration of industry and the rise of finance capitalism changed the face of American business and paved the way for the 20th-century experience.

POLITICS IN THE GILDED AGE

Politics during the Gilded Age was not a salubrious affair that inspired a wide range of great men to do great things for the benefit of the nation. Congress was a smoke- and alcohol-filled den where deals were struck, and the Senate was full of prominent state appointees who treated it as a private club for their enjoyment and self promotion. Often in this maze the needs of the public were left far behind.

Bribes and influence peddling were commonplace, and such corruption did not end with the Grant administration. Instead these practices became lasting period features. The Democratic and Republican parties were surprisingly evenly divided during these years, and each was tainted by scandal, although the Republican-dominated presidency remained largely above the most sinister practices and abuses. Elections were often shoddy occasions where fraud and voter manipulation were rampant at all levels of government. The parties did not seem to stand for much in the way of issues, and petty divides dominated most legislative action. Major issues surrounding the rapid industrialization, increased immigration, and the growth of cities received little attention and during the entire era only five major pieces of legislation reached the president. However the electorate was expanding and voter turnout was surprisingly high when compared to the present.

The White House entertained a stream of Republican presidents from Lincoln to Theodore Roosevelt, with Grover Cleveland being the only Democratic exception. Republicans, supported by Union veterans such as the Grand Army of the Republic, exploited memories of the Civil War and waved the "bloody shirt" during national elections to associate the Democrats with the Confederacy and the Civil War.

Republicans also benefited from the newly franchised former slave vote, but this was steadily undercut during the era as Reconstruction ended, and the south began its policies of disenfranchisement. The Republicans also assumed the mantle of a pro-business, pro-Protestant party, supporting high tariffs and a sound currency. There were reform elements within the party such as the Mugwumps who wanted to end the glaring corruption of the times, but their effect was not lasting. The presidencies during the Gilded Age were muted in comparison to the activist presidencies of the modern era, the result of custom as well as the limited talents of those holding office.

The Democratic power base was in the south, and for this reason at the presidential level they found it hard to compete. Although Republican Rutherford B. Hayes won the flawed election of 1876, which led to the Compromise of 1877, this did boost for a time Democratic prospects, particularly in the south. New Yorker Grover Cleveland managed to buck the Republican trend in 1884 and in 1892. Democratic Party city machines built a base among the newly arrived, largely Catholic and Jewish immigrants in the large northern cities. The party launched appeals to the working-class voters in these areas. Other than a generally anti–high tariff Democratic stance, and the occasional support of inflationary monetary policies, on most major issues there was little difference between the parties.

THE POPULISTS

The problems in agriculture were not appreciated by either major party, which would lead to the formation in the 1890s of a third political party, the Populists. The Populists formulated a more radical agenda for change than either the Republicans or Democrats. Monetary reform and an inflationary currency were embraced by the Populists as key issues.

The 1890 Sherman Silver Purchase Act reflected the monetary concerns of the era. Its enactment was a slight move away from a gold standard when it allowed silver to become a reserve base for the nation's currency. Democrats during William Jennings Bryan's 1896 campaign saw the gold standard as an issue and gained the endorsement of the Populist Party in the process. However this challenge was rejected, and Republican William McKinley won the presidential election. In turn the Populists, by joining with the Democrats, lost what effectiveness they had gained in 1892 when their candidate James B. Weaver gained over a million votes, or 10 percent of the popular vote. Some would argue that many of the Populist causes would later be incorporated in the Progressive Era reforms that came to shape both the Republican and Democratic parties before World War I.

The political issues that dominated the Gilded Age largely involved the tariff, reform of the civil service, and a tight money pro-business currency policy. The high tariff benefited American business and in theory protected jobs, and was a feature of Republican policy. Civil Service reform was proposed to eliminate some of the corruption found in the pursuit of government jobs and contracts. The Pendleton Civil Service Reform Act of 1883, signed by

President Chester A. Arthur, curbed some of the worst practices of the spoils system. By 1900 almost half of federal civil service jobs had been removed from the old practice of political rewards.

HINTS OF REGULATION

The approach to business and industry in the Gilded Age was wedded to a *laissez-faire* philosophy that saw too much government intervention as an obstacle to economic growth. However the power of the emerging corporations and the dominance of the railroads could not be ignored, and issues involving corporate restraint of trade brought about the first hints of regulation.

The Interstate Commerce Act of 1887 outlawed a series of unfair discounts that eroded competition. The Sherman Antitrust Act of 1890 also attempted to reverse certain business combinations that restricted or interfered with fair trade and the free market. After reviewing legislation, the Supreme Court essentially upheld federal regulatory authority, but reduced state attempts to cope with national corporations through state regulations.

Yet the court also maintained a generally pro-business interpretation of the constitution, which limited the impact of regulation and opposed excessive government intervention into workers' hours and union rights. Furthermore the 1896 *Plessy v. Ferguson* decision upheld the legality of separate but equal provisions in public institutions. This ultimately validated state segregationist and discriminatory policies that denied African Americans their full rights as citizens. The politics of the era was finally shaped by the Spanish-American War under the William McKinley presidency, which had great popular support and reflected America's new-found authority on the world stage.

IMMIGRATION

During the early decades of the Gilded Age most immigrants still arrived from northern and western Europe, and during the 1870s the Germans and Irish remained the most numerous. However by the 1880s more and more immigrants came from southern and eastern Europe. Over five million arrived in this decade, and they often were subject to systems of contract labor that promised a rich future. Transport improvements in steam shipping also made the immigrant journeys considerably more bearable. In addition the new immigrants—such as the Jews escaping Russian pogroms, and Greeks and Italians fleeing poverty and political unrest—frequently encountered resistance and prejudice because of their more observable cultural and physical differences.

Chinese labor also appeared in large numbers during this era. The Chinese were employed building the western railroads, and their presence caused increasing resentment, particularly as they undercut wages. Opposition would

Immigrants arriving at Ellis Island, which was the largest of 30 immigration stations opened by the federal government to process those who arrived by third-class passage or steerage.

eventually produce the Chinese Exclusion Act of 1882 to end what was seen as an overwhelming influx. Many Japanese joined the Chinese and migrated to America to take up various opportunities on the west coast; this too would eventually raise nativist objections which finally produced the 1905 Compact Agreement with Japan to curb further immigration.

The wave of America's western migration was also supplemented by Slavic and Scandinavian immigrants who took up farming in the Plains states. This helped fill the vast national interior to the extent that by 1890, over 17 million Americans lived west of the Mississippi.

After 1886 those immigrants arriving in New York were greeted by the Statue of Liberty, a gift from France that proclaimed a warm welcome and offered the promise of American freedom. Yet in reality many immigrants faced language and custom difficulties and oftentimes hostility. Their situation was often made worse by poor living conditions in the urban tenements. Immigrant numbers increased so rapidly that in 1892 a new processing center was opened at New York City's Ellis Island to deal with the volume. By the end of the era over 10 million new immigrants had arrived.

CULTURAL DEVELOPMENT

The industrial expansion of the Gilded Age also transformed the way Americans lived. Science and technology affected daily life and changed the very nature of American consumerism. Within these later decades gas, public sewage, water works with filtration systems, and electricity became available to many urban homes. By the 1890s horse-drawn omnibuses would eventually be replaced by electric street cars, and the internal combustion engine was steadily improved. In this regard Charles E. Duryea's efforts to improve the internal combustion engine in the 1890s set the stage for the automobile revolution in the early years of the 20th century. New York City also pioneered fast mass transit in the 1870s with the pneumatic subway. Boston followed with a similar mass transit subway system in the 1890s. Alexander Graham Bell's telephone, Thomas Edison's electric light bulb and his drive for a world of electrified products, James Eastman's box camera, and I.M. Singer's sewing machines made huge differences as to how people lived.

Companies such as Sears and Roebuck and Montgomery Ward opened the American market to mail order catalog sales. In the 1870s department stores like Wanamaker's in Philadelphia paved the way for a new type of marketing under one roof, and beginning in the same period, Frank W. Woolworth's 5 and 10 cent stores introduced lower price shopping with store branches spreading throughout the country. Procter and Gamble's Ivory Soap also became a symbol of the standardization of products and quality across the nation.

The Gilded Age also witnessed the growth of American professionalism with academic disciplines setting standards and defining and promoting study. The American Historical Association was founded in 1884, and William James's studies in pragmatism set the stage for the field of psychology, leading to the establishment of the American Psychological Association in 1892. Professionalism also entered the area of sports with the founding of the National Baseball League in 1876, followed by the American League in 1900.

Medicine followed suit with the growth of innovative sciences such as bacteriology, as well as new medical training schemes. The opening of the Mayo Clinic in the 1880s represented a more scientific approach to curing disease. Germ theory would eventually change the health of the nation. Accordingly, rubber gloves, used first at John Hopkins, became a standard feature of surgery for the containment of contagion.

The idea of healthy eating also emerged through the breakfast food revolution pioneered by the likes of John H. Kellogg, Will

An 1898 advertisement for Ivory Soap featured a pioneer's camp.

Kellogg, and Charles W. Post. Beginning in the 1890s cereals became a feature of the American diet.

The age's fine arts were dominated by the romantic and sentimental, and followed traditional realistic styles with a strong commitment to portraiture and the expanding and varied national landscape. The Metropolitan Museum (1872) and the Corcoran Gallery (1869) were established and made the public display of collections important.

Art remained highly dependent on the formal European academies, although American Impressionists such as Mary Cassatt gained prominence. Other reputations were established during these decades and included artists such as John La Farge, William Morris Hunt, James McNeill Whistler, Robert Henri, and John Singer Sargent, all of whom gained international recognition and in some instances successful European-based careers.

By the end of the Gilded Age the Art Nouveau movement had arrived from Europe, imported along with William Morris's Arts and Crafts style to shape national decoration and expression. Engineering triumphs such as the 1883 completion of John A. Roebling's Brooklyn Bridge symbolized the new industrial dynamic. Architecture was also changing, and by the 1890s firms such as McKim, Mead and White became dominant urban influences, as did Louis L. Sullivan, whose skyscrapers changed the look of American cities permanently.

Literature in the Gilded Age produced a flowering of talents and reflected a range of styles from the romantic to the realistic, with a significant rise in regional literature, highlighting American variety and dialects. Bret Harte wrote on western pioneer themes; Henry James explored personal relationships, artifice, and the difficulty in individual fulfilment; Mark Twain gained a worldwide audience with his coming of age novels humorously exploring American language and foibles; and William Dean Howells explored relationships and the day's social issues in a realistic manner.

In addition Stephen Crane's novels cast a realistic look at the Civil War and other aspects of American life. Besides the popularity of the novel, there were a wide range of other literary successes such as John Fiske's popularized American history, Charles M. Sheldon's imaginary speculations of Jesus returning to Gilded Age America, and much poetry, including the discovery of Emily Dickinson, James Whitcomb Riley, E.A. Robinson, and the final literary efforts of Walt Whitman and Herman Melville.

CONCLUSION

Change was a byword of the era and the changes that came often had both positive and negative connotations. The country's wealth increased dramatically, but was concentrated in a few hands. As a result of immigration the face of America changed, as did its overall population, which had surpassed 60 million. The abundant free land once available in the western heartland was gone at the era's end. The life of the migratory Native American became one tied to the reservation, and final resistance to American encroachment was crushed at the Battle of Wounded Knee in 1890, which marked the end of the Indian Wars.

The industrial growth created new cultural needs for a literate public and education at all levels became more important. More and more high schools appeared in the growing urban areas. Old universities expanded and new universities appeared on the scene to meet the career and professional needs of the modern state. American women were also being educated as never before. They increasingly entered the expanding employment market, and as the era's suffrage movement steadily reflected, women demanded equality and more from their lives.

Many of the Gilded Age's dilemmas were highlighted by Chicago's 1893 World Columbian Exposition. The exposition attracted over 27 million visitors and its displays introduced and promoted the new corporate America. Technology and a sense of a modern destiny, full of future possibilities, as well as new amusements, suggested a changed America. However the exposition overlooked the era's serious contrasts such as great wealth in the midst of poverty, racism, worker exploitation, and other social problems. The decades

The Palace of Mechanic Arts appears behind the obelisk in this photograph of the 1893 World's Columbian Exposition in Chicago, Illinois, which introduced or inspired many new technologies.

after the Civil War and Reconstruction unveiled a new world inhabited by many heroes and villains. It also ended America's status as an agricultural backwater. America at the end of the Gilded Age was a modern industrial power that would from this time on have a place on the world stage.

THEODORE W. EVERSOLE

Further Readings

Bartlett, Richard A. *The Gilded Age 1865–1900: Interpretative Articles and Documentary Sources*. Upper Saddle River, NJ: Addison-Wesley, 1969.

Cashman, Sean D. *America in the Gilded Age: From the Death of Lincoln to the Rise of Theodore Roosevelt*. New York: New York University Press, 1993.

Edwards, Rebecca. *New Spirits: Americans in the Gilded Age, 1865–1905*. New York: Oxford University Press, 2005.

Fine, Sidney. *Laissez-Faire and the General Welfare State: A Study in Conflict in American Thought, 1865–1901*. Ann Arbor, MI: University of Michigan Press, 1967.

Garraty, John A. *The New Commonwealth, 1877–1890*. New York: Harper-Collins, 1968.

Greenwood, Janette E. *The Gilded Age: A History in Documents*. New York: Oxford University Press, 2003.

Morgan, H. Wayne. *The Gilded Age: A Reappraisal*. Syracuse, NY: Syracuse University Press, 1968.

Schlesinger, Arthur M. *A History of American Life: The Rise of the City*. Vol. 10. New York: Macmillan, 1938.

Smythe, Ted Curtis. *The Gilded Age Press, 1865–1900*. Westport, CT: Praeger, 2003.

Trachtenberg, Alan. *The Incorporation of America: Culture and Society in the Gilded Age*. New York: Hill and Wang, 1982.

Wiebe, Robert H. *The Search for Order, 1877–1920*. New York: Hill and Wang, 1966.

Chapter 2

Family and Daily Life

*"We never know the love of our parents for us
till we have become parents."*
— Henry Ward Beecher

THE MOST IMPORTANT institution in American life during the Gilded Age was the family. Ironically by this time in history the family had lost (at least among some classes) its role as an economically productive unit or a means of maintaining order and control in society. As the fervor of American Protestantism waned during the Gilded Age and public schools became more common, the family also lost many of its religious and educational functions. Public and private institutions increasingly cared for the mentally ill, the physically disabled, and orphaned and abandoned children, tasks that had once been assumed by families. The American family increasingly became an institution dedicated solely to producing children, caring for the basic needs of everyday life, and providing love, comfort, and emotional support for its members. Not all families during the Gilded Age, however, were transformed in these ways, and some socioeconomic and ethnic groups were better able to meet this familial ideal than others.

THE MIDDLE-CLASS FAMILY

The first people to adopt this new model of family life were native-born, middle-class whites. During the Gilded Age, production became increasingly mechanized and moved work to mills and factories. As a consequence middle-class wives and children lost their economic functions because they could

19

A cast iron pot-bellied stove and an insulated wooden ice box. Despite requiring frequent maintenance, improved home appliances began to reshape the lives of middle-class women in the late 19th century, while often remaining out of reach of lower-class women.

no longer assist the man of the house. Adult, increasingly foreign-born laborers became the dominant factory worker, replacing young native-born men, who had once worked in small shops producing handmade goods. At the same time housewives lost the job of cooking for and laundering the clothes of apprentices and young artisans who had once lived in the family home.

Factory laborers now lived in boarding houses near their places of employment or, if married, in tenement houses in distinctively working-class neighborhoods. Furthermore as more and more products were mass produced, middle-class women found that the goods they had once manufactured and sold for cash—textiles, soap, and candles—were being replaced by factory produced goods or new technologies such as gas and electric lighting. The distance between the world of the home and the world of work also increased as middle-class families moved to the suburbs to escape the noise, dirt, and chaos of the cities.

By the Gilded Age, middle-class women had lost their economic function. Their job was no longer to produce or to assist in the production of goods for sale, but to assist their husbands in maintaining and reproducing the family's middle-class status. As husbands went to work at distant places of employment, wives stayed at home, striving to maintain the setting in which middle-class life was lived. Women also cultivated the manners, morals, and cultural knowledge that separated the middle class from the working class.

The most important task of the middle-class wife was raising children. When economic production moved outside the home, middle-class children no longer assisted in the manufacture of goods. Among the middle class, children were no longer regarded as economic contributors. Instead children were seen as helpless and innocent beings who required the love, devotion, and protection of their parents. Children were no longer valued as economic assets; they were a drain on family finances. However they were also valued as symbols of their parents' love for one another.

Middle-class women were expected to devote themselves entirely to the care of their children. They attended to their needs and keep them clean, happy, and safe. They inculcated in them the moral values that they thought enabled the middle class to thrive above the working class. They oversaw religious instruction, protected them from bad influences, and also taught manners and practiced the middle-class virtues of modesty, politeness, diligence, and self-control.

The importance attached to raising children and the time, effort, and dedication required for the task, together with the fact that raising children cost money that the children did not "repay" through economic contributions to the family, caused many middle-class couples to limit the number of children that they produced. During the Gilded Age middle-class adults were producing only three or four children instead of the average of seven children that families had produced at the beginning of the century.

Visitors were received in often expensively decorated front parlors, which might be furnished with a woolen carpet, a sofa, gentlemen's chairs with arms, and ladies' chairs without arms.

Child Abuse and the Society for the Prevention of Cruelty to Children

During the Gilded Age child abuse as a serious social problem was addressed for the first time. In earlier periods, patriarchal notions of the family had allowed parents to treat their children as they chose. In 1874 Etta Angell Wheeler, a woman doing missionary work in the working-class neighborhoods of New York City, heard of a young girl named Mary Ellen who was

Adults approach a judge on behalf of a young boy in a children's court around 1902.

being abused by her cruel foster parents. Her foster parents reputedly beat and burned her. They made her sleep on the floor and failed to provide her with adequate clothing. Outraged, Wheeler went to the police and demanded that they remove Mary Ellen from the home.

The police refused, maintaining that parents had the right to raise and chastise children as they saw fit. Wheeler then went to seek help from the Society for the Prevention of Cruelty to Animals. Wheeler also went to her husband, a newspaper man, who publicized Mary Ellen's tragic case. Pressured by public opinion, the police arrested Mary Ellen's foster mother and charged her with assault. She was found guilty and imprisoned for a year.

In the wake of this well-publicized case, a Society for the Prevention of Cruelty to Children (SPCC) was established in New York City, and other cities followed. Although these societies were supposed to search out all cases of child abuse, they concerned themselves primarily with working-class families, especially those that bore the least resemblance to middle-class families—immigrant families, families headed by single mothers, and families in which husbands were absent or unemployed. The definition of child abuse quickly expanded to include not just cases of beating or incest but "neglect" as well, which could consist of failing to provide children with adequate food and proper clothing, or leaving small children unattended when parents went out to work. By this standard, many parents, including those who loved their children and cared for them as best they could, were guilty of child abuse.

When child savers believed that they had detected abuse or neglect, the goal was to remove children from their families and place them with foster parents or in orphanages. Many New York City children were sent west on "orphan trains" and placed in the homes of midwestern farmers, where country air and farming would presumably improve their lives. Parents seeking their children were often unable to locate them. The SPCC became so feared that people commonly referred to it only as "the Cruelty."

One of the most important tasks of Gilded Age middle-class parents was educating children. As production became increasingly mechanized and the specialized skills of craftsmen were rendered obsolete, boys were no longer needed to serve long apprenticeships to prepare them for future occupations. Most middle-class jobs involved no physical labor or craft skills whatsoever. Young boys who were destined to become businessmen, bankers, salesmen, lawyers, or engineers had to be educated. Girls who were not expected to begin a career or work for wages also needed an education to make them suitable wives for educated men and knowledgeable mothers.

ATTRACTING MULTIPLE SUITORS

When thinking about their daughters, the primary concern of Gilded Age parents was that they become chaste, well-mannered young women capable of attracting multiple suitors. Once safely married, they would tend to their homes and raise children. Besides studying academic subjects, middle-class girls learned to sing, play piano, and dance. They studied the rules of etiquette, practiced their table manners, and learned how to carry themselves in public. Girls also supposedly learned how to manage a house in preparation for their future lives. In reality, girls often learned nothing more than how to make pastry and do fancy needlework.

Keeping house during the Gilded Age was no easy task. Every morning beds were aired and made. Chamber pots and slop jars were emptied, cleaned, and put back in place. Ashes from the stove and water from the basin at the bottom of the ice chest were emptied. Floors were swept and mopped. Tables were scrubbed and pots, pans, and dishes washed and put away. Carpets and rugs were beaten, furniture polished, and the numerous pictures, statues, and curios in the parlor carefully dusted.

Children were bathed, dressed, and fed. Food was purchased and three meals were prepared and served each day, and the kitchen was swept and cleaned after each meal. If the family lived in the city, the front steps were swept and washed on a regular basis. One day each week, housewives gathered the dirty clothes for mending and laundering. Delicate women's fashions were

This staged 1898 photograph captures an idealized vision of middle-class children.

sometimes completely dismantled and later sewn back together. Women then had to wash numerous shirts, pants, dresses, stockings, drawers, sheets, towels, and diapers, a task comprising more than a dozen separate steps that took all day. They then had to spend the next day ironing the sheets and clothes. Women were also expected to polish the stove, wash windows, polish silverware, and, at periodic times during the year, make new clothes for themselves and their children.

THE URBAN WORKING-CLASS FAMILY

Working-class families in the Gilded Age were quite different from middle-class families. The most important factors separating the two was the working-class family's more precarious financial situation and its location in the city. Some working-class men, who possessed skills that had not yet been rendered obsolete by machinery, earned enough money to support their families without assistance from other family members.

However most workingmen were not the sole earner of the family. Frequent layoffs in mills and factories meant that most working-class men were usually employed only one-third of the year. Lack of money to pay for basic necessities meant that many working-class women and children earned money to help support the family. The working-class family, therefore, could literally not afford to view its children as innocent beings who needed to be coddled and protected and whose days should be divided between school and play. Working-class women could not be sheltered from the coarse influences of the outside world and could not devote their time exclusively to caring for their children and managing their homes.

The wives of workingmen had a difficult task. They simultaneously maintained the home, raised children, and earned money to contribute to the family income. Flats in urban tenements were difficult to maintain. All water for cooking, bathing, scrubbing floors, and washing dishes and clothes had to be carried upstairs from pumps in the street or yard or from pumps or sinks in the basement of the tenement house. Afterwards, housewives had to carry the water down to the street again. Eager to maintain the order and cleanliness of their homes, working-class women had to fight a ceaseless battle against the dust, soot, and flies common in Gilded Age cities. Lack of kitchen space and the inability to afford ice chests meant that working-class housewives had to shop for food nearly every day. Coal to heat the cook stove had to be carried up flights of stairs and ashes carried down. When clothing needed to be washed, the working-class wife did not have the option of sending her laundry out to be done by someone else or hiring help. Water was hauled and heated; clothes were mended, scrubbed, rinsed, hung, and ironed; and waste water was disposed of all by the housewife herself.

Childcare was especially difficult for the working-class mother. Tenement flats were small and cramped, leaving little room for children to play. In addi-

Bath time in a cramped turn-of-the-century tenement. A woman washes a small child in a tabletop basin, for which water most likely had to be carried up from street level, around 1905.

tion there was always the danger of toddlers crawling through open windows and plunging to the ground below. While middle-class mothers could send children to play on the porch or in the yard, working-class mothers who sent their children outside to play knew that they were sending them to play in the streets. Streets in Gilded Age cities were dangerous. They were crowded with carriages, buggies, and wagons that often sped along at a ferocious pace. Many people, including small children, were injured or killed by speeding vehicles. If they wandered into the railyards, children faced danger from moving trains. Children who went swimming at the docks often drowned.

The difficulty of caring for children was compounded by the size of the typical working-class family. While middle-class couples deliberately limited and spaced the number of births, working-class couples found it more difficult. Lack of disposable income meant that working-class couples could not afford contraceptive devices. This left unreliable methods of birth control as the only options, and all required the willing assistance of the husband. Many working-class men who considered sexual potency as proof of their masculinity were unwilling to cooperate.

Although single working-class women commonly labored for wages outside the home, married women usually worked at home. Some women worked in their homes because they had small children to attend. Other women worked in their homes because their husbands considered it shameful for married

Contraception

During the Gilded Age people who wished to limit their fertility had many options. Condoms made from goldbeaters' skins (a skin prepared from a thin layer of animal membrane that was used in the manufacture of gold foil) were widely available, especially after the import duty on the skins was removed in 1873. Other condoms, popularly called "French safes," made from vulcanized rubber or fish membranes were also available. However men were often reluctant to wear them, and they frequently broke. Middle-class couples did not like them because of their association with the prevention of venereal disease and their use in brothels.

Rubber cervical caps and diaphragms were available for women. Women also used sponges and tampons soaked in supposedly spermicidal solutions. They also used contraceptive pessaries, small circular devices that were inserted in the uterus, made of bone, ivory, or metal with a small coil attached. Pessaries were usually prescribed for women with uterine disorders, which were often the result of difficult births. Pessaries had a contraceptive effect for reasons that physicians did not fully understand. Other women, who may have felt uncomfortable with contraceptives that needed to be inserted, douched with various substances that were believed spermicidal. Douche bags and syringes and the ingredients used in douching solutions could be purchased from druggists. Women who did not have access to contraceptive devices or could not afford to purchase them, especially rural and African-American women, relied on prolonged breastfeeding, withdrawal, the rhythm method, and various folk remedies, such as teas made from abortifacients like tansy and pennyroyal.

Americans continued to purchase and use contraceptive devices despite a series of laws passed in the 1870s and 1880s, collectively called the Comstock Laws, that outlawed the advertising of contraceptives and the shipment of contraceptive advice or devices through the mail.

Such laws were challenged in court on the grounds that they interfered with the right to free speech, but in 1877, in the case *ex parte Jackson*, the Supreme Court ruled that such restrictions did not violate the First Amendment. Despite the triumph of the Comstock Laws, the American birth rate declined during the Gilded Age.

With few good options, poor women still turned to knowledge of poisonous herbs like tansy.

Older boys, such as these young laborers in a North Carolina cotton mill, often left school; while younger boys earned income by shining shoes, selling newspapers, and running errands.

women to work outside the home. Italian immigrants, who began to arrive in the United States in large numbers at the end of the Gilded Age, often forbade their wives and older daughters to work outside the home. Women working outside the home implied that the male head of the family was failing in his efforts to support the family. It also brought the women into contact with unrelated men.

Other men, especially skilled laborers, disapproved of wives working outside the home because they feared women would take much-needed jobs away from men. It is not surprising then that working-class wives generally contributed to the family economy by doing paid work in their homes.

Families with space to spare frequently took in boarders. If the family did not have a spare bed to rent, boarders might share a bed with the children of the family. Others slept on couches, on top of cook stoves or sideboards, on or under kitchen tables, or on chairs placed together. Working-class wives cooked and washed clothes for boarders, while other working-class housewives took in mending and laundry for middle-class wives. Other women did piecework at home, sewing buttons and collars on men's shirts, assembling toys, rolling cigars, weaving baskets, or making paper flowers to adorn middle-class hats and bonnets. Some women watched other women's children while they worked outside the home. Others worked as janitors,

A woman and her 12-year-old niece in their tenement apartment in New York City making paper flowers on a school day in February 1912. Their work could bring in an extra dollar or two per week, and the woman also did janitorial work in the building.

sweeping and scrubbing hallways and stairs in the tenement house in exchange for reduced rent.

Working-class children assisted their parents in earning money. Older boys often left school to take full-time jobs. Some boys went into mills to act as their fathers' assistants. The support of their sons was often crucial to adult male workers; men with sons to help them could produce more in a shorter amount of time. Younger boys frequently earned money peddling goods in the streets, shining shoes, selling newspapers, making deliveries for merchants, delivering telegrams, and running errands for businessmen.

Girls also helped to provide for their families, but their ability to do so was limited by their sex. Fathers who allowed their sons to work often did not approve of working daughters. Although older daughters might work in factories or mills, parents preferred that daughters stay home to assist with housework and childcare. Some cities passed ordinances that legally prohibited girls from peddling on the streets. Younger girls were thus limited to assisting their mothers with piecework at home, returning finished piecework orders to factories, and bringing new materials home.

THE RURAL FAMILY

Families who lived on farms faced challenges similar to those that confronted urban working-class families. Shelter was often inadequate, steady income was not guaranteed, and schools did not always exist. Rural families often adopted strategies similar to those of the urban working class in order to overcome these difficulties.

Like the urban working-class family, the rural family relied on the labor of all members. Frontier wives not only assumed the usual wifely duties of cooking, cleaning, and washing clothing, but also frequently assisted with crops or animals. Women fed livestock and often helped their husbands with plowing, planting, and harvesting. On small ranches where owners could not afford to hire male laborers, ranchers' wives drove livestock. When husbands were absent from home, as they frequently were, women hauled water and chopped wood. If a woman's husband suffered an injury, became seriously ill, or died, she was expected to take over the running of the farm.

Wives also helped to support the family in ways that urban women did not. Distance from a town or railhead led frontier women to supplement the family's food supply through their own labor. Farm, ranch, and mining camp wives tended gardens and raised cows and chickens. They gathered wild greens, wild plums, and berries. Rural women, like urban working-class women, added to the family's income by selling their goods or services. If the family lived near a town or in a mining camp, the housewife might sell eggs, butter, or produce from her garden. Some women baked bread or pies to sell to unmarried miners who missed home-cooked meals. Women also mended and washed single men's clothes. Miners' wives, who could not directly assist their husbands with their everyday work, often made money in this way. Miners in particular needed help to supplement their income;

A rural family, including a boy holding onto a bull, posed for this photograph in front of their house constructed of blocks of sod in Custer County, Nebraska, in 1886.

many miners earned only half of the amount needed to support a family above the level of bare subsistence.

Children also worked to support the rural family. Girls helped their mothers with their housework, watched younger siblings, and assisted their mothers in baking and doing laundry. Children of both sexes helped their fathers to plant, plow, and harvest. They also milked cows, gathered eggs, weeded kitchen gardens, fed and watered livestock, and chased birds from the fields. On ranches, both sons and daughters learned to ride at a young age and often helped their fathers care for horses and drive or brand livestock. In mining camps, boys went to work in the mines at a young age, driving mules through the mine shafts or working as "breaker boys" who sorted coal. Boys and girls also helped to supply the family table by gathering berries and hunting for small game. Children were expected to learn these tasks at a young age.

TWICE THE NUMBER OF CHILDREN

Rural families continued to have large numbers of children at the same time that other families were limiting or attempting to limit births. Rural families commonly had twice the number of children typical of the suburban middle-class family. On the frontier, children were a valuable source of labor. Many rural people also married at an earlier age than people living in towns and cities, therefore they had more time to produce children. This was particularly true of miners, who reached their peak of economic productivity when they were in their 20s. As a result, miners usually had at least eight children. Many rural parents, however, wished to limit the number of children they produced, and fertility declined on the frontier just as it did in more settled regions. The constant burden of pregnancy, childbirth, and nursing made it difficult for rural wives to accomplish the many tasks that were expected of them on daily basis. Many frontier women gave birth attended only by their husbands, and others gave birth completely alone while their husbands went in search of help. Although the Comstock Laws limited women's ability to receive contraceptive devices or advice through the mail, many women did write about their problems to their female friends and relatives.

Another reason frontier mothers wanted to limit the number of children was the simple fact that children were a constant source of worry. Many hazards confronted rural children. Children fell in wells and creeks and drowned while drawing water. They often encountered snakes, wolves, mountain lions, and bears while hunting. A small child could wander away from the house and become lost in wheat fields or in tall prairie grass. On the prairie, wild fires, flash floods, and sudden snow storms threatened children's safety. On January 12, 1888, a sunny spring-like day, more than 200 people died when a blizzard struck the Great Plains. Entire families froze to death in poorly built shacks. Many of the dead were children caught in the storm while walking home from school. Many froze to death; others, unable to breathe in the constantly blowing wind,

Polygamy

During the Gilded Age, nearly all American marriages were monogamous. However some Americans entered into polygamous marriages. Perhaps the most famous polygamists were the Mormons. Among the Mormons, polygamy, referred to as "plural marriage," was considered a religious act and duty. Mormon men were encouraged to take multiple wives and have numerous children to assure themselves a larger portion of heaven. Men, however, were required to treat all their wives equally and to maintain each wife and her children in the same fashion. Men who could not afford to support more than one wife were advised to remain monogamous until their finances improved.

Mormon women entered plural marriages for various reasons. On the Utah frontier, while other women suffered from the absence of female companionship, Mormon women could find support and friendship among their sister wives. Sister wives could assist one another in performing the arduous physical tasks that life on the frontier often required. Sister wives could also help one another during childbirth and help with childcare. The requirement that men treat their wives the same meant that husbands needed to divide their sexual attentions equally among their wives as well. Some women enjoyed not having to be constant sexual companions to their husbands. Many women undoubtedly entered into plural marriages because of the belief that unmarried women would not enter heaven after death.

Mormons continued to enter into polygamous marriages despite the fact that the Morrill Anti-Bigamy Act of 1862 made polygamy a federal offense punishable by five years in prison. In 1882 the Edmunds Act deprived Mormons who continued to practice polygamy of their right to vote, serve on juries, or hold public office. In 1887, as part of a sixth attempt to achieve statehood, Utah's constitution was rewritten to make polygamy illegal. The Mormon Church soon declared that it would no longer sanction plural marriages. Despite this, many Mormons continued to enter into polygamous relationships, and Utah was not granted statehood until 1896.

Native American tribes also allowed polygamous marriages. In many tribes, especially those that relied on hunting and raiding, polygamy ensured that women and their children would not be left without support in the event of the death of the husband and father. Even in tribes that did practice polygamy, however, most marriages were monogamous; only very wealthy men could support more than one wife. As the Great Plains and southwestern tribes who practiced polygamy were increasingly confined to reservations during the 1870s and 1880s, Christian missionaries tried to break up polygamous marriages. Ironically the presence of the missionaries may actually have contributed to the practice of polygamy. As Christian missionaries took Native American children away to be educated at eastern boarding schools, some men took teenage girls as second or third wives, at the request of the girls' parents, in order to save the girls from school and keep them with the tribe.

An African-American woman doing laundry outdoors accompanied by several children on the grounds of a former plantation around 1887.

suffocated. One schoolteacher attempted to lead three of her students to the boarding house where she lived. Although the boarding house was less than 100 yards from the school, all three children died on the way.

THE AFRICAN-AMERICAN FAMILY

During the Gilded Age the vast majority of African-American families were rural families engaged in agricultural pursuits. The great African-American migration to northern cities would not begin until the early 20th century. Although some African Americans migrated west after the Civil War, most African-American families continued to live in the former states of the Confederacy. Here they were affected not only by their distance from urban areas and their occupation as farmers, but by their race and status as former slaves.

Most African-American families supported themselves through sharecropping or tenant farming. Too poor to buy their own land, and in some cases confronted by laws that forbade African Americans to own property, most African-American farmers, like most poor, white southern farmers, worked on the lands of wealthy white men. In some cases the men were their former owners. Tenant farmers paid rent for the right to live on and farm the land, while sharecroppers lived on and farmed the land in exchange for part of their crop. At the beginning of the planting season, tenant farmers and sharecroppers usually bought seed, food, and other supplies from country stores often owned by the men on whose land they worked. Typically, goods were purchased on credit with the understanding that the bill would be paid in full at harvest time. Quite often, however, farmers were unable to pay their bills. Unable to ever fully repay what they owed, African-American families often remained in debt for years, sometimes generations.

African-American farmers faced difficulties finding field labor. Men who wished to free themselves from the legacy of slavery sought to keep their wives and children from working in the fields. For many African-American men, freedom meant the freedom to protect one's family, especially one's wife, from performing hard physical labor. Unfortunately poverty forced many farmers to depend upon the work of women and children. In some families, fathers accepted assistance in the fields from their sons while wives and daughters contributed to the family economy in other ways. Many African-American women took in laundry. Many others took jobs as servants in the homes of white women, cooking, cleaning, and tending to their children. Many African-American girls took such jobs as well. African-American wives kept kitchen gardens and raised chickens. Children gathered wild berries and greens and hunted and fished.

African-American men and women had few other opportunities to earn money. Some men found work as craftsmen or opened their own shops. Some men found work in lumber camps and mines. Some women in the upper south found work sorting tobacco leaves. Better paid jobs, however, were usually reserved for whites, and most mills and factories would not hire African-American workers for fear that their white employees would refuse to work alongside them.

Earning enough money to keep their children out of the workforce was the goal of many African-American parents. In those parts of the south where schools for African-American children were available and in the north, parents strove to send their children to school and to keep them there as long as possible. In those parts of the south where public schools for African Americans were not available, churches often held classes for children and adults who wished to learn to read and write. In some parts of the south, the inability of African-American parents to provide adequately for their children could lead to the loss of children. In some southern states, laws required that county officials take African-American children from parents who could not suitably feed, clothe, and shelter them. Children whose fathers had died or were unemployed were subject to the same fate, as were children whose parents were not legally married. The children became wards of the county and were placed with foster parents who promised to care for and educate them. These foster parents were whites who provided the children with food and shelter and, in exchange, required the children to perform chores, such as working in the fields, tending livestock, doing laundry, scrubbing floors, and caring for white children. The children were legally bound to stay with their foster parents and provide them with free labor until adulthood.

African-American parents taught their children how to behave in public, especially around whites. Children were taught to be respectful of whites, to step out of the way when they saw a white person coming, and to address whites using formal titles. They were taught to maintain their dignity, to conceal feelings of anger or sadness, and to bear the many humiliations that everyday life offered them. Mothers were especially careful to guard their daughters' reputations. Girls were encouraged to be chaste and modest, and mothers refused to allow their daughters to spend time with or go walking at night with boys that they did not know well.

Maintaining their reputations and keeping their families together were crucial to African Americans. Memories of slavery, which had torn many families apart, led African Americans to try to strengthen and extend their kinship ties. Throughout the Gilded Age African-American men and women continued to search for spouses, children, parents, and siblings from whom they had been separated while enslaved. African-American couples placed great value on obtaining marriage licenses and gaining legal sanction for their relationships. Families maintained ties with distant relatives and cultivated "fictive kin" among the people who lived near them. Children grew up in the presence of numerous people whom their parents referred to as Aunt, Uncle, Sister, Brother, and Granny, even though they were not related to them by blood or marriage. Such fictive kin who, during slavery, had served as replacements for relatives who had been sold far away, now provided assistance by helping with housework, sharing food, and watching children when their parents were absent.

THE MEXICAN-AMERICAN FAMILY

The Mexican-American family underwent several important changes during the Gilded Age. As Anglo-American farmers and ranchers poured into California and the southwestern territories, many Mexican-American families found it difficult to continue their traditional way of life, raising small herds of cattle, sheep, or goats. As Anglo settlers came to dominate ranching, Mexican-American men were forced to look elsewhere for a source of income. Some hired themselves out as laborers working on Anglo-owned farms and ranches. Others took jobs as miners or railroad workers. Some men, unable to find steady employment, took to the road in search of work. Some were gone for months at a time.

With husbands gone for long periods of time, Mexican-American women often took over the role of head of the family. Many more Mexican-American families than Anglo-American families were headed by women. Mexican-American culture, however, cherished traditional gender roles which dictated

A Mexican family with a small child stand by their tent near Rocky Ford, Colorado, where they worked in the sugar beet industry after the turn of the century.

that women confine themselves to the home and to traditional gender roles. Women were thus limited in their ability to earn money. Many sold produce from their gardens. Others worked as *curanderas*, selling herbal remedies to those who needed them. Women often found themselves forced to depend on wages earned by their children and members of their extended families. Children's godparents often helped when the family fell on hard times. In the Mexican-American community godparents were more than friends who pledged to oversee the child's religious education in the event that parents were unable to do so. Godparents were expected to care for the child in the event of the parents' death and to provide financial assistance when necessary.

People who lived in extended families tended to fare better economically than those who did not. Despite the advantages to living in extended families, the number of extended families declined during the 1870s and 1880s. Economic pressures made it difficult to maintain large households, even with the income generated by multiple workers. Some Mexican-American women tried to support their children on their own, but, increasingly, families moved to mining camps to be with absent husbands and fathers, and other families went to work together as agricultural laborers.

The Gilded Age proved to be a challenging time for many American families, and during this period, families of various ethnicities and levels of wealth found themselves adjusting to new ways of life. European immigrants and their families adjusted to life in the working-class neighborhoods of industrial cities. Mexican-American families found themselves uprooted as old ways of life were destroyed. African-American families tried to adjust to life in the post–Civil War south. As members of the middle class established a new form of family life in the suburbs, frontier families attempted to adjust to life on the Great Plains. However all these families struggled with many of the same concerns: the ability of husbands to support their families, the amount and type of paid labor that should be performed by married women, the number of children to have and the best way to raise and educate them.

ANN KORDAS

Further Readings

Brodie, Janet Farrell. *Contraception and Abortion in Nineteenth-Century America*. Ithaca, NY: Cornell University Press, 1994.

Coontz, Stephanie, et al. *American Families: A Multi-Cultural Reader*. New York: Routledge, 1999.

Lyman, Edward Leo. *Utah History Encyclopedia*. "Statehood for Utah." Available online, URL: http://www.media.utah.edu/UHE/s/STATE HOOD.html. Accessed January 2008.

Mintz, Steven. *Huck's Raft: A History of American Childhood*. Cambridge, MA: The Belknap Press, 2004.

———, and Susan Kellogg. *Domestic Revolutions: A Social History of American Family Life*. New York: The Free Press, 1988

Nasaw, David. *Children of the City. At Work and At Play*. New York: Anchor Press, 1985.

Robinson, B.A. *Ontario Consultants on Religious Tolerance*. "Polygyny During the Nineteenth Century." Available online, URL: http://www. religioustolerance.org/lds_poly.htm. Accessed January 2008.

Ross, Susan M. *American Families Past and Present: Social Perspectives on Transformations*. New Brunswick, NJ: Rutgers University Press, 2006.

Strasser, Susan. *Never Done: A History of American Housework*. New York: Pantheon Books, 1982.

West, Elliott. "Children on the Plains Frontier." In *Small Worlds: Children and Adolescents in America, 1850–1950*. Elliott West and Paula Petrik, eds. Lawrence, KS: University Press of Kansas, 1992.

Chapter 3

Material Culture

*"So long as all the increased wealth goes to make sharper
the contrast between the House of Have and the House of Want,
progress is not real and cannot be permanent."*
— Henry George

THE GILDED AGE is often remembered as an age of material excess. Not only did the sheer numbers of everyday goods exceed those produced in earlier periods, so too did the complexity, specialization, and elaboration of common goods. Simplicity was not a hallmark of this time period in which the United States celebrated its economic prowess, material wealth, and cultural flowering. Objects of daily life reflect the impulse to project the appearance of wealth, abundance, refinement, and sophistication. Most of the material goods produced during this time period were intended for consumption by the middle and upper classes. The working class, however, also yearned for such objects and, as advances in mass production and the ability to secure inexpensive raw materials increased over time, less expensive versions of goods created for the middle class began to be accumulated and consumed by the working class.

HOUSING

During the Gilded Age there was a wide variety of housing. The prevalence of a particular architectural style was dependent on wealth and geographic location. Farmers in the Ohio Valley and along the eastern seaboard and people living in small towns throughout the country usually lived in houses that had remained relatively unchanged in their basic style since the colonial period.

Seven people, including three small children, pose with a horse-drawn wagon and a cow outside their dugout house in Oklahoma in 1909.

One type, called the I-house, contained two connected rooms on the first floor and two rooms on the second floor. The houses were framed with wood and covered with wooden boards or shingles. Gabled, or peaked roofs provided space at the top of the house in the form of an attic. Another common housing type was the cross or cruciform house. Such houses had between four to eight rooms on the first floor arranged in the pattern of a cross. A second story with a similar layout sat on top of the first. The first floor might be completely or partially surrounded by a porch. Cruciform houses and I-houses were generally plain in their exterior decoration. Homeowners often decorated the exterior with mass-produced woodwork, with boards placed vertically, horizontally, or diagonally to form a pattern. Such decorative embellishments were known as stickwork.

In areas where sawed lumber was scarce or expensive, rural people constructed housing from whatever was readily available. On the Great Plains where wood was scarce, people often took up residence in sod houses. Sod was cut from the prairie with plows and then cut up into large sod bricks, and stacked to form a single-story one-room house. Holes were cut in the sides for doors and windows. Poles were laid across the top of the walls and covered with sod strips or canvas wagon tops (or both) to form a roof. Sod houses, called soddies, had many advantages. They were easy and inexpensive to build, costing less than $3. They were also warm during the bitter prairie winters and cool during the scorching summers. Sod houses, however, also had many drawbacks. During heavy rainstorms and when winter snow melted, sod roofs often became saturated, leaking on the inhabitants inside. Sod walls and roofs also provided convenient nesting places for snakes and other forms of animal life. Despite their drawbacks, a sod house was infinitely superior to a dugout, essentially a hole dug into the sides of a hill. They were topped with poles or branches over which sod was placed. With no windows, dugouts were dark, gloomy places.

In the southwest, where neither wood nor sod was generally available in large amounts, residents constructed dwellings similar in design to sod houses using adobe bricks that had been made of a mixture of mud and straw and baked in the sun. People living in the southeastern part of the United States constructed houses of pine boards or logs. Many of these dwellings were "shot gun houses," more derisively referred to as "shot gun shacks." Shot gun houses consisted of a series of rooms arranged in a straight line so that if someone fired a gun through the front door of the house, the bullet could travel unimpeded in a straight line through all of the rooms and out the back door. Houses in the southeast might have a detached kitchen located in a lean-to behind the house so that the main dwelling could remain relatively cool in the summer months.

Although most people who lived in a given region lived in similar types of housing, city dwellers inhabited a variety of housing types. Many middle-class and wealthy city dwellers lived in townhouses built of brick or stone. Brick and stone were the preferred materials for city housing because of the constant threat of fire. San Francisco, where large numbers of buildings were built of wood, caught fire several times. The most common architectural style

A Hopi Native American at work building walls of mud and straw bricks for an adobe house in the southwest around 1905.

for townhouses was the Second Empire style. Second Empire houses, which imitated the townhouses of Paris, featured mansard roofs (raised roofs that turned down steeply in both the front and the back so that they completely covered the top floor of the house). Elaborate brackets beneath the eaves gave the appearance of supporting the roof. Second Empire houses were popular in cities because their roofs gave the impression that large houses were less massive than they seemed. The first floors of most townhouses were raised above ground and were reached by a flight of steps. Townhouse basements were partly above ground, and a basement door located in the front of the house could often be reached by steps leading down from the street. An extremely small front yard might be enclosed by a decorative wrought iron fence complete with gate.

Wealthy members of the urban working class often lived in simple I- or cruciform style houses built on city lots. Poorer members of the working class, of which there were many, occupied tenement houses that were usually located near their places of employment. During the Gilded Age when factory production boomed and large numbers of urban workers desperately needed housing, investors began to construct buildings specifically designed to serve as housing for working-class city dwellers. Many of these houses were "dumbbell tenements." The dumbbell tenement, which won first prize in an 1879 competition to design a model tenement, was between four and six stories high and had four flats on each floor. The two flats in the front that faced the street had four rooms each. The two flats in the back that faced the alley had three rooms each. Built side by side in rows, the houses were separated by air shafts, thus giving them the shape of dumbbells. None of the flats had indoor plumbing. The residents of each floor shared a toilet in the hall or an outhouse in the backyard. The very poorest of the poor lived in the cellars of tenement houses. Such places were dark, damp, and often filled with vermin.

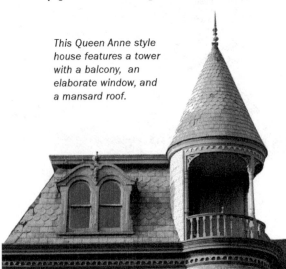

This Queen Anne style house features a tower with a balcony, an elaborate window, and a mansard roof.

In the outlying suburbs, middle-class families dwelt in large homes built in a variety of styles, most of which were variations on the cruciform pattern. During the Gilded Age the middle-class home became an elaborate construction. The technique of balloon framing, in which two-inch boards are nailed together to form a light frame to which siding could be attached, allowed for more creative housing designs. The ease of constructing walls meant that houses no longer had to be shaped like boxes or rectangles. Rooms could jut out from the regular floor plan. Overhangs could be built.

Second Empire style houses were popular in the midwest and in the northeastern states. Many of these houses featured towers capped with their own mansard roofs. Also very popular was the Queen Anne style. Queen Anne houses were asymmetrical in shape. Roofs were steeply pitched and followed an irregular line. Most had

A Queen Anne style house with a tower and bricks of at least two colors used for decoration.

bay windows and porches on the front of the house. Porches often extended around the sides of the house as well. Some Queen Annes had towers. The walls of wooden Queen Anne houses were decorated with shingles cut in a variety of shapes. Brick Queen Annes were decorated by varying the patterns of the bricks or using bricks of different colors. Front doors often featured large glass windows.

Houses belonging to middle-class or wealthy Americans usually contained a multitude of rooms which, ideally, were dedicated to specialized purposes. The first floor of the house contained the rooms in which the daily activities of the family were carried on. The space above the first floor was reserved for sleeping, bathing, dressing, and caring for children. The rooms to the front of the house on the first floor were considered "public" rooms. These were the rooms into which friends and visitors would be invited and entertained. As such, they were the rooms that were most elaborately furnished and decorated.

FURNITURE AND INTERIOR DECORATION

The interior of middle-class homes reflected the wealth and craze for consumption that characterized the Gilded Age. Immediately upon entering the house, the visitor was ushered into the front entrance hall, decorated to make an immediate impression. The walls were adorned with wallpaper. A large hall stand most likely dominated the space. Often elaborately crafted of heavy, dark wood such as walnut or mahogany, the hall stand held the coats and cloaks belonging to various members of the family. It might also contain a large mirror in which family members and visitors could check their appearance before venturing out into public. During the Gilded Age outward appearance, which reflected one's social status and wealth, was extremely important. The hall stand might also have a seat on which visitors could rest if they needed to wait for a member of the family. Beside the hall stand might be found an umbrella stand. A stand for receiving calling cards was also present.

From the hall, the visitor would most likely be invited into the parlor. Located at the very front of the house, the parlor was usually the largest and most elaborately and expensively decorated of all the rooms. The parlor walls

Calling Cards

Middle-class Americans in the Gilded Age considered their reputations and social standing of utmost importance. To maintain ties with the other members of their social circle, and to move upward into a more elite circle, middle-class women engaged in the ritual of calling. Middle-class women visited their acquaintances almost every day. One day a week, women remained at home to receive their own callers. Calling cards were an important part of this ritual. Calling cards were small, pasteboard cards printed with the owner's name written in a fancy script. Women's cards might be additionally embellished with images of decorative scrolls or flowers. All middle-class adults, both men and women, had their own calling cards, which were purchased at a local print shop. One of the hallmarks of Gilded Age adulthood was the ordering of the first set of calling cards.

When women arrived at the home of an acquaintance, they placed two of their husband's calling cards (one for the wife and one for the husband) and one of their own calling cards (for the wife only) on a tray held by the servant who had answered the door. If she wished to actually visit with the wife, the caller would bend the right side of the card. If she had come merely to thank the wife for a recent dinner party invitation and did not wish to actually see her, she would bend the upper right-hand corner of the card. The servant would then carry the cards to the mistress of the house. If the woman of the house were not at home, the visitor would leave calling cards on the card receiver in the front hall. If the caller also wished to leave a message for the family, she could do so using calling cards.

A bent lower left-hand corner meant that the caller was offering condolences for a recent death in the family. A bent upper left-hand corner meant that the caller was offering congratulations. A bent lower right-hand corner signified that the caller was leaving town for a while. If the caller left cards on behalf of a family member who had not come with her on the visit, the card would be left unbent to indicate that the card's owner had not come to the house in person.

were covered in factory-produced wallpaper that came in a variety of patterns and colors. Wallpapers in earthen colors (greens, russets, and browns) were common choices. Many people attempted to incorporate nature and things that reminded them of nature into their homes. Natural elements were also incorporated in the designs of the large woolen carpets in which parlor floors were covered. Carpets often featured floral and scroll designs. Earth tones, such as tan, brown, cream, olive, and terra cotta were popular. However bright greens, blues, yellows, and reds were also included in carpet designs.

THE PARLOR

The standard complement of furniture for a parlor consisted of a sofa, one or two gentlemen's chairs, and one or two ladies' chairs. Gentlemen's chairs had arms so that the man of the house could repose in comfort. Ladies' chairs did not have arms; a lady at repose was supposed to keep her hands folded neatly in her lap, and arms would also have made it difficult for a woman to arrange her skirts properly. Armless, straight-backed side chairs provided for additional seating as did overstuffed ottomans, foot stools, divans (backless sofas), and lounges (long, armless couches for reclining).

The center of the parlor was often occupied by a large, round parlor table made of a walnut, cherry, rosewood, or mahogany. The table often served as the resting place for the family Bible. While the Bible reassured visitors of the family's piety, the presence in the parlor of an organ or piano alerted callers to the family's good taste and sophistication. Glass-enclosed curio cases held collectibles such as souvenirs and postcards. Stereographs containing side-by-side images of the same scene or object photographed from slightly different angles were also displayed. Stereograph cards were viewed using a stereo-scope, a handheld device with a clip at the far end to hold a stereograph card and, on the end near the viewer, an eyepiece. When the viewer looked through the eyepiece, the images on the stereo-graph melded, and the image became three di-mensional. Large albums, prominently displayed on tables or stands, held collections of auto-graphs, photographs, trade cards, and *cartes de visite*. Collecting *cartes de visite*, pasteboard cards printed with photos of famous actors and actresses, athletes, and political figures, was a Gilded Age craze made pos-sible by advances in print-ing and photography that

A platform rocker with carved ornamentation in the Eastlake style, named for the British architect Charles Eastlake.

allowed for the swift, inexpensive mass production of photographic images. Although money was clearly needed to furnish a parlor in a manner acceptable to the middle class, working-class homes also had parlors. Because of a lack of space, especially in urban tenement house apartments, some working-class families used the parlor as a bedroom.

After the parlor, the most formal room in the house was the dining room. Dining rooms were the most masculine rooms in the house, perhaps because of the longstanding tradition of the husband and father as the principal provider of sustenance for the family. Not all families had houses large enough to set a room aside for the sole purpose of dining. Many middle-class families combined their dining room with their sitting room (also called the living room or the second parlor), an informal, "private" room at the back of the house where the family read, played games, and relaxed together. Sitting rooms were much less elaborately furnished and decorated than formal parlors.

Bedrooms were located on the second or third floor of the middle-class home. Bedrooms were simple, intended only for sleeping and dressing. Usually, the only furniture in a bedroom was a wooden four-poster bed, a dresser, a standing closet or armoire for storing clothes, and a washstand. Although middle-class homes set aside rooms for every possible purpose, very few

A stereoscope with a stereograph card placed in the clip at the far end. When a viewer looked through the eyepiece, the image would appear three dimensional.

This 1891 lithograph, depicting the assault on Fort Sanders on November 29, 1863, is typical of prints that memorialized the Civil War.

Art: Paintings, Prints, and Statues

Visual art was an important component of the middle-class parlor, which was usually decorated with an assortment of paintings, prints, and statues. Some paintings and statues may have been original works of art. Most, however, were inexpensive reproductions of famous works. The mass production during the Gilded Age of chromolithographs (colored prints produced using stones on which pictures had been etched) enabled people to collect reproductions of famous paintings. Contemporary artists, such as Winslow Homer, produced chromolithographs (more informally called chromos) as well. Sentimental reproductions of everyday life (contemporary life or life in the past) and religious scenes were popular. Landscapes also sold well. Chromos could be purchased for only a few dollars.

Small statues also decorated the middle-class parlor. Mass-produced copies of statues by sculptor John Rogers were particularly popular during the Gilded Age. Rogers's statue groups, made of plaster and between one and two feet in height, featured sentimental images of peddlers, plump babies, children at play and at school, and country folk enjoying themselves with simple pastimes. Plaster busts of famous people might also be displayed in the parlor or in the library if the family had enough space to set aside a special room for this purpose. Busts of historical figures such as George Washington and Napoleon, and famous artists and musicians like Beethoven were especially popular. Family pictures, whether photographs or painted portraits, were also displayed in the parlor, conveying to the visitor the family's concern with both its ancestry and its close ties to living relatives.

A ceramic pitcher and bowl set for washing one's hands and face at a bedroom washstand.

houses during the Gilded Age had rooms specifically allocated for bathing. Most people washed their hands and faces using ceramic pitchers and bowls that stood on bedroom washstands. When a full bath was desired, iron or tin bathtubs would be carried upstairs and filled with buckets of hot water that needed to be toted upstairs from the kitchen. Rubber bathtubs that were suspended from a frame like a hammock were also available and easier to store. The few houses that had running water might install a flush toilet in an empty closet, under the stairs, or in the attic or basement. Other middle-class families contented themselves with an earth closet. An earth closet was, as the name indicates, a closet or other space within the house. In the space was a seat with a hole in the middle. Solid and liquid waste passed through the hole into an enclosed container. The user of the earth closet then tossed dirt or charcoal into the hole to cover the recent deposit. Periodically, the contents of the box would be emptied. Earth closets never proved extremely popular, and most middle-class families, like working-class ones, relieved themselves in outhouses behind their dwellings.

COOKING AND EATING MATERIALS

Gilded Age kitchens were also furnished with the goods necessary to live a proper and prosperous life. Just as front halls, parlors, and dining rooms displayed the wealth, education, sophistication, and good taste of a family, the meals produced by the family kitchen and the utensils used to produce and consume them were intended to do the same. During the Gilded Age meals were more elaborate than they had been at previous times in American history, and, in order to produce such large and elaborate meals, housewives accumulated a variety of new tools and gadgets designed for specialized tasks. By the end of the Civil War, only the very poorest of American housewives or those who lived in extremely remote areas used fireplaces to cook. Cast iron cook stoves were now common in American kitchens, and they were more elaborate than the cook stoves that had first been produced in the 1830s and 1840s. Stoves, many of which could burn either coal or wood, had four to six holes on the stove top. This gave the housewife the ability to prepare a variety of dishes simultaneously. Pots and pans were required to fit snugly into the opening of the hole, and stoves often came with pots designed to fit the holes on that particular stove. Stoves might have one oven (for baking) or two (one for baking and one for warming food). Stoves also usually came equipped with a large boiler to heat water for bathing or cleaning. At the bottom of the stove was a drawer that collected the embers and ashes that were produced as the coal or wood burned. Like many other household furnishings of the Gilded Age, kitchen stoves were often lavishly embellished with nickel plating.

Middle-class kitchens in the Gilded Age were also likely to contain ice boxes or ice chests. These wooden chests held a lead-lined box containing one or more shelves. A separate area at the top of the chest held a large block of ice that usually weighed between 100 and 200 pounds. A basin at the bottom of the chest collected the melted water and had to be emptied regularly. Some ice chests had a door in the back of the cabinet. Ice chests were often placed with the door in the back of the cabinet facing a corresponding door in the exterior wall of the kitchen that opened onto the porch. Using these doors, the ice man could deliver blocks of ice directly to the ice chest without disturbing the family or dripping water through the house. A card placed in the window of the house informed the iceman how much ice the household required.

Although a wide variety of manufactured goods could be found in the Gilded Age kitchen, pantry, and dining room, the era's obsession with accumulation and display can perhaps best be seen in the astounding array of objects produced solely for the purpose of serving and consuming food at the dining table. For everyday eating, most middle-class families dined on plates made of earthenware, a relatively inexpensive form of ceramic dinnerware. The dinnerware was often plain or printed with designs in a variety of colors; a combination of blue and white was very popular. Porcelain dinnerware, often of French manufacture, was reserved for formal dinners and special occasions. Etiquette books of the period usually advised that housewives have a dinner service capable of serving 12 people and a variety of serving dishes. However it is doubtful that any but the most affluent homes had so many pieces of dinnerware.

A fireplace stove with ovens for baking and warming food.

CLOTHING

Despite the growth in mass production of other articles, most clothing continued to be made by hand by the housewife or by a professional dressmaker. Although ready-to-wear men's clothing was manufactured during the Gilded Age, women's and children's clothing, with a few exceptions, was not yet mass produced. Perhaps the largest obstacle to the mass production of women's clothing during the Gilded Age was the complexity of women's clothing during that period. The most popular style of dress was the princess style. Princess dresses had relatively flat fronts and full skirts that were gathered in the back. Over time, the style of these dresses grew increasingly long.

The middle-class woman needed several different types of dresses to see her through a day. A relatively simple morning dress would be worn while at home. However if it was the day that the housewife had set aside for receiving callers, the woman would change her morning dress for an afternoon dress in which to receive her visitors. Afternoon dresses were more elaborately trimmed and decorated than morning dresses and were made of expensive fabrics such as silk or satin. When women left the house, they wore even more elaborate attire. Visiting dresses were worn when the housewife went calling on her acquaintances. Promenade dresses, which had skirts that were raised a bit higher in back in order to make walking easier, were worn when a woman went for a stroll. Carriage dresses, designed for riding in wheeled conveyances, had long trains that trailed from the vehicle as it sped along. An entirely different wardrobe, all in black, was required for mourning.

Beneath the outer dress, Gilded Age women wore an additional set of clothing. The most crucial piece of underclothing was the corset. Formerly made by

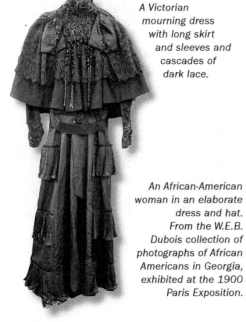

A Victorian mourning dress with long skirt and sleeves and cascades of dark lace.

An African-American woman in an elaborate dress and hat. From the W.E.B. Dubois collection of photographs of African Americans in Georgia, exhibited at the 1900 Paris Exposition.

hand, corsets in various styles were mass produced during the Gilded Age. In its most basic form, the corset was a fabric tube with long, narrow strips of bone or metal sewn inside the fabric around the entire circumference of the tube. Corsets had strings that, when pulled, compressed the waist, making it narrower. The strings were then fastened tightly in the back. During the Gilded Age, corsets grew longer, eventually reaching from the breast to the tops of the thighs; the form-fitting princess gowns of the era looked best on long, narrow bodies. Within this basic shape, a wide variety of corsets were available. Some were designed specifically for slim women; others were designed to accommodate the

A glamour photograph of the Gilded Age shows the extremes to which corsets were used to alter the figure.

bodies of heavier women. Lightweight models were made for summer wear. Maternity corsets allowed for extra fullness in the abdominal region. Corsets with removable breast panels were made for nursing mothers. Corsets could be simply made, or they could be decorated with lace and ribbons.

Under her outerwear, along with the corset, the middle-class woman usually wore a camisole, trimmed in lace and ribbons, and a pair of drawers. Over this, she would wear a petticoat that, like the camisole, was also adorned with lace and perhaps a ruffle along the bottom edge. During the Gilded Age, women no longer wore the voluminous layers of petticoats or stiff crinolines (stiff, bell-shaped skirts) that had been required by the styles of earlier eras; the princess style required a trim silhouette. The princess style did, however, require a bustle, a wire tubular structure worn atop the woman's buttocks. The extra volume was needed to hold up the fabric gathered in the back of princess dresses. As the size of trains diminished over time and less fabric was gathered at the back of the dress, bustles were replaced with small, horsehair-stuffed pads that provided only minimal elevation.

Although this was the ideal wardrobe for a Gilded Age woman, most American women did not own such a wide variety of dresses, and did not always adhere to the most recent fashions. Farm wives and working-class women might have one everyday dress and a fancier dress to wear on the Sabbath or on special occasions. Women on the western frontier might own only one dress that, because of their relative isolation, was no longer in keeping with the current fashions. Women who needed to engage in physical labor would not have worn princess dresses anyway. The snug waist and skirt and the train made it difficult for wearers of the princess dress to actually engage in

Three small boys standing in their velvet suits inspired by the Little Lord Fauntleroy *story.*

most forms of productive work. Old dresses were mended until they wore to pieces. Even then a thrifty housewife might try to save the dress by lining it with canvas from leftover wagon tops. Women who worked outside the home sometimes dispensed with dresses altogether and wore simple skirts and blouses instead. Working-class women also commonly dispensed with the corsets and petticoats that no middle-class woman would have dreamed of going without. Even poor and working-class women, however, could display some finery on occasion. African-American women were noted for the dresses that they wore to church on Sundays. Many African-American women wore dresses made of taffeta and other costly materials. Some wore dresses gathered in the back in the princess style.

Gilded Age girls dressed in fashions similar to those of their mothers. Little girls were made to wear lighter, more flexible versions of adult corsets called waists. When they entered adolescence, they graduated to adult-style corsets. Little boys dressed for everyday activities in miniature versions of working men's clothing—simple shirts and pants. Boys usually wore short pants until age 10 or 12. At this time they were allowed to wear full-length trousers. For formal occasions, boys dressed in suits with short pants and jackets. Under the jacket they wore a white shirt. Some boys' suits were quite elaborate in design. Following the publication in 1885 of the story "Little Lord Fauntleroy" by Frances Hodgson Burnett in *St. Nicholas Magazine,* a children's periodical, middle-class mothers attempted to dress their sons in the manner of the story's child hero. Mothers clothed their pre-pubescent sons in velvet suits with lace collars that were secured at the waist with colored sashes. Some mothers also tried to curl their sons' hair in imitation of Cedric, Lord Fauntleroy.

TOYS AND GAMES

The Gilded Age marked the beginning of the mass production and marketing of toys and games for children. A combination of wealth and romantic ideas regarding childhood during this period led many middle-class parents to present their sons and daughters with factory-produced toys and games that were designed to teach children values. Toy makers such as Charles Crandall, George Parker, McLoughlin Brothers, Milton Bradley, and Albert Schoenhut made use of new manufacturing processes to produce an abundance of toys and games. Newly invented processes that made possible the transfer and reproduction of brightly colored illustrations were used to embellish cards, blocks, and game boards, making them more appealing to children.

Toys and games that taught children about the value and use of money were popular. Gilded Age children owned mechanical banks and played card games like "Game of Banking" and "The Amusing Game of the Yankee Peddler" and board games like "The Amusing Game of the Corner Grocery" and "The Merry Game of the Country Auction." Also popular were toys that taught or reinforced literacy and games that were designed to assist children in acquiring the cultural knowledge expected of all educated people during the Gilded Age. Alphabet blocks were common toys for younger children. Card games such as "The Game of Letters" and "Alphabet Game" also drilled children in basic literacy. Older children could boost their literary skills by playing card games such as "Authors" and "Game of Poets." Card and board games also taught children about such subjects as art, botany, geography, and history. Miniature pianos and other toy musical instruments taught children about music. Some toys sought to reproduce the experience of going to school itself. Charles Crandall's "District School," which was first marketed in 1876, consisted of a floor plan of a typical school and movable figures that represented the students and teacher. The toy contained such realistic elements as books printed with real words and a boy sporting a dunce cap.

Other toys and games sought to improve children's religious knowledge and values. On Sundays many pious parents did not allow children to play with their everyday toys and games; playful, exuberant behavior was considered improper on the Sabbath. Games and toys with religious themes, however, were usually acceptable. Children might play with Noah's Arks and their assortment of animals. Even cards were acceptable if they were used to play games such as "The Scripture Game of Who Can Tell?" and "Grandma's New Testament Game." Ironically the same children who played with religious toys and games may also have played with games that ridiculed members of non-European ethnic groups and often invoked racist stereotypes.

GIRLS' TOYS

Although children of both sexes played with educational and religious games, many toys and games were gender specific, clearly intended for either boys or girls. Dolls and their accessories were the most common toys purchased for girls. In the Gilded Age, the most common manufactured dolls were fashion dolls, or "lady dolls," that were intended to teach middle-class girls about fashion and etiquette and to encourage them to practice their sewing skills. Fashion dolls had an adult appearance and their bodies had adult proportions. Dolls designed to look like babies were not common during the Gilded Age; most children had younger siblings and so could practice feeding, diapering, and rocking babies with the real thing. Some "baby dolls" were imported from France during the Gilded Age, but despite the name, they did not resemble children. Doll bodies, which were usually stiff and unbending, were frequently made of kid leather or bisque, and the heads were composed of painted metal or china. The most expensive dolls were made of wax and often appeared quite lifelike, until the child left the doll in the sun and it melted. Dolls' heads and bodies could be purchased separately, enabling mothers to sew their own doll bodies and affix factory-manufactured heads or to easily repair dolls whose china heads had shattered or whose wax faces had dissolved. Handmade dolls outnumbered manufactured dolls during the Gilded Age, however, and those girls who owned factory-made dolls often owned ragdolls as well.

Doll accessories, such as beds, miniature tea sets, and wardrobe trunks, were also manufactured, and some of the more expensive dolls came with elaborate wardrobes containing outfits for every occasion, including travelling, formal visits, and funerals. Most dolls, however, did not come with wardrobes, and clothing designed for dolls was not manufactured; dolls' clothes for the most part had to be hand sewn by girls and their mothers. Toy manufacturers also produced miniature iron stoves, tin pots and pans, wooden cupboards and kitchen tables, and wash tubs and wash boards for little girls.

BOYS' TOYS

While dolls and miniature cooking and cleaning equipment were intended for girls, toys specifically designed for boys were also produced by toy manufacturers. Boys' toys focused on transportation and construction. Miniature iron locomotives were popular toys. Some were steam powered; others could be made to move through a clockwork mechanism. Toy engines powered by steam were also available. Miniature tools and gardening implements allowed little boys to emulate grown men.

Outdoor games were also popular, and manufactured sporting goods were produced in large numbers. Many boys owned baseballs and bats. Steel-bladed ice skates were made for both male and female adults and children. "Ladies' skates" were identical to men's except for the addition of an extra strap that fit around the woman's ankle. The creation of the lawn by middle-class suburban homeowners ushered in the fad of croquet. Many companies manufactured croquet balls, mallets, and wickets. Some companies made wickets with candle holders so that the family's fun did not have to end at dusk. Many middle-class families also purchased nets and racquets to play lawn tennis and bows, arrows, and targets to practice archery.

Aquariums and Ward Cases

The aquarium, a container for keeping animals and plants that live underwater, became popular in the United States during the Gilded Age. Aquarium keeping was already popular in Great Britain and Germany. Gilded Age aquariums were made of a variety of materials and came in a variety of styles. Some were simply large glass bowls. Some had four walls of glass held together by a metal frame. Others had only one glass pane and wooden panels formed the other sides. The bottoms of some were made of stone. Aquariums stood on tables or stands and some aquariums were designed to hang from the walls. Keeping an aquarium was a difficult project before the 20th century. Electric pumps to aerate the water did not exist, so owners had to aerate manually by scooping water out of the tank into another receptacle, thoroughly mixing the water, and pouring it back in. This needed to be done frequently. Only someone with a significant amount of leisure time or who could afford a servant could keep an aquarium of any size. Despite the difficulty, enough aquarium owners existed in the United States to provide a readership for The New York Aquarium Journal, which began publication in 1876.

Ward cases were simpler to keep, and many Gilded Age families did so. Ward cases, which were invented by the British physician Nathaniel Bagshaw Ward in the late 1820s or early 1830s, were used to raise plants that could not otherwise survive in polluted industrializing cities. Ward cases consisted either of simple glass domes or more elaborate wooden cases with glass panes. Inside the cases, in which heat and moisture were produced by sunlight shining through the glass, Gilded Age Americans kept delicate plants such as ferns and orchids. Collecting and raising ferns was a Gilded Age fad that was so popular that it had its own name—Pteridomania.

Other new activities were also popularized during the Gilded Age, leading to the mass production and consumption of the equipment needed to engage in them. Rollerskating became popular, and as rollerskating rinks spread across the United States (Dodge City, Kansas, a remote cow town, opened its first rink in 1878), many Americans purchased rollerskates made of wood and metal. Bicycles with large front wheels and small rear wheels were owned by many men and boys during the Gilded Age. When, in 1884, the "safety" bicycle with wheels of equal size was created, bicycling became possible for women and girls as well. The creation in 1887 of bicycles without crossbars to impede women's skirts made it even more possible for women to partake of the new activity.

Taken together, all of these objects characterize middle-class Americans as solid, sober, respectable people. They were pious people who valued education and loved their children. They loved nature and the outdoors. They were sophisticated people with impeccable manners and good taste.

ANN KORDAS

Further Readings

Cable, Mary. *American Manners and Morals: A Picture History of How We Behaved and Misbehaved*. New York: American Heritage Publishing Company, 1969.

Cross, Gary. *Kids' Stuff: Toys and the Changing World of American Childhood*. Cambridge, MA: Harvard University Press, 1997.

Darwin County. "Pteridomania—The Victorian Fern Craze." Available online, URL: http://www.darwincountry.org/explore/000529.html?sid=fb. Accessed February 2008.

Formanek-Brunell, Miriam. "Sugar and Spite: The Politics of Doll Play in Nineteenth-Century America." In *Small Worlds: Children and Adolescents in America, 1850–1950*. Elliott West and Paula Petrik, eds. Lawrence, KS: University Press of Kansas, 1992.

Haywood, C. Robert. *Victorian West: Class and Culture in Kansas Cattle Towns*. Lawrence, KS: University Press of Kansas, 1991.

Malloy, Alex G. *American Games Comprehensive Collector's Guide*. Iola, WI: Krause Publications, 2000.

McAlister, Virginia and Lee McAlister. *A Field Guide to American Houses*. New York: Alfred A. Knopf, 1994.

McDannell, Colleen. *Material Christianity: Religion and Popular Culture in America*. New Haven, CT: Yale University Press, 1995.

Schlereth, Thomas J. *Victorian America: Transformations in Everyday Life, 1876–1915*. New York: HarperCollins, 1991.

Stevenson, Louise L. *The Victorian Homefront: American Thought and Culture, 1860–1880*. Ithaca, NY: Cornell University Press, 1991.

Strasser, Susan. *Never Done: A History of American Housework*. New York: Pantheon Books, 1982.

Summers, Leigh. *Bound to Please: A History of the Victorian Corset*. New York: Berg, 2001.

White, Shane and Graham White. *Stylin': African-American Expressive Culture from Its Beginnings to the Zoot Suit*. Ithaca, NY: Cornell University Press, 1998.

Williams, Susan. *Savory Suppers and Fashionable Feasts: Dining in Victorian America*. Knoxville, TN: University of Tennessee Press, 1996.

Wright, Gwendolyn. *Building the Dream: A Social History of Housing in America*. New York: Random House, 1981.

Chapter 4

Social Attitudes

"We ought not to allow a permanent aristocracy
of inherited wealth to grow up in our country."
— President Rutherford B. Hayes

CARL SANDBURG IN his poem "Chicago" notes that the city he loves is "stormy, husky, brawling." This is an apt description of the Gilded Age itself, especially of the attitudes of the people. It was stormy as the belief systems of the rich clashed with the poor, the radical with the conservative. It was husky in that it was a time when attitudes might be described as big, tough, and strong. And it was brawling in that violence between—or toward—groups often broke out. These qualities of the Gilded Age are evident in the impact of Social Darwinism on the relationship between industry and labor and on the attempt to moderate this clash through the Social Gospel. Women also struggled against socially held beliefs that they were solely domestic beings, belonging only in the confines of the home. And even though they were not able to totally overcome these chauvinistic attitudes during the Gilded Age, women began the progress toward equality. And despite the fact that this was a country largely of new immigrants, racist and discriminatory beliefs sometimes overwhelmed ethnic groups such as the Chinese. Others, who were attacked because of the color of their skin or because of their religion, fought back with varying degrees of success.

SOCIAL DARWINISM
Even perhaps more than Charles Darwin himself, the British philosopher Herbert Spencer—who coined the phrase "survival of the fittest"—was a seminal

thinker to Americans exploring and espousing the idea of Social Darwinism. Simply put, Social Darwinism is the application of the ideas of scientific evolution to the workings of society. The popularity of Social Darwinism was not entirely wrought by Spencer. There were American scientists and thinkers who added to evolutionary theory, including paleontologists Joseph Leidy and Othniel C. Marsh. And more importantly, there were those who effectively sold the idea in the press and in the classroom, including philosopher John Fiske, botanist Asa Gray, and especially sociologist William Graham Sumner.

Social Darwinism was reflected in some of the literature of the Gilded Age. Authors such as Stephen Crane, Theodore Dreiser, Frank Norris, and Jack

What Social Classes Owe to Each Other

William Graham Sumner (1840–1910) was an influential American academic, whose numerous books and essays on American history, economic history, political theory, sociology, and anthropology gave him a wide audience for his *laissez-faire* advocacy of free markets, anti-imperialism, and the gold standard. In *What Social Classes Owe to Each Other*, he questions the attitudes of social classes.

"We are told every day that great social problems stand before us and demand a solution, and we are assailed by oracles, threats, and warnings in reference to those problems. There is a school of writers who are playing quite a role as the heralds of the coming duty and the coming woe. They assume to speak for a large, but vague and undefined, constituency, who set the task, exact a fulfillment, and threaten punishment for default. The task or problem is not specifically defined. Part of the task which devolves on those who are subject to the duty is to define the problem. They are told only that something is the matter: that it behooves them to find out what it is, and how to correct it, and then to work out the cure. All this is more or less truculently set forth.

"After reading and listening to a great deal of this sort of assertion I find that the question forms itself with more and more distinctness in my mind: Who are those who assume to put hard questions to other people and to demand a solution of them? How did they acquire the right to demand that others should solve their world-problems for them? Who are they who are held to consider and solve all questions, and how did they fall under this duty?

"So far as I can find out what the classes are who are respectively endowed with the rights and duties of posing and solving social problems, they are as follows: Those who are bound to solve the problems are the rich, comfortable, prosperous, virtuous, respectable, educated, and healthy; those whose right it is to set the problems are those who have been less fortunate or less successful in the struggle for existence."

The pulpit of Plymouth Church in Brooklyn, New York, which Henry Ward Beecher turned into a national platform for his ideas through his popular and eloquent sermons.

London experimented with characters that were caught up in larger and darker social forces that were beyond their control. The forces of society, economy, and heredity prompted some people to question whether or not humans were capable of free will. Nature, above all other forces, was often depicted as random, detached, and entirely oblivious to the plight of man.

Darwin's theories were as much a shock to established religions in the United States as they were to established religions in England. Nevertheless Spencer, with the help of apologists, was able to win over many clergymen. Many of these clergy found ways to inform traditional views of religion with evolutionary theory. A prominent example was abolitionist Henry Ward Beecher, brother of Harriet Beecher Stowe, author of *Uncle Tom's Cabin*. He was pastor of the Plymouth Church in Brooklyn and ended up as a friend of Spencer.

In Spencer's philosophy, progress was not a concrete entity; you could not really see progress by the number of possessions you owned. Progress meant the movement toward heterogeneity, division of labor, and greater complexity. In his own words, from the conclusion of his article, "Progress: Its Law and Cause," progress is "the advance from the simple to the complex, through a process of successive differentiations." Furthermore in nature, there are and always will be winners and losers, the strong and the weak, and (for humans) the rich and the poor. It was the reality of nature itself.

Andrew Carnegie, a Scottish immigrant who acquired vast wealth through steel and the railroads, was one of the most important proponents of Social Darwinist theory.

Those thinkers that championed Social Darwinism believed that progress was necessarily slow, but positive. Abrupt and radical attempts at social change such as through socialism, militant labor unions, and Marxism were doomed to fail. In their view, taking from the rich to give to the poor would simply be an act of rewarding failure, and it would ignore the facts of birth: some people are born with the natural ability to succeed, and some are not. Only the slow forces of evolution could bring life to a better end. And the weak, no matter what was tried, would always fall by the wayside in failure.

INFLUENCE ON BUSINESS LEADERS

Critics of the theory believed that Social Darwinism could be used to justify harsh and unfair business techniques, including cornering markets and creating monopolies. There is a record of leaders of industry echoing the phrase "survival of the fittest" and embracing what historian Richard Hofstadter has called "social fatalism."

Railroad executive Chauncey Depew, for instance, said that rich and powerful guests at banquets in New York were a gathering of those who represented the survival of the fittest. John D. Rockefeller declared that growth of big business came about through the survival of the fittest as it worked through the laws of nature and God. James J. Hill, also a railroad executive, declared in an essay that the process of small railroads being gobbled up by larger railroads was an example of the weak being conquered by the strong in the battle for the survival of the fittest. But the most famous, and instructive, public pronouncement of the theory was probably in Andrew Carnegie's "The Gospel of Wealth."

In "The Gospel of Wealth," Carnegie—a Social Darwinist—is preoccupied with how to appropriate his surplus wealth. Carnegie admits that there can be great disparity in wealth, but that this disparity can be beneficial. He believes that great wealth in the hands of individuals can be positive for society. Wealthy homes, for instance, can be worthy and respectful repositories for all of the refinements of civilization, such as great books and great art. And while there are negative effects from competition and industrialization, there are positives as well, especially the fact that materially, even the working man is better off. He further writes, "And while the law may be sometimes hard for the individual, it is best for the race, because it insures the survival of the fittest in every department."

Carnegie goes on to say that it is logical and inevitable that some people—those with talent—are going to accumulate more wealth than others. And socialists, communists, and anarchists are simply attacking the foundations of civilization. Or, as he says, he is for evolution, not revolution. He sees these social radicals as trying to destroy individualism, private property, the right to accumulate wealth, and competition—all the things that

The Carnegie Free Library and Music Hall in Allegheny City, Pennsylvania. Among other works, Carnegie built 1,679 libraries across the United States, giving away 90 percent of his fortune.

are necessary for a country to be great and for the life of all to gradually improve.

Finally he returns to his primary question: what should he do with excess wealth and can he ameliorate the disparity of wealth? He rejects two approaches: first, giving all his wealth to his family after his death; and second, bequeathing his wealth to the public after his death. His solution is twofold. First the person of great wealth must lead by example. He must live a life of moderation. Second he must set up a trust to distribute his excess wealth in a beneficial way while he is still living. Carnegie is against indiscriminate charity; in fact he feels that the person of wealth must be totally in charge of the distribution. A main focus would be in giving money in a way that would help others to help themselves. This would include "free libraries, parks, and means of recreation" as well as works of art for public edification and enjoyment. All of this, rather than radical politics, would solve the problem of inequality between the rich and the poor.

Social Darwinists believed that one should not interfere with the natural order of things. Revolution in place of evolution was considered wrong because it elevates those that are less deserving or "fit." The economic counterpart to Social Darwinism is *laissez-faire* capitalism. *Laissez-faire* is a concept that began in the 1700s. By the time of the Gilded Age it meant the non-interference of government with economics. Obviously this belief in no government restrictions or interference with business would have been beneficial to those who believed in the creation of monopolies and unfair competition. Government interference, according to *laissez-faire* principles, violated the natural order.

The popularity of *laissez-faire* principles began to diminish toward the end of the Gilded Age with the Interstate Commerce Act (1887), regulating railroads, and the Sherman Anti-Trust Act (1890), which was supposed to break up monopolies. Most historians see both of these as mostly ineffective and agree that government regulation would not really begin in earnest until the early part of the 20th century.

THE SOCIAL GOSPEL

The Social Gospel can be seen as the antithesis of Social Darwinism. One of the central ideas of the Social Gospel is evolution, but it is God's evolution, and it is not only possible for humankind to participate in this evolution—an evolution toward the Kingdom of God on Earth—but also desirable. As Walter Rauschenbusch, one of the Gilded Age leaders of the Social Gospel wrote, it becomes imperative for people "to complete God's fair creation."

The Social Gospel was especially involved with promoting economic justice, particularly through labor unions. Aside from Rauschenbusch, there are two other prominent Protestant leaders of the movement: Washington Gladden and Josiah Strong.

Washington Gladden

A writer, a Protestant minister, and a driving force for the Social Gospel Movement, Washington Gladden was born on February 11, 1836, in Pottsgrove, Pennsylvania. Both of his grandfathers had been shoemakers. He grew up on a farm and at age 16 he was apprenticed to a newspaper publisher for four years and began a life of writing. At age 20, he left his apprenticeship to attend Williams College. He graduated in 1859 and was ordained in 1860 in the Congregationalist church. He began his religious life as the pastor of the State Street Congregationalist Church in Brooklyn, New York. In 1868 he published his first of 40 books, *Plain Thoughts on the Art of Living*. In 1871 he became the religion editor of the *New York Independent*.

His Social Gospel principles can be seen in one of his books, *Working People and Their Employers*, published in 1885. At all times his goal is to mediate what he calls the war between labor and capital. He begins the book first by praising labor and associating it with Christ the carpenter and laborer. Physical work, says Gladden, is as noble as mental work. But he also chides the worker for sometimes doing shoddy work and for making unreasonable wage demands on an employer when the employer is obviously in a state of financial weakness. And while Gladden is not against strikes, he is against violence and intimidation, especially against strike breakers. He also addresses the hatred of some workers for machines. Machines, he says, have many benefits and are not the evil that workers sometimes think they are. The factory or mine owner, on the other hand, must not live an immoderate life and then claim he has no money for wages. And instead of always living by the laws of blind profit, the owner must begin to moderate business practices with Christian principles.

The ultimate way out of the war between labor and capital, according to Gladden, is for the workers to combine their own capital into cooperatives to run their businesses. Unfortunately, writes Gladden, the American worker may not be ready for this yet and so an intermediary approach should be tried: profit sharing.

After serving as a pastor at two churches in Massachusetts, in 1882 Gladden began a 30-year stint at the First Congregational Church in Columbus, Ohio. In 1886 he attempted to diffuse a bitter strike by streetcar workers in Cleveland, Ohio. He spoke to a crowd of employers and employees on the topic of "Is It Peace or Is It War?" There he confirmed to the workers their right to strike. He also intervened in a street car strike in Columbus and argued for arbitration. Gladden also gave speeches on racial equality, including one in Atlanta where he met with W.E.B. DuBois. He was a member of the city council in Columbus, served as president of Ohio State University, and received an honorary doctorate from Notre Dame University for his public stance against the anti-Catholic American Protective Association. He died in Columbus on July 2, 1918.

Jane Addams, founder of Hull House, around 1913.

Josiah Strong was the most controversial of the three. Strong became passionately involved in missionary work and felt that English-speaking peoples were the superior ones to spread Christianity. He was, though, against greed and selfishness. And he wrote that white, African American, Native American, and Chinese were all of one blood, belonging to one family and to degrade one was to degrade all. He warned that crowded cities were a threat and that social justice was necessary to overcome this threat.

Washington Gladden wrote 40 books and numerous articles, many of which addressed the principles of the Social Gospel. He was a moderating force in what he called the war between capital and labor, but stood behind the right of workers to strike. Nevertheless he was against violence of any kind. His ultimate answer to the problem of economic injustice was worker cooperatives. He also supported profitsharing. For him, the principles of Christian love were essential to good relations between workers and owners. Gladden also argued against unrestricted competition and for a progressive income tax.

Walter Rauschenbusch, who was a theologian as well as a minister, was much more influenced by socialism than Gladden. One of the churches where he was a pastor was the Second German Baptist Church in the Hell's Kitchen section of New York City. There he gained a first hand experience of the trials and tribulations of the poor. To help in exposing the situation of the poor, he started a non-denominational organization called the Brotherhood of the Kingdom. They had yearly conferences where people from all over the country would deliver papers. The 1899 conference included such titles as "Industrial Cooperation," "The New Christian State," and "The Reign of God in the World." For Rauschenbusch, the Kingdom of God on Earth included "the sanctification of all life, the regeneration of humanity, and the reformation of all social institutions."

REAL WORLD MANIFESTATIONS OF THE SOCIAL GOSPEL

Determining the real effect of the Social Gospel during the Gilded Age is difficult. Unions had not yet come into prominence (only three percent of the work force in 1900 belonged to unions) and some say the Social Gospel did not really take effect until Franklin Roosevelt's New Deal. But two prominent examples of this kind of social consciousness are Hull House and the Salvation Army.

The Hull House was opened in 1889 by Jane Addams and Ellen Starr in a heavily immigrant neighborhood on the west side of Chicago. The idea for

Poor and homeless men in a Salvation Army shelter in early 20th-century England—such outreach activities inspired the founding of Hull House and the American Salvation Army.

Hull House was modeled after a settlement house they had visited in England. The English settlement house was run by students who tried to improve the life of the poor.

Addams and Starr began almost immediately to help educate the poor. They began a kindergarten and offered educational readings and lectures, many from famous Americans like Susan B. Anthony, Clarence Darrow, and Frank Lloyd Wright. The house was used for union meetings, and Addams and others helped to financially support workers during strikes.

The Salvation Army was started in England by William and Catherine Booth. They avoided the middle-class churches and began their ministry in the streets of London. They reached out to the poorest of folks, to the drunks, to the homeless, and to the prostitutes.

Eliza Shirley first introduced the Salvation Army to America in Philadelphia in 1879. In 1880 William Booth sent Shirley some help, eight people—one man and seven women. They held their first outdoor ministry in Battery Park in Manhattan. Despite being ridiculed at first, the Salvation Army was able in three short years to expand into 12 different states. The role of women as ministers was controversial and daring for its time.

ATTITUDES TOWARD WOMEN

Prior to industrialization society was primarily agricultural, and women were equal partners in the economic life of the family. Even in 1900 the typical farm wife still worked 10 hours a day in the winter and 13 hours a day during the summer. But the "proper place" for middle and upper class women in the Gilded Age was considerably different from earlier times and from the frontier and farm way of life.

The attitude of the majority of middle and upper class men (and even of many of the women) was that a woman's place was in the home. The husband was the sole breadwinner while the wife was the moral guardian of the family and remained at home. That was her domain; that, in the terms of the day, was her sphere. As Lucy Stone, one of the Gilded Age's strongest advocates for women's rights explained it, "The idea that [women's] sphere was at home, and only at home, was like a band of steel on society." Married women had no property rights and were generally barred from professions. Divorce laws, including the custody of children, favored men. But not all of the women during this period would accept this limited view, and they attempted to change the prevalent attitudes, primarily through the fight for the right to vote.

The first women's rights convention was held in 1848 in Seneca Falls, New York, and was led by Elizabeth Cady Stanton. There they drafted a "Declaration of Sentiments," which included the demand for suffrage. All of this went against the prevailing attitude of the time and the women were attacked in the press. A January 27, 1876, editorial in the *New York Times* stated that "no one of intelligence pretends to deny that universal suffrage involves very serious evils . . . ."

The women's movement was temporarily derailed during the Civil War. It picked up again in 1866 with the formation of the American Equal Rights Association by Elizabeth Cady Stanton and Susan B. Anthony in 1869, as well as the American Woman Suffrage Association, formed by Lucy Stone and founded in 1869. They eventually combined in 1890 to form the National American Woman Suffrage Association, which was led by Susan B. Anthony. Other prominent leaders included Ida B. Wells, Mary Church Terrell, Esther Morris, and Matilda Joslyn Gage.

Progress was slow. In 1875 the census showed that 544 women were categorized as physicians, surgeons, and medical service workers. This rose to 4,500 by 1895. Sometimes the victories were only local or by state. For instance, Michigan passed a universal municipal suffrage in 1893. They had passed a married woman's

Lucy Stone, the women's rights advocate and suffragette, in the mid-19th century.

The Tireless Ida B. Wells

A journalist, suffragette, and civil rights activist who tirelessly brought the truth to the rest of the country about lynchings in the south, Ida B. Wells was born into slavery during the Civil War on July 16, 1862, in Holly Springs, Mississippi. Her mother, Elizabeth Wells, a cook, lived on one plantation while her father, James Wells, a carpenter, lived on another. After the war, they were able to buy a house and reunite the family.

In 1878 a yellow fever epidemic struck and killed both her parents as well as four of her siblings. Her parents, before they died, had been caring for other sick members of the community. Wells kept the family together in her parent's house and began teaching.

Ida B. Wells around the time she wrote Southern Horrors: Lynch Law in All Its Phases.

In 1880 she moved to Memphis, Tennessee, searching for a better paying job. She took a job there as a teacher and soon became involved in protest politics. She famously tested the railroad segregation laws in Tennessee by sitting in the first class section and had to be physically removed from the train, while being jeered at by white passengers. This and the subsequent court cases associated with it gave her a chance to begin writing for the public as a journalist. It also cost her job as a teacher, and she invested some of her money in a newspaper, *Memphis Free Speech*.

1892 was a pivotal year for her, though a traumatic one. Three African American shopkeepers—friends of hers—were lynched. She organized a boycott and wrote a series of editorials on the injustice of it, as well as a scathing, uncomfortable analysis of why African-American men were being lynched, and called for African Americans to leave Memphis. Realizing that her life might be in danger for speaking out, she left town for Philadelphia. The next day her newspaper office was ransacked and destroyed.

She then lived in New York City for a while, writing for the *New York Age*. She also wrote a number of pamphlets giving a true statistical analysis of lynching and one of the most historically important and revealing works on lynching, *Southern Horrors: Lynch Law in All Its Phases* (1892). In 1895 she moved to Chicago where she met and married Ferdinand L. Barnett, a lawyer and the owner of *The Conservator* newspaper. She continued to write, lecture, and organize.

Ida B. Wells died on March 25, 1931.

The anatomical lecture room in a medical college for women in New York City in 1870. Five years later, the national census counted only 544 women physicians, surgeons, and medical service workers.

property act in 1858, and women were first allowed to attend the University of Michigan in 1870. Still it would be 72 years (until 1920) before women were finally given the vote by the federal government through the Nineteenth Amendment.

Attitudes of Americans towards new immigrants were often negative. The Chinese and Roman Catholics experienced great levels of discrimination during the Gilded Age. And, of course, discrimination and hatred toward African Americans in the south during the Gilded Age is well documented.

THE CHINESE

One of the leaders of the anti-Chinese movement was himself an immigrant, Irish-born Denis Kearney. Kearney came to the United States from Ireland in 1868 and settled in San Francisco, California. He became involved in politics and the workingman's association and became the leader of the Workingmen's Party, a socialist political party.

Kearney blamed the plight of the workingman on two groups: capitalists and Chinese immigrants. During his speeches he called for the lynching of business owners, and the destruction of their property. He blamed the Chinese for making jobs scarce and for helping the capitalists suppress wages. Kearney wanted the Chinese expelled from the United States. He began and ended his speeches by shouting, "The Chinese must go."

California at this time had enacted a number of laws discriminating against Chinese immigrants. Examples of overt violence toward Chinese persons began appearing. In Los Angeles, a mob lynched 15 Chinese people. Kearney and the anti-Chinese factions then led a charge to change the California State Constitution in 1879, with the ultimate goal of totally banning Chinese people from the state, a goal that never materialized. Delegates to the state constitutional convention declared that California was for white men only. And in 1882, the U.S. Congress, under pressure from California and a number of other western states, passed the Chinese Exclusion Act, the first American law to restrict a particular ethnic group from immigrating to the United States.

This caricature of a Chinese man celebrating a jail sentence for Denis Kearney ran in an April 3, 1880, newspaper.

ROMAN CATHOLICS

Roman Catholicism was the religion of many immigrants, especially the Irish and German, during the Gilded Age. Negative attitudes toward Roman Catholics had been around prior to this period. In a country whose population had been primarily Protestant, the flood of Catholic immigrants early in the century led to such things as the Know Nothing movement during the 1850s. This movement maintained that the Pope was going to take over the country, a belief that led to unsuccessful attempts to curb immigration. These sentiments then reappeared in 1891 with the founding by Henry F. Bowers of the secret society known as the American Protective Association.

The organization's technique was to try to persuade people to join by distributing pamphlets alleging, among other things, that Catholics had been directed by the Pope to massacre Protestants. It attempted to influence politicians, but the only two prominent politicians who openly supported it were Governor William O. Bradley of Kentucky and Congressman William S. Linton of Michigan. Its membership is estimated to have been less than a million people. It was opposed by the prominent Protestant clergyman Washington Gladden, who spoke out against it in the pages of *Century Magazine*, as well as by various politicians, including the Governor of Missouri, William J. Stone; the Governor of Wisconsin, George W. Peck; the Governor of Illinois, John P. Altgeld; and a number of senators, including Theodore

An 1852 advertisement for a short-lived anti-immigrant and anti-Catholic newspaper that was published in Boston and specifically targeted new Irish immigrants.

Roosevelt. While it failed as a political force, its attitudes, though in a much less extreme form, were prevalent, lingering until the 1961 election of John Kennedy as the first Roman Catholic U.S. president.

AFRICAN AMERICANS

Though discriminatory attitudes toward African Americans in the south are well documented, discrimination in the north is perhaps less known. In particular, African Americans were denied access to many labor unions, with the notable exceptions of the Knights of Labor and the United Mine Workers. Scholars have also pointed out that throughout all of the United States, African Americans were stereotyped in negative ways. One such type of stereotyping took place in the popular "coon song." In the "coon song" African Americans were characterized as lazy and ignorant. They were largely barred from the 1893 World's Columbian Exposition held in Chicago. This prompted Frederick Douglass and Ida B. Wells to boycott the exposition. Wells wrote a pamphlet to complement the boycott, *Why the Colored American Is Not in the World's Columbian Exposition.*

In the south, as soon as Reconstruction troops were withdrawn in 1876, Jim Crow laws—laws that created segregation—were enacted. Poll taxes evolved, effectively disenfranchising many. Vigilante justice flared, leading to lynchings and torture. The southern discrimination became so bad that it triggered an African-American diaspora to the west and north known as the Great Migration, beginning in 1870. Between 1890 and 1910 it is estimated that 250,000 African Americans left the south for the north, and about 35,000 more went west.

CONCLUSION

In 1886 near the end of the Gilded Age, the Statue of Liberty was placed in New York harbor. Emma Lazarus's poem, "The New Colossus," is inscribed on its plaque. Its most famous lines are: "Give me your tired, your poor,/Your huddled masses yearning to breathe free,/The wretched refuse of your teeming shore./Send these, the homeless, tempest-tost to me,/I lift my lamp beside the golden door!"

America, though, was and is more complicated than that sentiment suggests, and the Gilded Age, with all of its conflicts, is one example. Yet one of America's hallmarks, even between 1870 and 1900, is that it truly was and is a country evolving—even if the idea of evolution had to be redefined into something less harsh than Herbert Spencer's. Perhaps the Gilded Age was a period in history when the clashes were more severe, a bit too "stormy, husky, brawling." But the later periods of American history reveal a progression, humane though not perfect, toward the sentiments etched onto that plaque in New York harbor.

WILLIAM TOTH

Further Readings

Boller, Paul F., Jr. "The New Science and American Thought." In *The Gilded Age*. Ed. by H. Wayne Morgan. Syracuse, NY: Syracuse University Press, 1970.

Carnegie, Andrew. *The Gospel of Wealth and Other Timely Essays*. New York: The Century Company, 1901.

Desmond, Humphrey J. "The American Protective Association." In *The Catholic Encyclopedia*. New York: Robert Appleton Company, 1907.

Dorrien, Gary J. *The Making of American Liberal Theology: Idealism, Realism, and Modernity, 1900–1950*. Louisville, KY: Westminster John Knox Press, 2003.

Duster, A., ed. *Crusade for Justice: The Autobiography of Ida B. Wells*. Chicago, IL: University of Chicago Press, 1970.

Gladden, Washington. *Working People and Their Employers*. New York: Funk and Wagnalls, 1885.

Hofstadter, Richard. *Social Darwinism in American Thought*. New York: George Braziller, 1959.

Hopkins, Charles Howard. *The Rise of the Social Gospel in American Protestantism: 1865–1915*. New Haven, CT: Yale University Press, 1940.

Mintz, Steven and Susan Kellogg. *Domestic Revolutions: A Social History of American Family Life*. New York: The Free Press, 1988.

Ohio Historical Society. "Social Darwinism." Available online, URL: http://www.ohiohistorycentral.org/entry.php?rec=1528. Accessed February 2008.

Plante, Ellen M. *Women at Home in Victorian America*. New York: Facts On File, 1997.

Spencer, Herbert. "Progress: Its Law and Causes." *The Westminster Review*. (v. 67, 1857).

Chapter 5

Cities and Urban Life

"The larger a town becomes . . .
the greater will be the convenience available."
— Frederick Law Olmsted

DURING THE GILDED AGE American cities underwent major transformations. At the end of the American Revolution, most Americans lived in rural areas. Even within cities populations tended to be relatively small. Only one in 20 Americans lived in cities with populations over 2,500. New York City, the most urbanized city of the period, was home to only 22,000 inhabitants. Between 1790 and 1880 the number of American cities expanded from a mere 24 to 939, and the urban population climbed from 5.1 to 28.2 percent of the total population. Before the Civil War broke out in April 1861, there were 16 American cities with populations over 50,000 and nine with populations over 100,000. By 1900 38 cities claimed populations of more than 100,000, and more than 40 percent of Americans lived in cities of at least 2,500 residents.

Cities of the Gilded Age emerged largely in response to patterns of industrialization, and many cities sprang up along ever-expanding railroad lines. For the first time in American history large cities surfaced not only along the eastern seaboard and in the midwest, but also in the southwestern and far western sections of the United States.

REDEFINING AMERICAN URBANISM
Between 1865 and 1905 some 24 million individuals migrated into American cities. This population surge, coupled with expanding industrialization,

redefined life in urban America. Cities began growing outward, expanding into outlying areas. Improved forms of transportation made travel around city areas less difficult than in the past, and encouraged Americans to travel for both business and pleasure. Developers of the Gilded Age constantly sought ways to entice new people into large cities and employed a variety of methods to attract individuals fleeing big city life into surrounding suburbs.

The moniker "Gilded Age" was coined in part by writer Mark Twain (1835–1910), who referred to the fact that underlying the gilding of affluence, poverty and corruption were rampant in the United States of the late 19th century. Between 1870 and 1900 economic prosperity resulted in lavishly extravagant lifestyles for the wealthy, and a newly awakened social consciousness brought about improved standards of living for many members of the working class. The middle class rapidly expanded, averaging incomes between $500 and $2,000 a year. Yet despite its glamorous image, the Gilded Age was also a time of entrenched poverty, unhealthy living conditions, and hazardous work sites. The United States experienced industrial depressions in the 1870s and the 1890s that produced new levels of poverty, signaled a decline in trade unions, and promoted violence and urban disorder. In 1890 11 million families earned less than $1,200 a year. The other million American families were either affluent or comfortable, enjoying access to modern conveniences and technologies. The gap between rich and poor Americans remained wide throughout the Gilded Age. At the lowest end of the economic spectrum, city residents frequently lived in unsafe, overcrowded, unheated, and poorly ventilated tenements with no access to electricity or running water. Germs and diseases were able to flourish in these poor environments.

Urban populations throughout the United States continued a steady growth from the end of the Civil War until the Great Depression of the 1930s. By 1870, as technologies redefined life on the farm, Americans began forsaking life in small towns and on farms for life in large cities in order to take advantage of increasing opportunities in the factories, mills, and mines that were

Detail from a panoramic view of Duluth, Minnesota, in 1914, not long after its population increased from 3,300 to 33,000 from 1880 to 1890.

raking in huge profits as the pace of industrialization accelerated. The exodus of African-Americans from the rural south was particularly significant, with half a million African Americans migrating northward away from sharecropping, tenant farming, and discriminatory Jim Crow laws. At the same time improved transportation, particularly rapidly multiplying rail lines, brought widely separated Americans closer together than had been possible before the Civil War. By 1860 New York, Philadelphia, Baltimore, and Boston had been established as the major eastern cities of the United States. Much of the post-Civil War population growth took place west of the Appalachian Mountains as rail lines expanded toward the Pacific Ocean.

While the populations of all large cities continued to grow after the Civil War, the most significant growth patterns occurred in the midwest. In Chicago, for example, the population grew from 100,000 in 1860 and to more than a million by 1890. The city's population continued to expand, reaching 2,185,000 in 1910. Many cities that had been considered small before the war took on new significance with expanding industrialization. The population of Omaha, Nebraska, for instance, expanded fourfold in the decade following 1880. During that same period, Kansas City, Missouri, doubled its population, and the population of Minneapolis, Minnesota, more than tripled. Wichita, Kansas, grew from 5,000 to 23,000, and Duluth, Minnesota, increased from 3,300 to 33,000. In Alabama the population of industrial Birmingham increased by eight and one-half times.

URBAN POLITICS

The excesses of the Gilded Age provided an atmosphere that was ripe for abuses of government power. Political machines emerged that were capable of controlling state and local elections. They also proved a major influence on national elections. Party machine bosses chose their candidates carefully, supporting only those who toed the designated line. Votes were often awarded to the highest bidder, or given in exchange for political favors. Machine politicians attracted poor urban Americans by exchanging financial aid for votes. In New York, for instance, Democratic Boss William Marcy Tweed and his colleagues at Tammany Hall filled their own pockets while providing unprecedented social services. Tweed allotted 60,000 jobs to political supporters and increased New York City's debt to $70 million. He was convicted of fraud and extortion in 1873. At the opposite end of the political spectrum, Republican George B. Cox of Cincinnati, a former saloon owner, was involved in major urban reforms. Nevertheless he fixed elections and rewarded party faithfuls with city jobs.

Rather than setting a high moral tone for cities and states to follow, politics at the national level experienced rampant corruption during the Gilded Age. Ulysses S. Grant had emerged from the Civil War as a military hero. Once in the White House, Grant's administrative style allowed all forms of corruption

A lavish dining room in The Elms mansion on Bellevue Avenue in Newport, Rhode Island. The Elms was completed in 1901.

Urban Entertainment

During the Gilded Age, wealthy urbanites often sought out places where they could shut out the rest of the world. Social advisor Ward McAllister (1827–95) coined the term "The Four Hundred" to describe New York's affluent population of the late 19th and early 20th centuries. The ostentatious extravagance of "the 400" greatly contrasted with the poverty of many New Yorkers. With expanding industrialization, fortunes of $50 and $100 million were not uncommon among New York's urban elite. Some elite New Yorkers spent tens of thousands of dollars a year for entertainments, if not more, and employed half a dozen private chefs. One way of guaranteeing exclusivity was through "cotillion" dinners to which only acceptable members of elite society were invited. Other exclusive events included French-style *salons* in which vacationing socialites held court in places such as Newport, Rhode Island, each summer.

A lavish Newport evening would consist of the hostess receiving guests in a multi-room outdoor tent designed to hold 1,500 people. After being greeted, guests would be directed to a Japanese room that displayed Oriental art, tapestries, furniture, and cane houses all highlighted by Japanese lanterns. Tea would be served by young Japanese men in native clothing. The *pièce de résistance* of the tent would be the open-air ballroom lit by electric light. Dramatic effect would be achieved by two grottoes made of blocks of ice lit to resemble prisms in an illuminated cave. As the blocks dissolved, they would look like glaciers melting over rocks.

to flourish. He and members of his cabinet were accused of taking part in a number of corrupt deals, including the Credit Mobilier scandal, the Gold Conspiracy, the Whiskey Ring, and the so-called Salary Grab.

The affluence of the Gilded Age allowed state and local governments to design comprehensive budgets that offered public services ranging from police and fire protection, to government-owned utilities and improved transportation measures. Even so, sanitation was still primitive in many urban areas; and smaller cities were not always able to afford adequate public services. Reformists such as Herbert Welsh and Richard T. Ely were influential in bringing about more responsive city government.

An 1871 political cartoon entitled "The arrest of 'Boss' Tweed—another good joke" shows a sheriff patting Boss Tweed on the back.

Using European cities as models, Welsh and Ely offered elaborately detailed plans for urban reform. In response to their efforts, male and female reformers from New York, Brooklyn, Chicago, Boston, Baltimore, Minneapolis, Milwaukee, Albany, Buffalo, Philadelphia, and Columbus, Ohio, met in Philadelphia in 1894 to establish the Conference for Good City Government and develop strategies for fighting the negative influences of political machines. The group targeted the spoils system, which allowed politicians to place their cronies and political supporters in government jobs, as the area most in need of reform. The second area of needed reform was identified as the tendency to place national interests over those of individual cities. Conferees also advocated a plan for forming municipal parties that would place responsibilities for city governments in the hands of fairly elected local leaders, rather than under the control of national parties.

IMMIGRATION

Much of the industrial and economic growth of the Gilded Age was accomplished through the hard work of immigrants who came to the United States looking for opportunity and improved standards of living. The influx of immigrants into the country had begun around 1840, but immigration levels declined during the Civil War, before accelerating during Reconstruction.

A 1916 cartoon with Uncle Sam on a wall marked "Literacy Test" telling immigrants, "You're welcome, if you can climb it."

Between 1871 and 1901, 11.7 million individuals immigrated into the United States. By 1920 that number had reached 37 million.

About 90 percent of all American immigrants came from European nations, including Germany, Ireland, Italy, England, Scotland, Wales, the Austro-Hungarian Empire, Scandinavia, and Russia. Many of the immigrants who arrived at Ellis Island, New York, remained in the northeast, giving rise to large Jewish, Irish, and Italian communities. Many of the Irish and Canadian immigrants flocked to New England, while Italians and Russians headed for the middle Atlantic states. Immigrants from Germany and central Europe were more inclined to opt for the mines and industries of the midwest. Approximately 6.7 percent of American immigrants came from Canada, mostly from Quebec. By the 1890s these so-called "new" immigrants outnumbered "old" immigrants. Despite the influx of immigrants, the rate of foreign-born residents remained constant throughout much of the Gilded Age. In order to promote their own cultures, immigrants often clustered together, creating areas that became known by such names as "Chinatown" and "Little Italy."

Scholars have noted that throughout history, immigrants have been more inclined to settle in cities than in rural areas. This has been true in part because of greater employment opportunities in large cities. During the Gilded Age, the majority of new immigrants labored in industrial jobs, usually starting at the lowest levels. They often took on jobs that others would not take and were willing to work for lower pay than their American cohorts, frequently laboring under hazardous conditions.

By the 1880s nativism was on the rise in the United States in response to the changes wrought by persistent waves of immigration. Between 1880 and 1890, immigrants from Hungary, Russia, Italy, Austria, and Poland arrived in the United States in large numbers. Some Americans believed that immigrants from eastern and southern Europe, unlike those from other parts of Europe, were incapable of adjusting to American lifestyles because of the idiosyncrasies of their own cultures. The Immigration Restriction League and the American Protective Association were only two of the many organizations established to fight liberal immigration policies. The latter organization was motivated in large part by its anti-Catholic stance.

Attempts to limit immigration into the United States led Gilded Age politicians to enact restrictive legislation. Many of these attempts targeted the Chinese who numbered some 125,000 at the time, mostly concentrated in California. The first legislation, passed in 1875, attempted to limit only the immigration of Chinese women. Congress passed the Chinese Exclusion Act in 1882, banning Chinese laborers from entry into the country. Subsequently legislators attempted to restrict other immigrants, and began requiring a nominal entry fee. Contract labor was banned. Individuals with designated physical and mental conditions were denied entry, as well as those with criminal records and those who practiced polygamy, particularly Mormons. In 1892 the Ellis Island station in New York Harbor was established to serve as an entry point for most immigrants. Five years later, a controversial bill requiring literacy tests for all immigrants passed both houses of Congress. It was vetoed by President Grover Cleveland. The literacy requirement ultimately passed in 1917 when Congress overrode the veto of President Woodrow Wilson during World War I.

CITY PLANNING

Before the mid-19th century, the layouts of cities evolved chiefly in response to the market and actions of individual property owners. By the 1870s city planning was in its infancy. It was motivated not by politicians or architects, but by sanitarians and physicians who were determined to check the spread of infectious diseases. Through the efforts of such reformers, sanitary engineers began developing plans for comprehensive sanitation systems. Many cities conducted house-to-house surveys of all land areas located within their boundaries in order to identify problems and enforce legal stipulations. Early city planners also recognized the need to make parks available to urban residents to enable residents to enjoy fresh air and nature.

The 1893 Chicago World's Fair, which took place on the shores of Lake Michigan, was officially designated as the World's Columbian Exposition in honor of the 400th anniversary of Christopher Columbus's voyage to America. With its rich architecture that included urban plazas, domed buildings, towers, and classical revivalist buildings, Chicago was the ideal place for arousing interest in well-designed cities during the Gilded Age. The directors of the fair used the opportunity to provide Americans with a blueprint for moving into the 20th century. Over a six-month period, 27 million individuals visited the fair, including such notables as African-American lecturer Frederick Douglass, reformer Jane Addams, poet Paul Laurence Dunbar, writers William Dean Howells and Hamlin Garland, musician Scott Joplin, and attorney/writer Henry Adams.

After paying a $.50 admission fee, visitors entered the facilities through one of three entrances. Many attendees arrived first at the 55,000 sq. ft. Administration Building, a domed structure designed by New Yorker Richard M. Hunt. The Administration Building provided an introduction to the fair's 14

The domed Administration Building, which was designed by Richard M. Hunt of New York, was one of the many influential, yet temporary structures at the 1893 Chicago World's Fair.

white stucco buildings. One of the most popular structures at the fair was the Court of Honor, which was embellished by a reflecting pool, the MacMonnies Fountain, and the gilded statue *Republic*. Overall the fair highlighted 200 buildings, which had been designed to promote urban beautification.

The Chicago Exposition helped launch the City Beautiful Movement and encouraged city leaders throughout the United States to engage in city planning. The motivating force behind the movement was architect Daniel Hudson Burnham (1846–1912), who became known as the father of the City Beautiful Movement. In conjunction with his partner, Georgia-born John Wellborn Root (1850–91), Burnham was involved in rebuilding Chicago after fire ravaged the city in 1871. Burnham and Root's work on the development of Chicago's skyscrapers evolved into the Chicago School of skyscraper architecture, which exercised a major influence on multi-level structures erected in other large American cities.

Burnham's City Beautiful Movement emerged from his work as a director of the Chicago Exposition. His work was heavily influenced by the Beaux-Arts School popular in Paris, where many of the architects involved in the Exposition had been trained. Written in 1909, Burnham's *Plan of Chicago* proved to be a seminal work in the field of urban planning. His influence on Chicago's

Charles Mulford Robinson (1869–1917)

Journalist Charles Mulford Robinson became the first professor of civic design at the University of Illinois at Urbana-Champaign, at a time when Illinois and Harvard were the only two American universities teaching urban planning. Robinson's views on city planning were heavily influenced by the Columbia Exposition that took place in Chicago in 1893, which he described his 1893 report "The Fair of Spectacle." In 1899 Robinson took his enthusiasm for city beautification to the public in a series of essays written for *Atlantic Monthly*. The publication of his *The Improvement of Towns and Cities* in 1901 marked a turning point for the city beautification movement, and this work became the model for scores of beautification projects. Robinson followed this success with *Modern Civic Art; Or, The City Made Beautiful* in 1903. He believed that all cities should be carefully planned and suggested that factories should be moved out of American cities and into the suburbs. Instead of the over-crowded tenements that were common in the Gilded Age, Robinson advocated the building of model tenements.

Robinson contended that city planning should involve a joint effort by professionals by way of a commission made up of an architect, a landscape artist, a sculptor, an engineer, and one at-large-member who combined the interests of other professionals. Robinson insisted that all housing codes should be rigorously enforced. He took on an active role in urban planning in cities such as Detroit, Denver, Honolulu, Des Moines, San Jose, and Los Angeles.

architecture continued into modern times, as evidenced by the construction of Millennium Park early in the 21st century. The park's design included a concert pavilion and an expressway footbridge, and linked to Grant Park on the shores of Lake Michigan.

The tendency toward building enormous edifices after the Chicago Exposition led a number of large American cities to erect multi-level business complexes, which promoted urban growth. This tendency also resulted in the building of huge tenements in which scores of America's poor lived under stark and primitive conditions. On a more positive note, the influence of the Chicago Exposition and the City Beautiful Movement led to concentrated attempts to make urban areas cleaner and more pleasant. Throughout the United States small groups of concerned citizens began promoting beautification efforts. Reformers such as Charles Mulford Robinson, the author of *The Improvement of Towns and Cities* (1901), advocated urban beautification as the responsibility of all Americans.

Deadwood, South Dakota

Many western cities settled in the 19th century were established in response to the discovery of gold and silver. One such city was Deadwood Gulch, located in the Black Hills of South Dakota in an area covered with trees blackened by wildfires. Within a year of the 1875 discovery of gold in Deadwood, the population had expanded to approximately 10,000 people. Government officials tended to ignore claims of Sioux Indians that they owned the property where Deadwood was located. Law was virtually nonexistent, and saloons, gambling establishments, and brothels flourished. The Gem Theatre raked in profits of $10,000 each night. In response to the flourishing economy, miners sent for their families, and the first school was opened. Chinese immigrants were attracted to Deadwood, and they soon forsook the mines for laundries and grocery stores. Fee Lee Wong became the city's first Chinese herbalist.

Wild Bill Hickok's monument in Deadwood, South Dakota, in 1891.

Deadwood was home to such well-known Americans as Wild Bill Hickok and Calamity Jane. According to local legend, Wild Bill Hickok was murdered on August 2, 1876, by Jack McCall, a cross-eyed drifter, who shot him twice in the head as he played cards at a salon, one of 76 such establishments in Deadwood. McCall was set free after convincing a judge and jury that the shooting was justified by the fact that Hickok had killed his brother. McCall was later rearrested and convicted after it was proved that he had never had a brother. He was hanged. At Mount Moriah, on a sleep slope above the city, the graves of Wild Bill Hickok and Calamity Jane continue to attract visitors to Deadwood.

In response to the unprovoked murder, Deadwood's city leaders set up a town council, built a jail, and appointed Canadian Seth Bullock as sheriff. In 1878 a fire destroyed much of Deadwood's business district. New buildings of brick and stone were designed to withstand future fires. In 1883 a massive flood destroyed most of the original buildings that had withstood the fire. When the town was rebuilt, it established a new identity as a haven for working men and their families. Chinatown continued to flourish, and the Chinese hired two police officers and established a fire-fighting team. Among the lawless, opium dens also flourished. In 1895 Seth Bullock built a large pink and white sandstone hotel, which still stands.

CITY LIFE

Life in cities often proved a challenge to Americans who had previously lived in areas with dispersed populations. Crime rates were high in many urban areas, and many people felt the loss of personal space keenly. Some Americans, on the other hand, enjoyed the excitement of city life, particularly relishing access to greater educational and cultural opportunities. With downtown areas becoming increasingly devoted to business enterprises, more affluent Americans moved away from downtown areas, spawning suburban areas around all major cities. Urban residential areas were often left to the poor, who crowded together in tenements and ghettos. Because many of the poor were immigrants, small pockets of various cultures developed in large cities throughout the United States.

In response to demands to reduce the normal workday from 10 or 12 hours to eight, many Americans were free to enjoy more leisure time. In response, an entertainment industry surfaced to fulfill the demand for diversions and new experiences. More affluent Americans enjoyed lectures, museums, and concerts, many of which were sponsored by various churches. Families also began taking regular vacations for the first time during the Gilded Age. In 1872 Yellowstone, largely in Wyoming, became the first national park. As others were built, state and national parks continued to attract large numbers of visitors each year.

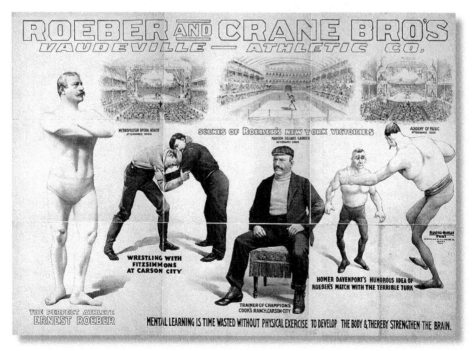

An 1898 poster for Roeber and Crane Brothers' Vaudeville-Athletic Co. advertised wrestling matches as mass entertainment, and promoted physical exercise.

The Great Chicago Fire

On Sunday, October 8, 1871, what became known as the Great Chicago Fire destroyed much of the city. According to traditional accounts, the fire started when Bessie, a cow being milked by Mrs. Patrick O'Leary, kicked over a lantern and set the O'Leary house on 137 DeKoven Street on fire around 9 P.M. In the absence of adequate firefighting equipment, the fire raged out of control, reaching Chicago's business district by 1:30 A.M. and continuing to spread. The fire still blazed the following day when it reached Fullerton Avenue. The fire was finally put out around midnight on Monday by a pouring rain. By that time 300 residents had lost their lives and another 90,000 were homeless. Property damages were evaluated at $200 million.

Recent research into the fire has theorized that the fire was started not by a cow, but by a comet, identified as Biela II, which allegedly set off a number of fires around Chicago on that same night. Writer Mel Waskin, for instance, uses eyewitness testimony to discredit the legend of Mrs. O'Leary's cow, contending that no phenomenon other than a catastrophic comet can explain the fact that stone buildings melted throughout Chicago and hot sand rained from the sky as far away as Wisconsin during the Great Fire.

A Currier and Ives print shows crowds escaping on the Randolph Street Bridge during the 1871 Chicago fire, which destroyed about 40 percent of the city.

The sale of books flourished during the Gilded Age, and so-called "dime novels" and "penny dreadfuls" placed reading matter within the price range of most Americans. Detective novels, westerns, and romantic adventures were perennially popular. In order to keep the memory of these genres alive, Stanford University has made such series as *Boys of America, Happy Days*, and *Beadle's New York Dime Library* available to modern readers via the World Wide Web. The dime novels, which were geared toward young working-class Americans, were available in a variety of locations, including news stands and drug stores. Eight-page "story papers," containing multiple illustrations, targeted family audiences.

A new emphasis on physical activity in the Gilded Age resulted in large numbers of urban Americans taking up activities such as bicycling, walking, and baseball. In some cities baseball clubs were established to give wealthy American males the opportunity to support their favorite teams while they drank alcohol and gambled. Other popular entertainments included vaudeville for the general audience and peep shows for those who sought out more earthy entertainments. While alcohol consumption continued to be high, early reformers had already begun insisting that unlimited access to alcohol frequently produced drunkenness and irresponsibility.

In many areas, April 1 was declared Settlement Day, and urban residents traveled around the city to settle all debts incurred during the previous year. The event also provided ample opportunities for entertainment, and Americans gathered on streets and sidewalks, as well as in banks, stores, and pubs to socialize. During the Gilded Age, fundraising was often combined with entertainment, and bake sales, rummage sales, and bazaars allowed large groups to interact with their families, friends, and neighbors.

WESTERN CITIES

Many American cities that thrived in the Gilded Age evolved from mining towns, including Boise, Idaho, and Helena, Montana. In California, San Francisco, which was the fastest growing city in the late 19th century, became known as the gateway to the American mining industry. Similarly, Denver, Colorado, which had begun life as a trading station, experienced an exploding population. The trend in population surges soon spread to smaller western cities. For instance, in Washington State, the population of Spokane climbed from 350 to 20,000 and that of Tacoma expanded from 1,100 to 36,000.

Most of Denver's early residents lived in farming and mining communities, and city leaders recognized the advantages of providing urban services in outlying areas. As a result, between 1850 and 1880, the city's population grew from a few families to 35,000 residents. By 1890, Denver boasted a population of more than 106,000. Lawlessness thrived in many western cities, providing vast opportunities for gamblers, thieves, and con artists, and for the attorneys who represented them. Even business owners who saw themselves as honest

Buying fish in a market decorated with Chinese lanterns on a Chinatown street in San Francisco, California, in 1906. By this time, Chinatowns existed in multiple cities across the United States.

were quick to take advantage of extensive demands for food, lodgings, and supplies, and prices rose astronomically. San Franciscans, for instance, paid as much as $40 for a quart of whiskey, and eggs sold for $1 each. Because lodgings were scarce, landlords could demand $8 a night for each cot they were able to pack into a single room.

Providing fire fighting services was one of the most important responsibilities for cities of the Gilded Age. Because houses were often built of wood and lit only by candles, fires were common. Once started, fires frequently spread to other areas because of inadequate firefighting capabilities. Fires devastated large areas in both Chicago and San Francisco. Around 40 percent of Chicago was destroyed by fire in 1871. San Francisco was particularly vulnerable to fire because it was largely a city of quickly constructed wooden structures. Between 1849 and 1851, six major fires devastated parts of the city. In May 1851, 22 blocks containing some 2,000 structures were destroyed. Each time San Francisco was rebuilt, distinct architectural styles were used, giving the city a constantly changing appearance.

Urban life was often composed of diverse communities. San Francisco, for example, was composed of a number of communities that represented distinct classes and ethnicities. The population of Telegraph Hill, for instance, was largely Latin American, Italian, and French. Working-class Irish residents populated Potero Hill. Germans clustered on Montgomery Street. Chinatown, still one of the most popular areas of San Francisco, was settled in the mid-19th century on what residents called Sacramento Street. The Chinese referred to the street as *Tong Yan Gai* (China Street) and put up colorful decorations reflecting their own culture. The laundry business attracted many Chinese immigrants. By 1871 there were 2,000 Chinese laundries in San Francisco. After cable cars were introduced in the city in the 1870s, Nob Hill became the home of many affluent San Franciscans.

The growth of western cities such as San Francisco was emblematic of the urbanization of the U.S. population in the Gilded Age because it was driven both by immigration and by native-born workers following the opportunities brought by industrialization. The growth of Gilded Age cities brought their new residents jobs and access to education and culture, but also forced formerly rural people to adjust to crime and cramped living conditions, problems reformers and planners were already at work on. During this period, patterns of segregated communities of the rich and poor and ethnic enclaves in the cities also strengthened and mirrored divisions in the population as a whole.

ELIZABETH R. PURDY
ARTHUR HOLST

Further Readings

Armstrong, Ellis L., ed. *History of Public Works in the United States 1776–1976*. Chicago, IL: American Public Works Association, 1976.

Atchison, Rena M. "The Perils of Unrestricted Immigration." *Annals of American History*. Available online, URL: http://america.eb.com/america/article?articleId=386365&query=cities+1870-1900. Accessed February 2008.

Calhoun, Charles W. *The Gilded Age: Perspectives on the Origins of Modern America*. Lanham, MD: Rowman and Littlefield, 2007.

Daniels, Roger. "Immigration in the Gilded Age: Change or Continuity," Available online, URL: http://www.oah.org/pubs/magazine/gilded/daniels.html. Accessed February 2008.

Klein, Maury and Harvey A. Kantor. *Prisoners of Progress: American Industrial Cities, 1850–1920.* New York: Macmillan, 1976.

Mohl, Raymond A. ed. *The Making of Urban America.* Wilmington, DE: Scholarly Resources, 1988.

———, and Neil Betten. "The History of Urban America: An Interpretive Framework." *The History Teacher* (v.3, 1970).

Monkkonen, Eric H. *America Becomes Urban: The Development of U.S. Cities and Towns, 1780–1980.* Berkeley, CA: University of California Press, 1988.

Monti, Daniel J. *The American City: A Social and Cultural History.* Malden, MA: Blackwell, 1999.

Mumford, Lewis. *The City in History: Its Origins, Its Transformations, and Its Prospects.* New York: Harcourt, Brace & World, 1961.

Perret, Geoffrey. "The Town That Took a Chance." *American Heritage* (v.56, 2005).

Peterson, Jon A. *The Birth of City Planning in the United States, 1840–1917.* Baltimore, MD: Johns Hopkins University Press, 2003.

Reps, John W., "Head Notes: Charles Mulford Robinson, Improvement in City Life: Aesthetic Progress." Available online, URL: http://www.library.cornell.edu/Reps/DOCS/robin_01.htm. Accessed February 2008.

Riefler, Roger F. "Nineteenth-Century Urbanization Patterns in the United States." *The Journal of Economic History* (v.39, 1979).

Rishel, Joseph F. *American Cities and Towns: Historical Perspectives.* Pittsburgh, PA: Duquesne University Press, 1992.

Rose, Julie K. "Welcome to the Fair." Available online, URL: http://xroads.virginia.edu/~ma96/WCE/introduction.html. Accessed February 2008.

Stanford University. "Dime Novels and Penny Dreadfuls." Available online, URL: http://www-sul.stanford.edu/depts/dp/pennies/home.html. Accessed February 2008.

Smith, Carter. *The Riches of the West: A Sourcebook on the American West.* Minneapolis, MN: Lerner, 1992.

Staeger, Rob. *The Boom Towns.* Broomall, PA: Mason Crest, 2002.

Sukkoo, Kim. "Urban Development in the United States, 1690–1990." *Southern Economic Journal* (v.66, 2000).

Warmer, Sam Bass. *The Urban Wilderness: A History of the American City.* New York: Harper and Row, 1972.

Waskin, Mel. *Mrs. O'Leary's Comet, Cosmic Causes of the Great Chicago Fire.* Chicago, IL: Academy Chicago, 1985.

Welsh, Herbert. "A Definite Step toward Municipal Reform." *Forum* (April 1894).

Chapter 6

Rural Life

"The cowboy's life is a dreary, weary one,
He works all day to the setting of the sun."
— Anonymous Cowboy Song

THE GILDED AGE was a time of expansion for the United States, most visibly in the rapidly industrializing cities, but also in rural areas, where agriculture expanded and new areas were settled. The Gilded Age altered rural life for many as the remaining open lands of the country came under cultivation, railroad lines were extended, and the Great Plains were fenced. Life in rural areas improved for some, but large numbers, especially in the south, became trapped in the system of sharecropping and struggled to meet even basic needs.

From 1870 to 1900 American agriculture doubled: the number of farms increased from 2.66 to 5.74 million, their total acreage increased from 407.735 to 841.202 million, and crop production increased proportionally. Livestock nearly tripled, with 24 million cows and 25 million pigs in 1870, and 68 million cows and 63 million pigs at the end of the century. The most dramatic expansion took place in the Great Plains, the last major agricultural frontier, where the 50,000 farms in Kansas, Nebraska, and the Dakotas blossomed into 400,000 farms by century's end. Still mostly wild grasslands at the end of the Civil War, by the start of the 20th century the Great Plains had become the nation's wheat belt and a major source of its cattle.

While the rural population of the country doubled in that time, the urban population tripled, as did the number of cities with a population over 50,000. Fifty thousand may not sound like a significant population to modern readers,

Farmers used smokehouses such as this one to preserve their own meats.

but this was the age before the skyscraper increased population density, before the automobile, subway, and public bus allowed people to live further from their workplaces. In 1870 some of the cities of roughly that size included Lowell, Massachusetts; Charleston, South Carolina; Indianapolis, Indiana; Providence, Rhode Island; and Syracuse, New York.

Thanks to the Second Industrial Revolution, the value of manufactured goods quadrupled over the period, while the value of agricultural products only doubled. Still the Industrial Revolution brought rural residents many benefits as well—not only advances in farming. Barbed wire greatly eased the expense and labor of fencing, and factory-made goods available by mail simplified daily life. Also the hygiene and comfort of indoor plumbing, and easily available clothes, furniture, toys, and tools, generally cheaper and higher-quality than what had been available in the past, made life easier for rural people. The transformation from self-sufficient family unit to nuclear family of consumers was hardly overnight; it took generations. Even in 1900 more than half of a farming family's goods and food were still produced on the farm.

THE FARMER'S TAX BURDEN

Farmers had never been fully self-sufficient and had always needed cash to pay their taxes, but the second half of the 19th century—especially the reforms of Reconstruction and the burgeoning Progressive Era—increased that tax burden through the institution of free public schools, state subsidies to railroad companies, and other government services and debts. Newly restrictive herd and game laws, many of which had been enacted in order to make subsistence difficult for newly freed slaves, were just as harsh to poor rural whites, for whom wildlife may have provided most or all of their meat and protein. This was especially true in the South, where those laws were most likely to have been passed and where most southerners—rural or otherwise—were in debt because of the toll of the Civil War and Reconstruction. Cotton remained the cash crop there and in fact boomed after the war. The new railroads made it easier to get crops to market, and new fertilizers shortened the growing season, making it possible to grow cotton in colder climates.

It took years for the rural south to adapt to a new labor system after slavery ended, and what developed was the system of sharecropping. Under

Barbed Wire

A French invention in the 1860s, barbed wire was further developed in the Gilded Age by various midwestern and southwestern innovators. The major brand was produced by the Superior Barbed Wire Company, which had been founded by sauerkraut-salesman-turned-cattle-rancher Isaac Ellwood. Ellwood first patented his own hand-twisted barbed wire before discovering the superiority of his competitor Joseph Glidden's wire, which was twisted by using a coffee mill. A sensible businessman, Ellwood abandoned his own design and bought Glidden's rather than try to compete with a product he knew was better.

In addition to its military application as a barrier to deter infantry and cavalry, barbed wire allows for fast, cheap, and effective large-scale fencing by unskilled laborers. Wire fences can be rolled up and transported easily, and need fewer tools and manpower for their installation. Unlike traditional fences, they are well-suited to temporary uses and easy to reuse, and they can be manufactured and distributed at a fraction of the shipping cost of a reinforced timber fence. The thick wire is twisted into sharp points at regular intervals and strung between fence posts in lieu of the traditional wooden slats. The pain of the barbs is sufficient to deter livestock and wild animals without doing them real harm, and without requiring that the fence be strong enough to withstand trampling.

Ellwood and Glidden went into business at just the right time. As all those open-range ranchers started to buy up land for diversified fenced-in ranches, there were hundreds of thousands of acres that needed to be fenced in—much of it in the Great Plains, a part of the country defined by its lack of native timber. At the same time, the expansion of the railroads—which passed through private land, much of it home to livestock, in addition to indigenous wild animals—created a huge demand for fencing, since the railroad companies were legally required to fence off the right-of-way in order to keep animals off the tracks. Barbed wire was erected faster even in parts of the country with ample timber, and required less frequent replacement.

Hundreds of barbed wire patents were filed, but Glidden's remained the most successful throughout his lifetime, and he held a number of positions while Ellwood expanded his ranching empire. Their company eventually, through a series of the sorts of mergers and reorganizations typical of the period, became the U.S. Steel Corporation. Barbed wire also reduced the usefulness of the riding horse, which is much more sensitive to the pain of the barbs than cattle. The use of barbed wire across the wide open spaces of the west hastened the obsolescence of the U.S. Cavalry.

The invention of barbed wire with its numerous sharp points led to the rapid fencing of the Great Plains.

Local merchants and mail order outfits supplied items that could not be made on the farm, but if many supplies had to be bought on credit, the debt could lock farmers into a cycle of poverty.

sharecropping—which had been in use with white laborers before the war in Mississippi counties where slaves were scarce—the landowner pays the laborer with a share of the crop. The basic principle of sharecropping is not much different from a salesman working on commission. It was beneficial for landowners during and after Reconstruction because they were cash-poor. But the specific implementation of it was often designed to punish freed African Americans and restore, to as great a degree as possible, the institution of slavery. In order to guarantee that they would have the number of laborers they needed at harvest time and other critical junctures, they often instituted binding contracts requiring a worker to remain with them for a year or more, and since the employer owned the property, they could evict employees at any time. Further, there was little oversight to make sure the sharecropper received the portion of the crop to which he was entitled—and in the case of free African Americans, they had few options if they felt they had been cheated. For an African-American worker to challenge a white employer was to risk not only his job and home, but the prospect of future employment and retribution. Poor whites did not fare much better.

The sharecropper purchased or rented his equipment, draft animals, seed, and fertilizer from the landowner if he could not provide them himself, and few could. Those who did were usually called "share tenants," and were recognized as having limited property rights. If the sharecropper could not pay with cash, he did so by reducing his eventual share of the crop, or going into debt to his employer. Further debt was incurred since the sharecropper would receive no portion of the crop—or his profit from selling it—until harvest, and in the meantime he had to clothe and feed his family. Even those sharecroppers not under long-term contracts were usually forced by circumstance to continue working where they were, even if they had been cheated by their employer and expected to be cheated again.

Still, debt or no debt, mistreatment or no mistreatment, being a sharecropper at least meant steady work, and employers could not cheat everyone, nor deny them everything. It was not a life anyone would choose, except in comparison to the uncertainty of seasonal work, or the slavery that had preceded the Civil War. So for many it was the best available option, and for many African Americans it was at least a step up from where they'd been—just a far cry from what they'd been promised. Like slavery, though, it was a system from which there was rare exit. Sharecroppers could not earn enough to purchase their own land and equipment, and after paying off the debts they'd run up on credit, they rarely had enough cash to do more than pay their taxes and other basic expenses—they lived paycheck to paycheck, year to year, with so little chance of improvement that few even had it in mind.

Instead, their children married young and had children of their own, because the sooner you started a family, the sooner that family could help you with the work. Though young children might be an economic burden, in the long run it paid to have children—the older ones could take care of their siblings, and in the labor-intensive lifestyle of the sharecropper, the labor of teenagers made up for the cost of raising them. They were not expected to send their children to college, and school-age children often left school early or missed substantial amounts of it in order to help with the harvest.

Sharecropping was not limited to the postbellum south. The labor needs of Reconstruction may have blown air on the ember of sharecropping, but it spread quickly across rural America, and not just among existing landowners. New farms were built in the Arkansas and Mississippi deltas, and in Oklahoma and Texas, where Mexican-American farmers were typically the

A family living on a rented farm with six acres of tobacco in Hebbardsville, Kentucky. The boys had delayed school for weeks to help work the farm.

Root Beer

Though it developed at the same time as commercial soft drinks—which were commonly sold as nerve tonics, health remedies, and the like—root beer is a fundamentally rural drink in much the same way that Coca-Cola (first marketed to urban workers in Atlanta) is fundamentally a city drink. Before it was manufactured commercially, root beer was a product made in the home, primarily from ingredients that could be foraged, making it virtually free but for the effort involved.

Like gin, cola, or even beer, root beer consists of a primary flavor note with a number of secondary flavors in order to bolster and accent the main flavor, or to personalize a particular recipe. The key component in root beer is the bark of the root of the sassafras tree, which is easily dug and rubbed off. Typically, the rest of the ingredients include other tree products—such as cherry or birch bark—along with spices, citrus peel, and one or more ingredients from the anise/licorice group. The ingredients are simmered or steeped like tea, or extracted by some other method, depending on preference or family tradition. Alcoholic root beer—which is lower in alcohol than beer or wine—is made by fermenting that root beer brew with sugar and yeast, much like traditional beer. Non-alcoholic root beer is simply combined with carbonated water, or with just enough yeast to naturally carbonate the water without producing significant amounts of alcohol. In both cases, the sweetener is often molasses or some other unprocessed sweetener, which was significantly cheaper and more plentiful for rural Americans at the time.

Alcoholic root beer was often used as a cough syrup or to treat other ailments, much as herbal teas are used medicinally around the world. Both forms were of course also consumed as a treat, and after commercial soft drink manufacture became a major industry, pharmacist Charles Elmer Hires began selling his root beer first as a powder to be mixed at home, and in 1893 as a bottled soda. It was Hires who started calling it "root beer." In American homes, especially in the south, it was often "root tea" or "sassafras tea."

Variants of root beer were made in parts of the country where sassafras is not native. In New England, the inner bark of the birch tree and its distilled sap were used to make birch beer. In the west, the sticky roots of the sarsaparilla vine were used to make sarsaparilla. Both tend to be more minty and cooler than sassafras root beer.

An 1857 poster advertising Bristol's Sarsaparilla framed with a border of sarsaparilla vine.

work force, as well as in the former Confederacy. More confined to the South was the crop-lien system. The war and Reconstruction had left southern landowners and small farmers in debt, and they found themselves relying on credit to a greater degree than before, in order to purchase the goods they needed from local merchants, who, in turn, had often purchased them on credit from wholesalers in northern cities. Since slaves were no longer available as collateral, southern merchants let farmers—and share tenants, and sharecroppers in less frequent cases—promise a portion of their crop, which the merchant then sold at harvest, using the proceeds to pay off the debt and interest.

The goods the merchants were selling were already marked up in price because they had bought them on credit themselves, and the northern wholesalers were not exactly generous with their credit terms. On top of that mark-up, the interest the merchants charged farmers and tenants was as high as 60 percent—and rarely less than a third. These would be criminal amounts today and were often condemned as usury at the time, but landowners kept entering into the agreements because they felt they had no choice—and being in that situation, of course, was an additional motivation to mistreat or take advantage of their sharecroppers. The crop-lien system also affected what the landowner chose to plant. Cash crops were virtually

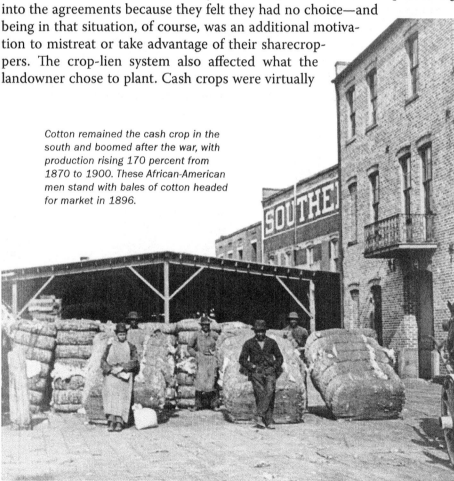

Cotton remained the cash crop in the south and boomed after the war, with production rising 170 percent from 1870 to 1900. These African-American men stand with bales of cotton headed for market in 1896.

all that made sense, in order to maximize the chance of having money left over after paying off debt at the end of the harvest.

In the long run, this situation was untenable. Sharecropping would persist into the 1930s, when New Deal reforms did away with it. But in the Gilded Age, the forced focus on high-profit crops like cotton kept southern agriculture from falling into complete disrepair. Between 1870 and 1900 production of cotton rose 170 percent. It was a nonperishable crop, and suitable for shipping long distances, which meant there were more markets for it than for easily damaged produce with a short shelf life. Many farmers committed to growing cotton or founded new cotton farms in formerly inhospitable areas after the war, when prices were high. Later in the century prices dropped, but they—especially small farmers—tended to stick to cotton anyway, because it was what they knew. The predominantly rural south was hit especially hard by this dependence on cotton. In 1900 the per capita income among southerners was only half that of northerners.

Southern business leaders decried this dependence and correctly predicted its outcome, but the climate, soil, and native parasitic insects of the south are not conducive to raising cattle or grain—the agricultural staples of the midwest, Texas, and the Great Plains—and only toward the end of the Gilded Age had refrigerated freight trains opened up winter markets in the north for southern produce. Southern farmers remained—to a greater degree than their

Crowds of people and tents set up outside a land office the day of a land run in Oklahoma (possibly Guthrie). The settlers were awarded claims in former Native American lands.

northern colleagues, who had a steadier and greater supply of cash—lashed to the hand-plow instead of the tractor, dependent on semicaptive manual labor passed down from father to son. Throughout the period and continuing after its end, southern farms remained smaller on average than American farms as a whole; too small to make their owners prosperous, or even what contemporary Americans would have considered lower middle class. Few farmers in the south were comfortable. They struggled, they expected to struggle, and they had no means to escape their struggles.

FILLING THE EMPTY SPACES
Meanwhile the rest of the country was not yet fully populated, its settlement having not yet caught up to the great expansions of the 19th century. The Homestead Act had been passed in 1862 by President Lincoln, but was slow to have effect. The act gave title of 160 acres of public land (the vast land owned but unused—and in many cases, uncharted—by the federal government) to any white adult who had built on it and farmed it for five years, and was used to encourage Americans to settle the western territories and states by providing opportunity to whoever was willing to work for it. There were a lot of problems with the Homestead Act. In some areas 160 acres was not enough for a viable farm, but it was one of the factors that succeeded in driving people west. Because of irrigation difficulty in so much of the undeveloped area, the 1877 Desert Land Act was further passed to sell land in 640-acre lots at $1.25 an acre to anyone able to irrigate it within three years.

Later—on five separate occasions from 1889 to 1895—the government opened up former Native American lands in what is now the state of Oklahoma, and awarded lots in "land runs," in which the first would-be settler to arrive was given the claim to the lot. The land runs were enormous events. The towns of Oklahoma City and Guthrie, each with a population in excess of 10,000, were created literally in an afternoon. Half a dozen newspapers and five banks opened in Oklahoma City by the end of the next month. Only boom towns surrounding discoveries of gold had ever grown as quickly.

At the same time, the two Morrill Land-Grant College Acts—in 1862 and 1890—transferred federal lands to the individual states in order to establish colleges that "without excluding other scientific and classic studies and including military tactic, [would] teach such branches of learning as are related to agriculture and the mechanic arts." The 1890 act further required that in each state, there be such colleges available to members of all races—whether that meant individual colleges for whites and African Americans, or desegregated colleges. The first act bestowed land and the second distributed cash, hence the term land-grant college for such schools created in the Gilded Age by these acts. In 1887 the Hatch Act dictated the creation of agricultural experimentation stations, at least one in each state, to be maintained by those land-grant schools. These stations were to study problems relevant to their state, in the areas of soil,

In this engraving, men take advantage of a locomotive to shoot a running herd of bison on the line of the Kansas-Pacific Railroad in 1871.

crops, livestock, and other agricultural applications. The resources of the land-grant colleges were used to directly benefit farmers, in large part in response to the many hardships they suffered in these decades.

SETTLING THE GREAT PLAINS

In 1870 the Great Plains were barely settled, compared to the other large regions of the continent. Twenty years later the Census Bureau declared the frontier closed, the country so thoroughly settled that there were no significantly empty spaces left.

Settlement of the Great Plains region was slow to start. Americans and their European forebears had been skeptical of the fertility and viability of such great swaths of land without trees, which was seen as a sign that the region had trouble sustaining plant life. That skepticism preempted any motivation to overcome the region's other obstacles to white settlement. The nomadic Native American tribes of the region posed a greater threat than the village-based tribes of other areas, and so few of the rivers were navigable that transporting goods to and from Great Plains settlements was difficult, expensive, and unreliable, making self-sufficiency even more necessary. The lack of timber made home construction a challenge and limited fuel supply. And everyone heard horror stories about those who did settle there: the grasshoppers that infested homes, eating cloth and grain; the hellish summers and punishing winters; the tedium of breaking through tough Plains sod, knotted together with thick tangles of grass roots, in order to plant; the dry years when the rain barely provided enough water to survive on; the cyclones and blizzards; and the then-millions of wild buffalo that roamed the Plains, a great unknown for the farmer worried about the safety of his crops.

The 19th-century revolution in railroads solved the transportation issue, providing a means faster and often more direct than riverways. The Indian Wars and large-scale buffalo hunting, which reduced herds millions strong to less than 1,000, reduced the indigenous threats. From 1870 to 1900 major campaigns were fought against the Apache, the Comanche, the Modoc, the Lakota, the Nez Perce, the Bannock, the Paiute, the Cheyenne, the Shoshone, and the Ute. While there were major American defeats, the Native Americans were for the most part considered "pacified." These were among the most significant American military campaigns of the era. Their main effect on rural American life was simply to make it more palatable for settlers.

Cattle ranching proved the most notable means of turning grasslands into income. Open-range cattle ranching had been used by Americans settling in Texas in the decades before the Civil War. There was so much excess grassy land that, unlike the ranches in the east that were fenced or penned in, livestock could be allowed to roam free on public and private land. Much of this livestock was—or became in a couple generations—wild, and included cattle, hogs, and horses. Ranches were usually diversified: livestock was ranched and crops were grown as well. Oats and other feed were grown in order to feed the domesticated horses, and ranches were built near year-round streams, but the cattle were allowed to roam wherever they pleased, including on neighboring lands. Cattle were branded with the symbol of their ranch, and every fall and spring the ranch hands gathered together for the roundup. During a roundup, all the cattle were rounded up and separated by brand, with calves born since the last roundup branded by their mother's ranch. Young males were castrated and then the herd was set free again. Steers—castrated males—gain weight

The tools of a cowboy's trade, such as this braided bullwhip used to control livestock, have become icons of the west, along with the romanticized image of cowboys themselves.

BRANDS OF
PIONEER CATTLEMEN
OF MANATEE COUNTY

Cattle were branded with the unique symbols of their ranches, such as these.

more quickly than bulls, and are less rowdy and aggressive.

In the fall roundup, after the herd had had time to fatten up over the lazy summer, a number of steers and mature females, or heifers, were separated from the herd and prepared for the drive to market. Another joint effort involving cowboys from all the ranches, the cattle drive brought the cowboys and their herd from the ranch to a cowtown set up along the railroad so the cattle could be loaded onto train cars and sent to market. The journey could take a few days, in the case of fairly lucky cowboys, or a few weeks through wide-open spaces where the herd was vulnerable to sudden storms, Native American raids, or rustlers. Larry McMurtry's Pulitzer Prize winning novel *Lonesome Dove* is generally regarded as an accurate account of a cattle drive, if not necessarily a typical one. Despite their association with the "Wild West," ranchers and cowboys had little to do with the world of gunslingers, riverboat gamblers, bank robbers, bandits, and Indian Wars. They were fundamentally businessmen, as tied down to their jobs and routines as bankers or salesmen. A cowboy had a day-to-day life that involved more alone time, just a man on his horse surveying the range, than if he worked in a city—but he made up for it at the round-ups and drives.

In this 1917 photograph, a young boy on a horse drives a small herd of cattle and a few calves to town in Lawton, Oklahoma.

Open-range cattle ranching quickly became an important part of the economy and culture of the Great Plains, from which cattle were shipped to St. Louis and Chicago, where meat packers in turn marketed their beef to urban consumers in the east. The modern reliance on beef as a major part of the American diet stems in no small part from this period. Pork and chicken had long been the staples in the south, while seafood was the typical fare in coastal towns from Mobile to Maine. It's no coincidence that the hamburger was invented and popularized in this era, back east.

Plains ranching hit a bump in the late 1880s, when dry summers and freezing winters reduced herds by about 15 percent, with some ranches losing half their cattle. Ranchers began claiming land under the Homestead Act and using it to build farms to grow hay and other feed, rather than depending purely on the open range approach. The Timber Culture Act allowed homesteaders to double the size of their claim if they planted 10 acres of trees, so this also became a common practice. States and towns, meanwhile, flat-out lied in their propaganda promoting their region, claiming special properties to their soil, or a near-magical climate that ensured temperate summers and mild winters—all in an effort to attract more settlers.

By the 1890s, one of the most dramatic expansions of American agriculture was complete. The Great Plains were crisscrossed with railroads and new barbed-wire fences. Those formerly wild grasslands, once inhabited mainly by Native Americans, were now supplying the nation with much of its grain and cattle. It remained to be seen whether this great build-out of farms would prove to be sustainable in the face of changing weather and market conditions, or whether, like sharecropping, it would one day become untenable, forcing settlers to migrate once again.

BILL KTE'PI

Further Readings

Arrington, Leonard J. *The Mormon Experience: A History of the Latter-Day Saints.* Chicago, IL: University of Illinois Press, 1979.

Bogue, Allan G. *From Prairie to Corn Belt: Farming on the Illinois and Iowa Prairies in the Nineteenth Century.* Chicago, IL: University of Chicago, 1963.

Cobb, James C. *Away Down South: A History of Southern Identity.* New York: Oxford University Press, 2005.

Danbom, David B. *Born In The Country: A History of Rural America.* Baltimore, MD: Johns Hopkins University Press, 2006.

Dykstra, Robert. *The Cattle Towns.* Lincoln, NE: University of Nebraska Press, 1968.

Fite, Gilbert. *The Farmer's Frontier: 1865–1900*. New York: Holt, Rinehart, and Winston, 1966.

Flynn, Charles L., Jr. *White Land, Black Labor: Caste and Class In Late Nineteenth-Century Georgia*. Baton Rouge, LA: Louisiana State University Press, 1983.

Foley, Neil. *The White Scourge: Mexicans, Blacks, and Poor Whites in Texas Cotton Culture*. Berkeley, CA: University of California Press, 1997.

Foner, Eric. *Nothing But Freedom: Emancipation and Its Legacy*. Baton Rouge, LA: Louisiana State University Press, 1983.

Frazier, Ian. *Great Plains*. New York: Penguin, 1989.

Lanza, Michael L. *Agrarianism and Reconstruction Politics: The Southern Homestead Act*. Baton Rouge, LA: Louisiana State University Press, 1990.

Malin, James C. *The Grasslands of North America: Prolegomena to Its History*. Lawrence, KS: James C. Malin, 1956.

Sitton, Thad, and Dan K. Utley. *From Can See to Can't: Texas Cotton Farmers on the Southern Prairies*. Austin, TX: University of Texas Press, 1997.

Webb, Walter Prescott. *The Great Plains*. Boston, MA: Ginn and Company, 1931.

Woodman, Harvey. *New South–New Law: The Legal Foundations of Credit and Labor Relations in the Postbellum Agricultural South*. Baton Rouge, LA: Louisiana State University Press, 1995.

Chapter 7

Religion

*"Gimme that old-time religion,
It's good enough for me."*
— Anonymous, classic revival song

THE THIRD GREAT AWAKENING of American history continued throughout the Gilded Age as it had since the 1850s, injecting a religious awareness into many aspects of life. In particular, with the first strains of progressivism becoming stronger, the Third Awakening religious movements focused on worldly concerns, more than personal salvation. Famine, poverty, crime, and corruption were all targeted, and temperance movements found new supporters. Although the period is regarded as particularly active for Protestants, the number of new sects and movements was at least as significant as any activity within the existing groups. Movements like Reform Judaism, the Ghost Dance, and the "Lost Cause" in the south are among the most important of the era.

It was a time of increased intellectualism, not only in the secular world, but among the pious as well. An evangelical preacher from the same part of Massachusetts as Calvin Coolidge and Jonathan Edwards, who had spearheaded the first Great Awakening, Dwight Moody was raised in the liberal Unitarian church, but converted to evangelical Christianity at age 18 and joined the Congregational church. Though he was active throughout the Civil War, it was during an 1872 trip to England that his preaching really came alive, and in fact he had more personal impact abroad than he did in the United States. But back home he founded both the Northfield School and the Northfield Mount

101

A portrait of Dwight Moody, founder of the Moody Bible Institute, in 1900

Hermon School, as well as the Moody Bible Institute on Chicago's North Side. The institute was founded as a center of Bible study to train the laity in revivalism and evangelical belief, and would soon become a major evangelical publisher as well as an educational program.

Charles Russell, who'd been raised in the Presbyterian and Congregationalist churches and had spent his teen years examining Eastern religions after a crisis of faith, was the central figure of the premillennialist Bible Student Movement. In the 1870s he and Nelson Barbour, a Millerite Adventist, published various pamphlets on the imminence of the Rapture and Christ's return. When the Rapture did not occur in April 1878 as the two had predicted, they argued for several years over the implication of their error, with Barbour eventually recanting most of his previous beliefs about prophecy. Russell's ministry grew in popularity, meanwhile, and he published a number of books outlining the future of the world as he had deduced it from Biblical prophecy. By the end of the century, newspapers were syndicating his sermons nationally, helping to popularize premillennialism in the public imagination even as many church authorities criticized his views as heretical, alarmist, or simply unfounded.

In contrast to many of the revivalist figures such as the popular Billy Sunday, Russell's approach was intended to be scholarly. He emphasized not the pageantry of sermons, but a rigid approach to Bible study.

THE GHOST DANCE
The Ghost Dance was a religion that grew out of the Paiute of Nevada and was popularized among the Lakota Sioux. The Nevada Paiute are actually more closely related to the Shoshone than to the southern Paiute, and call themselves the Numu, which like many self-identification terms means simply "the people." One of their spiritual activities was the "round dance," in which the community danced around the leader of the ceremony in a circle, often in combination with trance states and prophecy. They had little contact with white settlers until the middle of the 19th century, when raids, rapes, and retaliations became common. Whites also deliberately introduced smallpox to the Paiute population.

A Paiute man named Wovoka was born in Carson City in 1856, and may have been the son of the assistant of a Paiute prophet named Hawthorne Wodziwob, who preached a message he claimed was given to him by the dead: they would return to their loved ones soon. When Wovoka's father died in

1870, he was taken in by David Wilson, a local rancher and devout Christian, and started using the name Jack Wilson. Little else is known about him until the 1880s. Like Jesus, Wovoka steps out of the picture for the bulk of his youth and coming of age, as he formed a religion for himself that combined elements of the Paiute beliefs he had been raised with and the Christian faith he came to know. His Ghost Dance, inextricably tied to Native American/white relations, is very much a syncretic faith. Syncretic faiths are founded by blending two or more discrete systems, in this case the Native American and Christianity.

At some point in the 1880s, Wovoka began preaching a simple message of love and morality, little different from what would be heard in the pulpits of any small-town church. That changed when he claimed to have received a vision from God during the January 1, 1889, solar eclipse. In the vision Wovoka stood with God in Heaven and looked upon his ancestors living happy full lives, in a beautiful land flourishing with life. God told Wovoka that if the people lived lives of peace and love, they would be reunited with their loved ones in Heaven. God gave him the ritual of the Ghost Dance, and appointed him "deputy of the west," while President Harrison remained "deputy of the east."

Like some early Christians, Wovoka interpreted this Heaven as a state attainable on Earth without needing to die, a holy condition the world could attain. The five-day ritual of the Ghost Dance could sweep away the evils of the world and bring back the golden age. The Ghost Dance was inherently millenarian—concerned with the imminent transformation of the world—like many Christian movements of the time. He began teaching it immediately, focusing mainly on the Paiutes in his area.

The Ghost Dance practice spread to other tribes, losing something in the translation. Somewhere along the way, by the time it reached the Lakota Sioux in the following year, the injunction to peacefully coexist with the whites was lost, and the "washing away of the evil" was interpreted to mean a return to a world before European settlement—and a return of the buffalo. The Lakota also wore Ghost Shirts, which seem to be a Lakota Ghost Dance adaptation of the endowment garments of the Church of Latter-Day Saints, who had also had contact with both the Ghost Dance and the Lakota. Ghost Shirts supposedly protected their wearer from violence, especially gunshots. When

A caricature captioned "A Millerite Preparing for the 23rd of April" shows a man hiding in a fireproof safe in preparation for Christ's return.

Frederic Remington created this illustration of a Ghost Dance of the Oglala Sioux in Pine Ridge, South Dakota, in 1890.

the federal government broke up the Sioux reservation into smaller reservations, violating an earlier treaty, performances of the Ghost Dance increased, worrying some agents of the Bureau of Indian Affairs. More troops were deployed, and at the end of 1890, Sioux leader Sitting Bull was arrested for failing to stop the Ghost Dance. A Sioux man shot at the arresting soldiers, prompting retaliation. Sitting Bull and his son Crow Foot were both killed in the firefight.

Less than two weeks later, the Wounded Knee Massacre was started when a deaf Sioux man refused to relinquish his weapon to American soldiers and a weapon was discharged accidentally in the struggle. Over 150 Sioux, mostly women and children, were killed, along with 25 American soldiers.

THE LOST CAUSE

The Lost Cause of the Confederacy is sometimes described as a literary movement in the south following the Civil War, but "literary" is unnecessarily limiting. It would be more accurate to describe it as a philosophical trend, a notion pervading southern thought, as southerners of all stripes struggled with regional identity and the need to reconcile the values of the traditional antebellum society with the changes wrought by Reconstruction and especially the defeat of the Confederacy. Southern identity had been so tied up in religion—as religion in the south had been so inextricably linked to regional

Christian Youth Groups

Sunday school services focusing on introductory Bible studies and moral teachings had been offered by some churches since the 18th century, and in the 19th century were especially common among Protestant churches near the frontier, where Native American, immigrant, or illiterate children might not otherwise be exposed to church teachings, and in urban areas where the laity was well-to-do and children could be expected to be literate and able to read the Bible rather than having it read to them. As the Industrial Revolution brought more and more young men to the cities and set them to working six-day weeks, and as more and more secular activities became available to them on the weekends, churches began to reach out to them, and to the demographic most likely to falter in church attendance: young people past the age of children, but too young to have children of their own.

While many of these outreach groups had an educational aspect, they were more than an extension of Sunday school. The Young Men's Christian Association (YMCA) and the Young Women's Christian Association (YWCA) were both Christian youth outreach groups at their inception, and continued to operate as such throughout the 19th century. Beginning in the 1880s with the Young People's Society of Christian Endeavor, evangelical Christian youth groups became more and more popular, and young men and women would remain an important part of the evangelical demographic from that point forward. These groups tended to refer to themselves as youth ministries, and oftentimes went a step beyond Bible study to conversion efforts and youth-run social events open to the public in hopes of attracting new members to the word of God. Collegiate campus ministries, often student-run, would follow in this mold.

Later in the decade, more denominational youth groups followed, particularly the Lutheran Luther League and the Methodist Epworth League, both of which were formal associations of local denominational youth groups spread out across the country. After-school programs were sometimes offered, as were trips to other cities or to Europe organized and chaperoned by adult sponsors. Youth groups meshed well with revivalism, as both played into the overlap between religion and entertainment, and youth groups provided a permanent base for young people after a revivalist preacher got them fired up.

identity—that the Lost Cause was as much a religious movement as anything else, even when it was not phrased that way.

Was a victory over the southern military a victory over southern ideals? Southern clergy described southerners as a chosen people, and the south as God's favored America. The north was not simply less moral, it was less religious and the center of atheism and secularism. The Lost Cause

An image of Robert E. Lee used on a tobacco label in 1865 captured southern sentiments.

portrayed Confederate heroes like Robert E. Lee, Stonewall Jackson, and Jefferson Davis as moral paragons compared to the moral bankruptcy of the northern aggressors. They, and Lee especially, acquired an almost divine mystique, the saints and martyrs of the overwhelmingly Protestant south. A famous anecdote reported in Charles Reagan Wilson's examination of the Lost Cause, *Baptized in Blood*, has the niece of Father Abram Ryan, a Lost Cause poet, explaining that the Yankees had crucified Jesus Christ.

Joining and participating in a local church became part of the southern obligation, marking the south and the southerner from the growing secularism of the north. Southern churches were generally less interested in social reforms than those in the north, and more interested in the state's enforcement of moral law. Heaven and Hell, good and evil, became more important, not less, in this prolonged period of self-examination for the southern nation. Classic hymns were even rewritten to incorporate references to the Confederacy, and the southern Methodist church adopted "Let Us Pass Over the River, and Rest Under the Shade of the Trees"—a hymn named for the last words of Stonewall Jackson.

Since southerners believed God was on their side in the Civil War, the Confederacy's loss raised the question of how a just cause could fail in a universe governed by an omnipotent deity. One of Ryan's poems, "The Prayer of the South," offers one answer:

> *Ah! I forgot Thee, Father, long and oft,*
> *When I was happy, rich, proud, and free;*
> *But conquered now, and crushed, I look aloft;*
> *And sorrow leads me, Father, back to Thee.*

REFORM JUDAISM

The Reform movement began among Jews in Germany in the early 19th century, incorporating a good deal of secular and Protestant-like thinking into Judaism. In fact, with the abandonment of mandatory circumcision, the denial of divine inspiration of the Torah, and the change in appearance to ceremonies and vestments, many of the changes were explicitly modeled after German Protestant practices, to help Jews fit in better. Some charged that Reform aimed to de-emphasize the Jewishness of Jews, and with Judaism as tied into ethnic identity as matters of faith, this led to a great many disagreements. Many Reform Jews denied that Jewishness held any ethnic meaning: Germans were Germans, they would have it, and Judaism was a choice that could be adopted or abandoned, like Protestantism or liberalism.

Reform Judaism explicitly rejected the idea of a Jewish state, and generally disassociated itself from the idea of the personal Jewish messiah, preferring to speak of a messianic age, a figurative interpretation of the old prophecies. None of these ideas were new, and many of them had been advanced time and again throughout the Middle Ages—but the Reform movement was organized, dedicated, and (relatively speaking) popular, and its demystifying approach, emphasizing moral be-

A man and a boy celebrate the Jewish New Year in New York City in 1907.

havior over supernatural proscriptions, was very compatible with prevailing 19th-century attitudes.

Many of the German immigrants to the United States were Reform Jews, and throughout the middle of the 19th century their numbers had grown, especially in urban centers. One by one various Jewish congregations began to adopt Reform principles, and the center of Reform shifted to the United States. The Philadelphia Conference (1869) and the Pittsburgh Conference (1885) outlined the tenets generally recognized by Reform theology, followed by the Central Conference of American Rabbis that was formed soon after:

- The potential for moral and philosophical truths in other religions, though Judaism presented "the highest conception of the God-idea."
- The validity of monotheism, and its compatibility with modern scientific research. Reform Judaism was arguably the first major denomination to explicitly and sincerely embrace the scientific community of the 19th century and beyond, with no qualifiers or appeals to divine inspiration.
- The moral laws of Mosaic tradition, as applicable to modern civilization.

- The lack of necessity for the many Jewish laws regarding ritual purity, which were dismissed as a product of their time, no longer relevant to the modern Jew.
- The nature of Judaism as a religious community, participation in which is a matter of personal choice, not an ethnic identity.
- The validity of some Christian and Muslim ideas.
- The immortality of the soul and the divine nature of the human spirit. Beliefs in bodily resurrection, Hell, and an afterlife of reward or punishment were all condemned as ideas from outside Judaism.
- The duty of a religious community to do its best to address the problems of its contemporary society, such as the maintenance of justice and the root causes of poverty.

THE ETHICAL CULTURE MOVEMENT

The son of a German rabbi, Felix Adler founded the Ethical Culture Movement (ECM) in 1876, and like many of the non-revival movements of the time, its focus was on ethics. All religions included ethical truths, ECM said, and following ethical principles was the path to wisdom and enlightenment. ECM makes no appeals at all to supernatural authority and no claims about the existence of a god or gods or any afterlife—an unusual stance in Western religions (but common among Eastern ones). Ethical Societies were established to fulfill the same basic functions as churches, providing Sunday sermons and moral instruction, as well as providing a center for charitable efforts and ceremonies like weddings. The first Ethical Society, in New York City, established the country's first free kindergarten. Other Ethical Societies were instrumental in advocating legal aid services, the National Association for the Advancement of Colored People (NAACP), and organizations to aid and protect children. Adler was a member of the Civil Liberties Bureau, the precursor to the American Civil Liberties Union.

THROW YOUR BURDENS ON THE STRONG WHO CAN BEAR THEM. DO NOT COME WITH THIS SPECIOUS PLEA IN THE NAME OF HUMANITY. TO ALLOW LITTLE CHILDREN TO BE EXPLOITED FOR THE SAKE OF THE FEW DOLLARS WHICH THEY CAN CONTRIBUTE TO THE FAMILY EARNINGS.

FELIX ADLER.

A plea to parents to keep their children from child labor from Felix Adler around 1913.

THE LATTER DAY SAINTS

After Reconstruction, Congress became more active in pursuing the abolition of polygamy, which many Republicans before the Civil War had spoken of in the same breath as slavery. The 1874 Poland Act shifted jurisdiction over the prosecution of polygamy to federal courts instead of the Mormon-controlled territorial

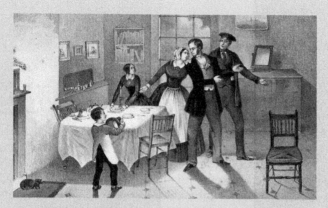

This 19th-century print dramatizes a wife's attempt to influence her husband to stay home rather than drink.

Temperance

Though not all Christians were opposed to alcohol, and not all temperance supporters were motivated by religious reasons, there was a general link between the two. Temperance activists were nearly always women, who in most parts of the country had been the "guardians" of religion throughout most of American history, especially in the south, where men could drink and carouse and brawl on Saturday nights so long as they were tamed and brought to church by their wives on Sunday mornings. Even when women were not moral authorities—men were still the ostensible church leaders—they were the custodians of those authorities' mandates. And few ministers would have been foolish enough to go against the grain of the women in his parish.

Many Temperance groups formed during the 19th century, from the political (the National Prohibition Party and the suffragist/abolitionist American Temperance Society) to the fraternal (the Templars of Honor and Temperance was a secret society devoted to abstinence). But like abolition, plural marriage, and abortion in the next century, the issue was not explicitly religious, but drew religious proponents.

The Women's Christian Temperance Union, perhaps the largest and most influential temperance group in the years leading up to Prohibition, linked Temperance with family values. Drinking threatened the safety and welfare of the family, and was the common cause of domestic violence. Christian groups tended to use the same logic to describe drinking as they did to describe sin, though there is no specific Biblical proscription against alcohol itself. This rendered "drinking in moderation" as nonsensical as "theft in moderation." Interestingly the Women's Christian Temperance Union did not accept Catholics or Jews as members, though it had no specific denominational affiliation. The violently anti-Catholic revival of the Ku Klux Klan also supported Temperance.

The Preacher and the Crusader

Henry Ward Beecher (1813–87), the preacher, and Anthony Comstock (1844–1915), the crusader, crossed paths during the Gilded Age and epitomized some of the forces at play in American religion.

An anti-obscenity advocate responsible for decades of censorship in American letters, Comstock began his decency crusade in the early 1870s, launching raids against Manhattan booksellers who sold erotic books "under the table." He made his first major case in 1872 in his attempt to suppress an account of an affair between minister Henry Ward Beecher and one of his parishioners. His tactic was to employ an 1864 law prohibiting the distribution of vague "obscene" publications and images through the U.S. mail. Comstock requested a copy of the book using a pseudonym, and then filed suit. Comstock acted as a national censor for the next 40 years, trying to suppress the work of authors including D.H. Lawrence and Theodore Dreiser.

Beecher was the brother of famed author Harriet Beecher Stowe who wrote *Uncle Tom's Cabin*. Beecher was seen at his best in the pulpit and he was known as a preacher of love without peer. Thousands of worshipers flocked to Beecher's enormous Plymouth Church in Brooklyn. Abraham Lincoln (who said of Beecher that no one in history had "so productive a mind") was in the audience at one point, and Walt Whitman visited him. Mark Twain went to see Beecher in the pulpit and described the pastor "sawing his arms in the air, howling sarcasms this way and that, discharging rockets of poetry and exploding mines of eloquence, halting now and then to stamp his foot three times in succession to emphasize a point."

The 1875 adultery trial in which Beecher was accused of having an affair with a married woman (and parishioner) was one of the most famous American trials of the 19th century. According to historian Michael Kazin, "His career took place during what one scholar has called the Protestant Century, when an eloquent preacher could be a sexy celebrity, the leader of one or more reform movements and a popular philosopher—all at the same time."

courts that had previously abstained from enforcing the law. The 1882 Edmunds Act further prohibited "bigamous cohabitation," so that no proof of marriage was required for prosecution. Polygamous marriage ceremonies were held in secret, and documentation was difficult, if not impossible, to obtain.

However the federal government overplayed its hand. The act also barred polygamists, including former polygamists, from holding public office or

A Mormon man posed on a porch with his six wives in 1885, after Congress had passed two acts trying to end the practice of polygamy, but before it attempted to dissolve the church entirely.

voting, required juries of non-polygamists in order to keep their influence out of the courts, and nullified prior elections in the Utah Territory, requiring new elections to be held under these new conditions. The act was also used against single people and monogamously married couples who simply believed in the plural marriage doctrine. In response Mormons stood fast by the practice of polygamy, and that same year, Brigham Young's successor John Taylor announced that polygamy would henceforth be required of all priests. Five years later, Congress went even further. It forcibly dissolved the Church of Jesus Christ of Latter-Day Saints, replaced local judges with federal judges, put the federal government in control of school curriculums, and denied women the right to vote (they had been granted suffrage by the Utah government in 1870).

To provide some sense of the scale and seriousness of the conflict over polygamy, half of the inmates of Utah prisons at this time had been convicted of polygamy or polygamous cohabitation. Many church leaders lived in hiding, communicating with their community by secret means. If not for the example so recently and so tragically set by the Confederacy, secession might have been a serious proposition. John Taylor died in 1887, and his 80-year-old successor, Wilford Woodruff, remained in hiding from federal marshals while making overtures to the Republican Party in hopes of finding some compromise. The federal government would not yield.

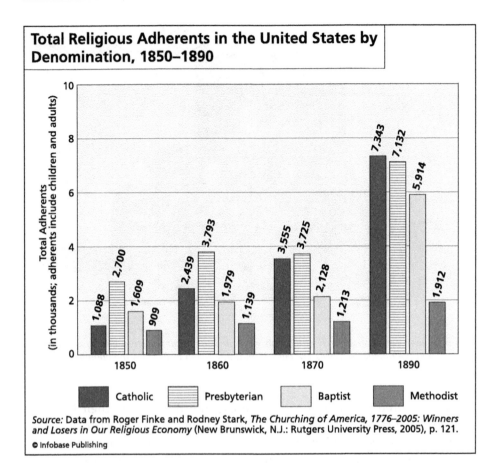

Total Religious Adherents in the United States by Denomination, 1850–1890

Total Adherents (in thousands; adherents include children and adults)

1850: Catholic 1,088 | Presbyterian 2,700 | Baptist 1,609 | Methodist 909
1860: Catholic 2,439 | Presbyterian 3,793 | Baptist 1,979 | Methodist 1,139
1870: Catholic 3,555 | Presbyterian 3,725 | Baptist 2,128 | Methodist 1,213
1890: Catholic 7,343 | Presbyterian 7,132 | Baptist 5,914 | Methodist 1,912

Legend: Catholic, Presbyterian, Baptist, Methodist

Source: Data from Roger Finke and Rodney Stark, *The Churching of America, 1776–2005: Winners and Losers in Our Religious Economy* (New Brunswick, N.J.: Rutgers University Press, 2005), p. 121.

© Infobase Publishing

Finally in 1890 Woodruff issued a manifesto, the intent and import of which he said had been revealed to him divinely, in the manner such manifestos were to Mormon leaders, ending the practice of plural marriage. The church would no longer sanction them, and members were explicitly directed to abide by the marriage laws of their state, wherever in the world they might happen to be. Existing marriages were not required to be dissolved. Most likely, Woodruff hoped that the church would continue to fight for the right to plural marriage, and it's possible he continued to support secret marriages, either as an individual or in his position as the president of the church. But in any case, this was the concession the federal government needed. Bit by bit over the rest of the decade, Utah's rights were restored, and the territory was granted statehood in 1896, which Woodruff happily lived to see. Utah promptly reinstated the right of women to vote, in its first year of statehood.

Though most of the Mormon splinter groups founded in the first generation were short-lived, some continued to thrive in the Brigham Young era and beyond. The Church of Christ was founded by David Whitmer, one of the three witnesses to Joseph Smith's golden plates, and who claimed to be Smith's proper successor. The Church of Christ, sometimes called the Whitmerites to differentiate them from other groups called the Church of Christ, was reorganized in Richmond, Missouri, in the 1870s. Whitmer published several pamphlets, and the small church survived his 1888 death, publishing its own version of the Book of Mormon as well as a regular religious periodical called *The Return*.

The Church of Jesus Christ remained consolidated in Kansas and Pennsylvania, with a claim of succession from Joseph Smith through Sidney Rigdon (his running mate in his presidential campaign, and as important to the early Mormons as Smith) and his follower William Bickerton. Unlike many Mormon groups, especially those that formed after 1890, the Church of Jesus Christ rejected plural marriage—as well as all scriptures other than the Bible and the Book of Mormon. *Doctrine and Covenants* and *The Pearl of Great Price*, books associated with other Mormon movements, were explicitly condemned, and church structure more closely resembled that of many Protestant groups.

The Community of Christ formed as Mormon groups organized themselves around Joseph Smith III, who had still been a child when his father died. The community remained in Illinois, and over time developed a number of theological differences from Brigham Young's church, notably, the absence of *The Pearl of Great Price*, the use of Joseph Smith's Inspired Version of the Bible instead of the King James translation, and a rejection of plural marriage and the various temple ceremonies of the Latter-Day Saints church.

CONCLUSION

During the Gilded Age, the country was growing more diverse, and diverse religious viewpoints abounded. Immigration helped the number of Catholics in the country rise to levels never seen before. Other groups, such as Native Americans, Jews, and Mormons, underwent important changes and reforms in the era. Despite internal turmoil, some religious movements in the late 19th century came to look outward and share concerns over social issues, such as famine, poverty, racism, child labor, crime, and corruption, that were affecting the lives their followers and, most visibly, the many new urban dwellers. Religious-minded reformers, like those before them who worked for the abolition of slavery, proposed social reforms such as temperance, and would only grow more vocal in the Progressive Era.

BILL KTE'PI

Further Readings

Arrington, Leonard J. *The Mormon Experience: A History of the Latter-Day Saints*. Chicago, IL: University of Illinois Press, 1979.

Bordin, Ruth. *Woman and Temperance: The Quest for Power and Liberty, 1873–1900*. Philadelphia, PA: Temple University Press, 1981.

Brown, Dee. *Bury My Heart at Wounded Knee*. New York: Owl Books, 1991.

Givens, Terry L. *The Latter-Day Saint Experience in America*. New York: Greenwood Press, 2004.

Hardy, B. Carmon. "That 'Same Old Question of Polygamy and Polygamous Living:' Some Recent Findings Regarding Nineteenth and Early Twentieth-Century Mormon Polygamy." *Utah Historical Quarterly* (v.73/3, 2005).

Jensen, Richard. *The Winning of the Midwest, Social and Political Conflict, 1888–1896*. Chicago, IL: Chicago University Press, 1971.

Kaplan, Dana Evan. *American Reform Judaism: An Introduction*. New Brunswick, NJ: Rutgers University, 2005.

Kehoe, B. Alice. *The Ghost Dance: Ethnohistory and Revitalization*. New York: Thompson Publishing, 1989.

Meyer, Michael A. *A Response to Modernity: A History of the Reform Movement in Judaism*. Detroit, MI: Wayne State University Press, 1995.

Nadell, Pamela S. *Conservative Judaism in America*. New York: Greenwood Press, 1988.

Osterreich, Shelley Anne. *The American Indian Ghost Dance, 1870 and 1890*. New York: Greenwood Press, 1991.

Robinson, Stephen E. *Are Mormons Christians?* New York: Bookcraft, 1991.

Chapter 8

Education

"In schools for children, it ought to be a
leading object to teach the art of reading."
— *McGuffey Reader* 1879

ONGOING INDUSTRIALIZATION IN the Gilded Age created the need for a better-educated population, and the education system was revamped and professionalized during this time. Urban areas gained more high schools to serve the emerging working class in the cities. At the same time, vocational training grew, new universities were founded, and education extended to more people than before, including some women. Like other advances in the Gilded Age, however, not everyone benefited. Nonwhite students were routinely denied access to better facilities, and some of the patterns of discrimination that solidified in the Gilded Age would plague the U.S. educational system for generations to come.

THE TEACHING PROFESSION

In 1870 the National Teachers Association changed its name to the National Education Association. This indicated a shift toward recognizing education as a profession that demanded formal training. The Normal School movement that had begun in the 1830s continued its growth. Normal Schools trained teachers to view their job as a calling, and trained them not only in teaching methods, but also in manners and morals. In contrast, schools of education within universities tended to focus more on a functional view of teaching as based in the acquisition of specialized knowledge within a discipline. This difference

Plessy v. Ferguson and Education

The particulars of the 1896 *Plessy v. Ferguson* case dealt only indirectly with American schools, but its general effect was to institutionalize educational injustice for generations of African Americans.

The case centered around a man named Plessy who was traveling through the state of Louisiana. He claimed to be "seven-eighths Caucasian and one-eighth African blood," and in New Orleans, he boarded a train car restricted to white passengers. When the conductor asked him to leave and he refused, he was arrested and jailed. An 1890 Louisiana law allowed for "equal but separate accommodations for the white, and colored races" on railroads. Lower Louisiana courts upheld the right of the parish to arrest Plessy on the basis of violating this law. When the case came before the Supreme Court, the plaintiff argued that his constitutional rights, as guaranteed by the Thirteenth and Fourteenth Amendments, had been violated.

The majority of the court justices ruled that it was acceptable for states to legislate enforced separation of the races, based on past legal interpretations of the wording of the Fourteenth Amendment of the Constitution. In citing cases for support, the majority opinion mentions the establishment of "equal, but separate" schools "for colored children" in Boston and the District of Columbia. A specific case mentioned is *Roberts v. City of Boston* (1849), in which it was decided that school committees could establish "separate schools for children of different ages, sexes and colors, and that they might also establish special schools for poor and neglected children." The irony of basing a decision upon this state statute was that it was enacted well before the passage of the Thirteenth and Fourteenth Amendments.

The justices drew a distinction between political equality and social equality: "If the civil and political rights of both races be equal, one cannot be inferior to the other civilly or politically. If one race be inferior to the other socially, the constitution of the United States cannot put them upon the same plane." In arguing that the courts did not have the power to impose social equality upon the states, the Supreme Court opened the doors to almost 60 years of social segregation based on race. It would take many years, and dozens of court cases, before it was demonstrated that separate public facilities were inherently unequal by nature of their standards for racial segregation.

In his dissenting minority opinion, Justice Harlan refused to overlook the implications of the segregation of citizens by race: "What can more certainly arouse race hate, what more certainly create and perpetuate a feeling of distrust between these races, than state enactments which, in fact, proceed on the ground that colored citizens are so inferior and degraded that they cannot be allowed to sit in public coaches occupied by white citizens? That, as all will admit, is the real meaning of such legislation as was enacted in Louisiana." Harlan's words proved prophetic and the case was overturned in *Brown v. Board of Education* (1954).

in approaches to training created a gap between Normal School students trained by teachers with classroom experience, and college teachers trained in systematic and quantitative approaches to education. Over time the collegiate approach won out, as its proponents had both the prestige of college degrees and the benefit of educational research to back their arguments.

Societal expectations that women were best suited to care for children contributed to the feminization of the teaching profession. By the turn of the century the vast majority of elementary teachers were women, but the vast majority of school administrators, board members, and college faculty members were men. This gender gap within the teaching profession dem-

Five students and a teacher posed outside this school in Brush, Colorado—95 students were absent and working in beet fields.

onstrated a tension between increased professionalism of the teaching field and stereotypical gender roles of the time. As women took charge of more classrooms, questions of authority and oversight led to an increasing divide between teachers and school administrators. College teacher training programs often refused or sharply limited admission to female applicants, fragmenting the educational workforce. By the turn of the century, school administrators in many areas of the country paid male teachers more than females, on the simple justification that men would not accept such low pay for their labor.

After the Civil War ended, increasing numbers of public schools became coeducational, simply because it was the most economical option in running the schools. The flood of immigrant students led to school overcrowding and poor working conditions for teachers, especially in urban areas. Over the next three decades the National Education Association (NEA) became an important force in improving the living and working conditions of teachers. However its membership included relatively few classroom teachers before the turn of the century. Most NEA members were principals, superintendents, and district and state education employees. Teachers' rights would become an important focus of the organization by the early 1900s.

All teachers were expected to adhere to strict codes of behavior, dress, and personal morality. Women were not allowed to continue teaching after they were married. The average salary for a female teacher in 1880 was $54.50 a year; for male teachers, it was $71.40. In Springfield, Missouri, in 1881 teachers

A teacher presents a lesson on Native American culture to a class of white students in an elementary school in Washington, D.C., in 1899.

were required to start each day of school with readings from the Bible. Other school board rules of the time indicate that teachers were expected to govern students' speech and conduct, to win parents' cooperation in running their classrooms, and "to govern their pupils by the moral influence of kindness, and by appeals to the nobler instincts of their nature."

THE SCHOOL DAY

In the late 1800s, most students began school in the early morning, took a midday break to return home for lunch, then returned to school until late afternoon. In some schools, students brought their lunches from home if they lived more than three miles away. The school year schedule was sporadic, and was often based on agricultural cycles in rural communities. In Waterford, Virginia, in the 1880s, students attended a one-room schoolhouse. They studied reading, writing, penmanship, spelling, math, history, and geography. They used small notebook-sized blackboards called "slates" to practice their writing and spelling. School supplies were very expensive, and students would often use a single book and pencil for a full school year. Students also wrote using fountain pens and inkwells during penmanship practice. *McGuffey's Readers* were popular textbooks from which students learned practical and moral lessons. Maps and globes were used to learn about world geography. Students of all ages were expected to do chores around the schoolhouse to learn practical skills in addition to their academic lessons. Cleaning the blackboards, sweeping, chopping wood for the stove, and cleaning erasers were among the typical tasks of schoolhouse maintenance.

Teachers used several forms of classroom management to work effectively with students of multiple ages and ability levels. When a classroom contained multiple grade levels, a teacher usually designated an area of the classroom to work actively with a small group of students while the rest worked quietly on other lessons. Some activities crossed grade levels, such as singing, reciting the "Pledge of Allegiance," and penmanship practice. Other activities were more ability-specific, such as math. Students who progressed quickly were given work appropriate for their abilities in a subject, regardless of age; the "grade level" of a student was relatively unimportant. Discipline methods were left largely up to individual teachers. They ranged from verbal reprimand to the wearing of "dunce caps" and even to corporal punishment. Special activities at school might include recitation days, spelling bees, or "lightning" math and geography contests.

TALES OUT OF SCHOOL: CHILD LABOR

When examining education during this time period, it is important to remember that not all children had access to education, even though in most areas of the country a free public education was available. By the 1890s the Industrial Age was in full swing. Factories, mines, mills, and agriculture were so eager for unskilled labor that several industries employed children full-time. In 1890 1.5 million children under the age of 15 were working in full-time industrial positions for wages.

In the first few decades of the 20th century, laws would be passed in every state mandating public education for children up to the age of 16. Before the turn of the century, though, children were prized workers for several reasons. They worked for less pay than either men or women. Their families needed their incomes to survive. Their small size, particularly

A young African-American boy selling the Washington Daily News *on the street.*

Boys working with various tools in a shop class at the Tuskegee Normal and Industrial Institute in Alabama in 1902.

their small hands, made them ideal workers in spaces crammed with intricate machinery. Child employees were easier to manage, less likely to unionize, and thus less likely to strike or cause work stoppages. Thus children were put to work instead of going to school, in both urban and rural areas. Educational opportunities for these children were in short supply.

Social reformers like Jacob Riis, Florence Kelley, and Jane Addams made these children's hardships public and campaigned for reforms in child labor laws. Riis, in his 1890 book *How the Other Half Lives*, described child labor wages in New York City: "Sixty cents is put as the average day's earnings of the 150,000 [child workers], but into this computation enters the stylish 'cashier's' two dollars a day, as well as the thirty cents of the poor little girl who pulls threads in an East Side factory, and, if anything, the average is probably too high." Still those wages were essential to their families' survival. Working-class children were viewed as important contributors to the family economy, whether on the farm or in the factory.

MANUAL EDUCATION

An educational idea that grew increasingly popular after the Civil War was the philosophy of "manual education." The precursor to today's vocational education, manual education was intended to train students to use their hands and eyes, in addition to the intellect. The first manual school in the country, the St. Louis School of Manual Education, opened in 1879. It was founded by

Booker T. Washington

One of the most prominent African Americans of his generation, Booker T. Washington (1856–1915) was the founder of a school in Alabama that became Tuskegee University. Born a slave in Virginia in 1856, he and his family were freed by the Emancipation Proclamation of 1865. He became a house-boy for the Ruffner household in his early teens. Mrs. Ruffner allowed him to pursue an education in his spare time, and he excelled in school. At the age of 16, he enrolled in a new Normal School, or teachers' college, in Hampton, Virginia, which had been founded for the purpose of training African-American teachers. After completing his studies there, he attended Wayland Seminary in Washington, D.C. By the age of 25, he had completed sufficient training to become the principal at a new Normal School planned to open in Alabama.

The Tuskegee Normal and Industrial Institute opened in 1881. In addition to training African-American teachers, the school also provided vocational training in areas including carpentry, farming, cabinetmaking, printing, and masonry. Washington's educational philosophy emphasized such practical education with the goal of putting African Americans into the jobs available to them at the time. His philosophy contrasted with W.E.B. DuBois's philosophy of a classical liberal-arts education for a "talented tenth" of African Americans.

In an 1895 speech, the "Atlanta Compromise," at the Cotton States Exposition, he outlined his beliefs regarding education and race issues. He believed that through education, emancipated African Americans could raise themselves morally, spiritually, and economically, without assistance from government. In his view, becoming educated and economically independent were the most important steps African Americans could take toward social equality: "It is important and right that all privileges of the law be ours, but it is vastly more important that we be prepared for the exercise of these privileges. The opportunity to earn a dollar in a factory just now is worth infinitely more than the opportunity to spend a dollar in an opera-house." Washington believed the rights to work and to own property were more important than voting rights for African Americans in the short term. Washington's position made him unpopular with African-American activists who wanted to push for more radical changes in law and government, since they worked actively for an end to Jim Crow laws and other tools of legal segregation.

Booker T. Washington addressing a large crowd outdoors.

Calvin M. Woodward, and only admitted boys. In manual schools, classes in mechanical drafting, shop work, and woodworking were added to the usual classwork in math, reading, and science. Rather than train students for specific technical careers, manual classes were intended to introduce students to the use of basic tools that they could use in a variety of industries.

By giving students an introduction to basic mechanical principles, and an understanding of basic engineering, proponents argued that manual school

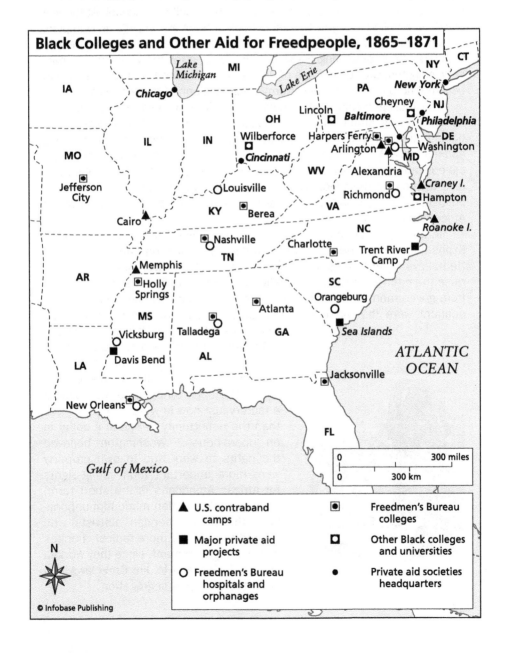

Black Colleges and Other Aid for Freedpeople, 1865–1871

U.S. contraband camps

Major private aid projects

Freedmen's Bureau hospitals and orphanages

Freedmen's Bureau colleges

Other Black colleges and universities

Private aid societies headquarters

0   300 miles
0   300 km

ATLANTIC OCEAN

Gulf of Mexico

N

© Infobase Publishing

students would be better prepared for working-class careers. Critics of the manual school movement believed that this type of education catered to industry and would interfere with the proper role of schools, which was to provide intellectual and moral development. Public discussion of the manual education movement marked the beginning of an era in education in which educators and philosophers would struggle to define the proper mission of public school education. Should schools prepare students for practical careers, develop their intellectual capacities, teach them the responsibilities of citizenship, or get involved in their moral and religious formation? As public schools

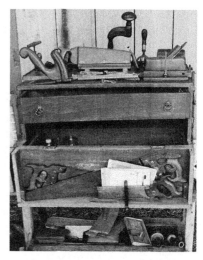

Manual schools gave students training with woodworking tools, among other practical skills.

opened and expanded across the country, the arguments over their missions and goals continued into the 20th century and beyond.

HIGHER EDUCATION: UNIVERSITIES AND COLLEGES

The Land Grant Act of 1862, the First Morrill Act, was put into effect during the 1860s and 1870s as land-grant colleges were formed across the states and territories for agricultural and mechanical arts education. Most of these land-grant colleges today are now public state universities. The Land Grant Act did not preclude classical liberal arts education, but instead emphasized the need for higher education that included training "to promote the liberal and practical education of the industrial classes on the several pursuits and professions in life." The recognition that advanced skills and methods were needed created new opportunities in the world of agricultural and technical trades. As the country continued to industrialize, men who could improve the design of farm and industrial equipment and increase production efficiency were in great demand.

Women's colleges continued to expand in number during these three decades. Although more opportunities were provided for higher education, the majority of colleges and universities remained closed to women. Between 1870 and 1900 women's colleges founded in the northeast included Wellesley (1870), Bryn Mawr (1885), and Barnard (1889). Most of these colleges began as "female seminaries," but eventually distanced themselves from Christian theological grounding. Their curriculum varied widely. Some were meant to offer the same academic rigor as men's colleges, while others served primarily as

Early Childhood Education and Industrialization

In the last third of the 19th century, public school education generally began around the age of six. In Europe educators such as Germany's Friedrich Froebel and Switzerland's Johann Pestalozzi began working with young children in the hopes of influencing their success in future years. Froebel believed that children's moral development could be influenced through controlled play, especially when they were very young. Pestalozzi tested his educational ideas first in an orphanage and later in two schools, where he generated the theory that teachers should work with young children to help them develop "accurate and intelligent observation of common objects and the forces of nature." While these theories were taking root in Europe, in the United States, early childhood education would develop first out of economic necessity; it would take until the 1920s for educational theories to be developed and tested in U.S. kindergartens.

The first attempts at early childhood education in the United States were private "infant schools," which first emerged in the early 1800s. These schools opened in conjunction with nearby factories dependent on female workers. At the beginning of the industrial era, women's labor was seen as useful or even essential to the economy, particularly in urban areas. In the 1820s working-class parents took advantage of the schools in order to become dual-wage-earning families. Opposition from social and church leaders in the 1830s, though, led to the schools' closure. Different reasons were given for opposition to early childhood education. Some thought that attending "infant school" caused too much mental stimulation, which could lead to mental illness in adulthood. Others wanted to preserve traditional gender balance within households, and believed that mothers belonged at home with their children.

Infant schools became primarily for poor children of working mothers, and most decreased rapidly in quality, becoming waystations for basic care. Some state governments even provided pensions so that mothers of young children would not have to work. Most of the infant schools closed by the end of the 1830s. These closures did not drive working-class women back into their homes, as many had hoped. Instead working women were left to patch together their own care and education arrangements for children under the age of six. Traditional gender arrangements in which mothers stayed in the household and cared for the children largely persisted in middle and upper-class households through the Civil War era.

During and after Reconstruction, private kindergartens and nursery schools opened across the United States, with the goal of providing early childhood education to children too young for public schooling. These schools differed from the infant schools of the 1820s, since their primary pupils were upper-class white children. These schools focused on basic skills training with the aim of preparing students to learn reading and writing.

ladies' finishing schools. Catholic and Protestant churches in various regions of the country also founded women's colleges to meet the educational needs of the growing population. In the south several colleges opened that specifically targeted African-American women. Bennett College in North Carolina, founded in 1873, and Spelman College in Georgia, founded in 1881, remain open today.

The New England Association of Schools and Colleges (NEASC) was founded in 1884. Until that time, the question "what is a college?" had no clear answer. With the explosion of colleges and universities founded in the second half of the 19th century, it became necessary to establish definitions for various types of colleges, and standards for accreditation. Accreditation is a peer review process in which an institution evaluates its educational goals, standards, and mission, and then seeks outside judgment to confirm that it is achieving those goals and that its standards are equal to comparable institutions. The NEASC was the first of several regional accrediting associations that assessed member institutions, pinpointed their strengths and weaknesses, and made suggestions for improvement. A college could win accreditation status for a period of seven to 10 years, after which it had to go through the process again to prove it was maintaining its quality. Other regional accrediting associations organized across the country. The end result was an improvement in the quality of higher education, as colleges worked to meet peer review standards for their faculty, facilities, and curricula.

In 1890 the Second Morrill Act was put into place, providing funding for state agricultural and vocational colleges across the southern states. During the period of secession, southern states were ineligible to receive the land-grant

This photo of seven young Native American children, some still in traditional garb, was taken before they entered school at the Hampton Institute in Hampton, Virginia, in 1899.

Native American students in a sewing class at the Bismarck Indian School in North Dakota after the turn of the century.

benefits of the First Morrill Act of 1862. The funding for this bill enabled 16 historically African-American colleges to become land-grant public schools, including Alabama A&M University, Southern University and A&M College, and Virginia State University.

NONWHITE STUDENTS AND EDUCATIONAL ACCESS

In 1875 Congress passed the Civil Rights Act, barring racial segregation in all public accommodations. That act was later ruled unconstitutional by the Supreme Court in 1883. Much educational policy concerning the education of racial minorities would be tested through the state and federal court systems. As the south emerged from the Civil War and struggled through Reconstruction, the racism underlying post-slavery tensions became evident in the redesign of public school systems. African-American children were sent to public schools with comparatively few resources, low-quality facilities, and poorly trained teachers. Although schools were scarce at first in most areas of the south after Reconstruction, the ex-slaves' huge demand for learning, literacy, and the chance at a better life created a clear need for more schooling. Northern-trained teachers were sent to the south throughout Reconstruction to aid in educating this newly eligible population. When Reconstruction ended in 1876, though, many of these well-intentioned efforts came to an end, as their funding sources dried up. In Georgia, for example, estimates are that less than 10 percent of eligible African-American children could actually attend public schools after the end of Reconstruction, in spite of laws mandating their attendance.

In the mid-1870s reservation schools were funded by Congress and established on Native American reservations to educate tribal members. These schools had the goal of assimilating Native Americans through English-only education and Christian indoctrination. The day schools were unsuccessful, and by the late 1870s, reservation and off-reservation tribal boarding schools were developed. The reformers believed that separation of children from their parents and from their tribes would result in the quicker acquisition of English skills, acquisition of a Christian moral framework, and elimination of tribal languages and religious practices.

The boarding schools required students to live away from their families 12 months a year. Upon arrival, the students were given new haircuts and new names, and forbidden to speak their tribal languages. Native boarding school education focused on reading, writing, and practical skills such as sewing, cooking, and washing clothes. In the summers the girls were forced to be domestic servants for local European-American families, while the boys worked as unpaid farm laborers. It would take until the 1920s before Native Americans were declared U.S. citizens, and the practice of forcibly separating children from their parents would end.

Immigrants to the United States from China and Japan also faced huge obstacles to full participation in society. In 1882 Congress passed the Chinese Exclusion Act, which suspended immigration rights for ethnic Chinese people for 10 years. The Chinese Exclusion Act was renewed every 10 years until 1902, when it was extended indefinitely. The law was finally repealed in 1943.

CHAUTAUQUA MOVEMENT

The Chautauqua movement was an adult education movement with Christian religious overtones, highly popular in the late 19th and early 20th centuries, and is still in a form of operation today. The Chautauqua movement brought entertainment and culture to rural communities, with speakers, teachers, musicians, entertainers, preachers, and experts of the day. Former President Theodore Roosevelt was quoted as saying that the Chautauqua movement is "the most American thing in America." Lectures were the main service of the Chautauqua movement. Topics included current events, travel, and stories, many with a dose of comedy. The most popular Chautauqua speaker was William Jennings Bryan, with his populist and evangelical message that addressed topics such as temperance. Christian instruction, preaching, and worship were an integral part of the Chautauqua experience. The Chautauqua movement was founded by Methodists, but being nondenominational was a Chautauqua principle from the start, and prominent Catholics also took part.

CONCLUSION

While the U.S. educational system suffered growing pains in the last decades of the 19th century, these struggles would prove to be just the start. The country's population continued to rise and education expanded further. The arguments over the mission of public schools and what constituted fairness in education that began in earnest in the Gilded Age would never cease being relevant, and even central to the nation's identity.

HEATHER A. BEASLEY

Further Readings

Adams, David Wallace. *Education for Extinction: American Indians and the Boarding School Experience 1875–1928*. Lawrence, KS: University Press of Kansas, 1995.

Anderson, James D. *The Education of Blacks in the South, 1860–1935*. Chapel Hill, NC: University of North Carolina Press, 1988.

Barton, Rhonda. "Native Students Balancing Two Worlds." *Northwest Education* (v.9/3, 1994).

Berube, Maurice R. *American School Reform: Progressive, Equity, and Excellence Movements, 1883–1993*. Westport, CT: Praeger Press, 1994.

Coleman, Michael. *American Indian Children at School, 1850–1930*, Jackson, MS: University Press of Mississippi, 1993.

Gitlin, Andrew. "Gender and Professionalization: An Institutional Analysis of Teacher Education and Unionism at the Turn of the Twentieth Century." *Teachers College Record* (v.97/4, 1996).

Grosenbaugh, Richard. Transcription of 1881 Springfield, Missouri School Board Rules for Teachers. Available online, URL: http://richgros.com/Education/Rules.html. Accessed May 2007.

Kliebard, Herbert M. *The Struggle for the American Curriculum 1893–1958*. New York: Routledge, 2004.

National Association of State Universities and Land Grant Colleges. Available online, URL: http://www.nasulgc.org/Default.htm. Accessed May 2007.

Newman, Mark. *Agency of Change: One Hundred Years of the North Central Association of Colleges and Schools*. Kirksville, MO: Thomas Jefferson University Press, 1996.

Riis, Jacob. *How the Other Half Lives: Studies Among the Tenements of New York*. New York: Penguin Classics, 1997.

Plessy v. Ferguson, 163 U.S. 537 (1896). Available online, URL: http://www.findlaw.com. Accessed May 2007.

Saracho, Olivia N. and Bernard Spodek. "Children's Play and Early Childhood Education: Insights from Educational Theory." *Journal of Education* (v.177/3, 1995).

Schickedanz, Judith A. "Early Education and Care: Beginnings." *Journal of Education* (v.177/3, 1995).

Washington, Booker T. *Up From Slavery*. New York: Signet Classics, 2000.

Chapter 9

Science and Technology

*"Machinery is now recognized as
essential to cheap production."*
— David A. Wells

THE FINAL DECADES of the 19th century are remembered largely in terms of the growth of the steel industry and the railroads, and the development of the great combinations of companies known as trusts that dominated entire industries. While it is true that the Gilded Age was the time of Andrew Carnegie and Cornelius Vanderbilt, it was also the time of Thomas Edison and Nikola Tesla, when electricity first found practical application beyond the telegraph. While heavy industry may have been the most visible aspect of Gilded Age science and technology, the more subtle development of electricity laid the scientific and technological foundations of the 20th century. And seemingly unnoticed, the seeds of the digital age were planted in the solution of a constitutional dilemma. The Gilded Age was a time of contrasts and contradictions, struggling to retain the genteel culture of the 19th century even as technological change propelled it toward the 20th century. Great wealth stood amid crushing poverty, shameless in the contrast between rich and poor. But at the same time people were beginning to ask questions about the best way to live, planting the seeds of change.

THE NEW STEEL NATION

The Gilded Age marked the beginning of a new kind of steel industry. The steel industry of the Civil War era was based upon the Bessemer converter

Workers rest on construction apparatus for one of the Brooklyn Bridge's four woven steel wire supporting cables. The steel was made to very high quality specifications for the time.

and primarily produced rails for the growing web of railroads that bound the far-flung nation together. While the Bessemer converter was notable for the speed with which it turned great volumes of pig iron into steel, that very speed was also a grave limitation. Bessemer steel was not high-quality, and while it was adequate for the railroad, it lacked the strength to substitute for wrought iron and cast iron in structural applications.

By the last decade of the 19th century, a new steelmaking process was imported from the newly united German Empire. The Siemens process used an open-hearth furnace with a system of gas recirculation, known as a regenerative furnace, to cook the iron into steel slowly, rather than in a single enormous blast of compressed air as in the Bessemer process. The resulting steels had far greater strength, which made them suitable for rolling into the I-beams of structural steel.

Several factors were driving America's cities toward vertical growth. Particularly in New York, built on an island, prime city real estate was becoming increasingly scarce, and thus expensive. As a result, builders grew increasingly interested in making efficient use of the vertical dimension. The development of the safety elevator by Elisha Otis, and its subsequent improvement by the company he founded to make it suitable for commercial

The Brooklyn Bridge

Although the leaders of New York City were stubbornly resistant to the innovative building technologies introduced by the Chicago school of high-rise construction, they welcomed a new and innovative method of constructing bridges. The concept of the suspension bridge was not new. The Inca Empire had built footbridges across enormous chasms in the Andes by suspending them upon cables of thick rope. In the industrial age it became possible to produce large suspension bridges supported by cables of woven wire and capable of carrying multiple lanes of vehicular traffic.

Detail of the Brooklyn Bridge showing the connection of smaller cables to a main suspension cable.

In 1870 John Roebling, a German-born engineer who developed a system for spinning wire rope on site, accepted the commission to build a suspension bridge across the East River, connecting Brooklyn and Manhattan. He had previously been successful in building a suspended aqueduct, but this project was far more daunting. The towers that would support the cables had to be built in the water of the East River, necessitating the construction of the largest wooden caissons (pressure vessels used in construction) ever built. Furthermore, the supporting cables would be made of steel wire, with some of the most demanding specifications for the quality of material to that time.

The construction of the Brooklyn Bridge seemed cursed at times. More than two dozen workers died in the process of building the bridge, and scores more were left crippled. Roebling himself died of tetanus as a result of having a foot crushed in the course of construction. His son Washington Roebling took over the project, only to be left disabled by decompression sickness. He convalesced in an apartment overlooking the East River and supervised the bridge's construction with the aid of a telescope, while his wife Emily served as his liaison officer on site.

When it opened on May 24, 1883, it was the longest suspension bridge in the world. Its main span measured 1,595 ft. (486 m.), and its total length including approaches was 6,532 ft. (1,991 m.). Every dimension, from the thickness of its four cables of woven steel wire to the height of its two granite towers, was record-setting. Later architects would break all of those records, but the fact that the Brooklyn Bridge did it first and has remained in service since that time has made it a historic milestone.

The Home Insurance Building, with two additional floors that were added later.

and office spaces, as well as industry, made vertical growth feasible.

In Chicago the first modern skyscraper was constructed, the nine-story Home Insurance Building. The first floor was to house a bank, while the upper stories were to be subdivided into many small offices. Because artificial lighting was still considered grossly inferior to natural lighting, it was necessary to find a way to keep the supporting piers as small as possible in order to permit large window apertures. There was simply no traditional means of construction with brick and stone that could produce a structure that tall without piers so thick that the windows would be tiny slits like those in a fortress.

Architect William Jenny provided the answer with an internal steel frame in which the lintels over the windows would be extended to connect with the vertical supporting columns on either side. He was able to subdivide the weather-related expansion and contraction of the metal columns into a manageable amount for each section. While this steel framework supported the floors, the stonework or brickwork of the exterior walls became a skin hanging from them rather than an integral part of the structure. This change permitted the exterior cladding to become purely ornamental, suspended from the external skeleton.

Chicago architects soon developed the steel-skeleton high-rise into a distinctive school of architecture. However in New York City this style of architecture met with intense hostility. New York building codes continued to mandate thick external walls, even in buildings with internal structures of steel, creating a "cage" style of construction in which the walls bore their own weight while the steel skeleton only bore the weight of the internal contents. So little allowance was made for the strength of this new material that it accrued only a weak economic advantage. Even as late as 1900, architect William Birkmire struggled to convince New York city planners that these thick walls were unnecessary, and in fact were an impediment to building tall steel structures.

THE TELEPHONE

While the steel industry was rapidly changing the skylines of America's cities, a Scottish immigrant who had made his life's work the teaching of the deaf was busy changing the way Americans communicated over a distance. The telegraph had become an important part of the American landscape, and many businesses depended upon it or such telegraph derivatives as the stock ticker and the gold indicator. However it was generally accepted that the human voice would remain out of the realm of electric transmission.

Alexander Graham Bell's interest in the nature of sound grew from his efforts to teach deaf people audible speech, using a system of "visible speech" developed by his father. However his work was expensive, and the charities of the day concentrated mostly on providing basic maintenance for the disabled, rather than rehabilitation services. As a result Bell was interested in inventions that might bring him money to further his work.

By the second half of the 19th century, the problem of multiplexing telegraph lines was becoming a consuming interest to the telegraph companies. If one could make each wire carry several signals at once, the bandwidth of the telegraph company's existing network would be multiplied for far less money than stringing the equivalent number of additional lines. Thomas Alva Edison, still a young man of unproven reputation, had developed early duplex and quadruplex telegraph systems, able to send two and four messages respectively, but further multiplexing eluded him.

Bell, using his knowledge of sound, was hoping to develop a system that would place each signal on a different frequency, a concept known as the harmonic telegraph. Throughout the middle of the 1870s, Bell had struggled to build his device with the assistance of Thomas A. Watson, a skilled machinist. Their work was spurred on by the knowledge that Elisha Gray, an engineer at Western Electric, was working on similar theories. While adjusting the reeds

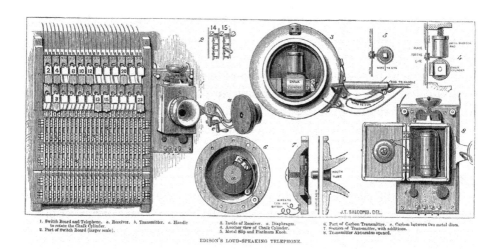

1. Switch Board and Telephone. a. Receiver. b. Transmitter. c. Handle
   to rotate the Chalk Cylinder.
2. Part of Switch Board (larger scale).

3. Inside of Receiver. a. Diaphragm.
4. Another view of Chalk Cylinder.
5. Metal Slip and Platinum Knob.

6. Part of Carbon Transmitter. a. Carbon between two metal discs.
7. Section of Transmitter, with additions.
8. Transmitter Apparatus opened.

EDISON'S LOUD-SPEAKING TELEPHONE.

Thomas Edison found a solution to the problem of a commercially viable telephone receiver with his carbon-button transmitter, shown in the telephone diagram above, along with a switchboard.

of the experimental apparatus, Bell happened to pluck one of them and was astonished to hear the same note being produced at the other end of the system. If his apparatus could transmit a tone, might it be possible to make it produce more complex sounds, even a recognizable human voice? The harmonic telegraph was abandoned in favor of a new idea, which would become the telephone.

For months their work produced only vague sounds. The rhythm of speech could be recognized, but nothing intelligible. On the basis of those preliminary results he filed for a patent, which was allowed on March 3, 1876. However a working device had yet to be realized. On March 10, 1876, Bell and Watson were working on a new transmitter design. By some accident Bell splashed some of the acid from the apparatus onto his sleeve. In his astonishment, he called out, "Mr. Watson, come here. I need you." The words, captured by the instrument in his workroom, were transmitted to Watson's room with astonishing fidelity. For the first time, a recognizable human voice had been transmitted.

However Bell's device, with its messy and potentially dangerous cups of acid, was not practical for consumer use. Were the telephone to have been used like the telegraph, by expert operators, it would have been acceptable, but Bell envisioned a device that would enable people to communicate over a distance from the privacy of their own homes. For the first commercial telephone service, inaugurated in 1877, he developed a magneto system that was marginally acceptable. However it used the same unit for both speaker and receiver, necessitating the user moving it from mouth to ear as the conversation went back and forth. Furthermore the reception was extremely poor, with so much static that once the novelty value of the telephone wore off, it would soon lose its charm.

The solution to the problem of a commercially viable telephone receiver was ultimately provided by Edison, who developed the carbon-button transmitter. Small and compact, it could be manufactured cheaply and reliably, allowing telephone receivers to have dedicated speaker and microphone elements. Soon a small industry sprang up of kerosene lamps burning continuously for the sole purpose of collecting lampblack in their chimneys to be formed into carbon buttons. Carbon-button microphone technology proved so satisfactory that it would be the primary telephone receiver material for nearly a century.

THE PHONOGRAPH

Bell's work on the telephone also inspired Edison to work on a device of his own. Recalling his early work in recording telegraph signals for ease of transcription, he began to wonder if a technology similar to that of the telephone might make it possible to not merely transmit the human voice, but capture it for posterity. From this work came the phonograph, and in early December of 1877 he demonstrated it to the astonishment of his loyal laboratory assistants.

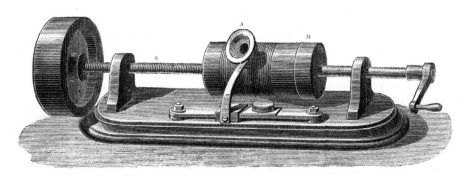

This early Edison cylinder phonograph recorded sounds on the rotating cylinder when one turned the crank on the right.

The original Edison phonograph was a primitive device, employing a layer of tinfoil wrapped around a cardboard cylinder as the recording surface. To record, one mounted a blank cylinder upon the device and turned the crank while speaking loudly into it. The diaphragm would cause the stylus to engrave the tinfoil with a helical groove representing the vibrations of the sound waves. To replay it, one then put the stylus at the beginning of the groove and turned the crank. If the crank was turned at the same speed as it had been during the original recording, the reward was hearing one's own voice speaking from the mechanism. Edison, ever the practical joker in spite of his growing reputation as a wizard of invention, enjoyed shouting back at his own recordings as he played them during public demonstrations.

Not only were the early cylinder records fragile, but they had so little capacity that they could hold only a brief song or poem. As a result of these limitations, the search began for a more robust medium for recording. Because of the fragility of stretched tinfoil, a thick coating of wax soon took its place, although it too was susceptible to damage. On a hot day one's entire collection of sound recordings could easily melt into uselessness. Furthermore cylinders took a great deal of space to store, much of which was air volume. A more compact storage medium was highly desirable.

Even as early as 1877, while Edison was still working on the initial concept that would become the phonograph, he briefly entertained the idea of recording on a flat disk with spiral grooves on each side. However it proved far more difficult to develop a mechanism to move the stylus in a spiral, while maintaining the smooth rotation of the turntable upon which the disk rested. As a result he became increasingly wedded to the cylinder phonograph, and continued to cling to it even at the turn of the century when practical disk record players began to appear. It was an unfortunate pattern of obstinacy that would be repeated at several points in the life of an otherwise eminently practical man.

THE LIGHT BULB AND ELECTRIC MOTOR

With the success of the phonograph, Edison's associates suggested that he could profitably turn his inventive talents to electric lighting. At the time the most common forms of artificial illumination involved combustion, producing wan, flickering flames with their attendant smoke and fire hazards. The arc light used electricity to produce a brilliant white light suitable for illuminating streets, but its glare was too powerful for any but the largest of indoor venues. If one could find a way to subdivide that fierce light into small units comparable to a gas lamp, but without its hazards, one could reap enormous profits. Edison set to his work with a will in 1878, predicting that he would develop a working electric lamp within a year.

The actuality proved far more frustrating, for while Edison had the basic theory down pat, the practicalities proved more difficult. The problem lay in finding a filament that would glow without burning through long enough to be useful to the consumer. In typical Edison fashion he tackled the problem by systematically examining every possible fiber until he found one that lasted in 1880. By that time, many of his backers were rapidly losing patience with his promises that failed to deliver.

Once Edison had a working light bulb, he set forth in the 1880s to create an entire electrical system in order to use it. He quickly realized that it would not be practical to run pairs of wires from the central generator to each lamp individually, particularly if one were to electrify an entire neighborhood rather than a single home such as his early efforts with the mansion of J.P. Morgan. As a result Edison developed the system of feeder circuits to distribute electricity to individual buildings, where it could be further subdivided into smaller circuits.

Even as Edison was enjoying success with electric illumination, Nikola Tesla was struggling with the problem of developing a practical electric motor. Michael Faraday had demonstrated that, just as one could generate electricity by moving a magnet through a coiled wire, one could also use electricity passing through a coiled wire to deflect a magnet from its usual north-south orientation. By extension one could use this phenomenon to turn a motor, thus using electricity not only to create light, but also to do work.

Just as the realization of the electric light bulb had been frustrating to Edison, the practical electric motor proved elusive. Early electric motors used commutators and brushes to keep the motor turning when alternating current reversed itself, but these lost energy through friction and sparking. Tesla believed that if only he could find a way to utilize alternating current directly, he could create a new kind of motor that would be far more efficient, and could be built far larger than previously thought possible.

While Edison solved problems by throwing everything conceivable at them until something stuck, Tesla preferred to work the theory through in his head until he was satisfied with it, and only then construct the realization of his ideas. However, the electric motor proved a difficult problem for even his formidable

Electric Currents

The success of Edison's electric light bulb and Tesla's polyphase electric motor led to a rapid expansion of the electric industry. That expansion led to ferocious acrimony over the form the new electric grid should take. Edison was a firm believer in direct current (DC). To his mind, DC was a safe, friendly current suitable for use in homes, while alternating current (AC) was a treacherous system that should be restricted only to industrial applications, if used at all. Edison was firmly convinced that AC was a killer.

Tesla's motor depended upon the ever-shifting direction of AC for its efficiency and versatility. Furthermore, AC had major technical advantages, particularly in long-distance transmission. With a DC distribution system, electricity could not be transmitted more than a mile before resistance losses made it impractical. As a result, a complete DC power grid would require a small generating station be located every few city blocks, requiring a small army of fuel trucks to supply them. By contrast, AC could be generated in bulk wherever it was most economical, shipped across the country via high-voltage lines, and then stepped down to appropriate voltages for household use.

As the question of which current should become the standard became heated, it became increasingly personal in Edison's mind. He could not forget that Tesla had left his laboratory to work for Westinghouse. Edison raised alarms about the safety of alternating current and set forth to prove his allegations about AC by using it to kill a series of animals. He also designed the electric chair as a means of executing condemned criminals with electricity. Although Edison was actually an opponent of the death penalty, he would not pass up any opportunity to portray AC as a killer. Despite problems, the electric chair became a standard method of execution for decades to come, until replaced by lethal injection. In the end, all Edison's efforts to portray AC as a killer lost to the simple fact that AC lent itself to economies of scale. Once the Niagara Falls hydroelectric plant came online and could transmit AC all the way to New York City, DC was permanently relegated to those few applications where portability requirements made a power cord impractical.

EXECUTION BY ELECTRICITY, SHORTLY TO BE INTRODUCED IN N. Y. STATE.

On August 6, 1890, convicted axe murderer William Kemmler became the first person executed by electric chair—on the third try.

The three direct current generators at the power station of the Pratt Institute in Brooklyn, New York, date from 1900 and are among the oldest steam-powered generators in the United States.

intellect to solve. In 1880 he endured a devastating psychological breakdown in which he became hypersensitive to even the slightest sound, yet his mind raced ahead on his dream of a motor without commutators and brushes.

In 1882 while Tesla was walking in a park, he finally realized the solution. He grabbed a stick and drew a diagram in the dirt, the first realization of an electric motor that would use alternating current. In order to actualize it as a practical system, Tesla needed backers. His search brought him to America, where he briefly worked for Edison. However that pairing ultimately failed, and he instead found a more amicable backer in the form of George Westinghouse, an industrialist who had built his fortune on his air brakes for railroads and was looking for ways to invest his wealth in further invention. Tesla was able to convince Westinghouse that the polyphase motor was the foundation of an entire electrical system, one that was worth substantial investment.

THE DIGITAL COMPUTER

The invention of the digital computer is commonly ascribed to Charles Babbage. Although in the "Analytic Engine" he described the first general-purpose digital computer, it remained a theoretical construct. Lack of funding, along with harsh limitations on the materials and machine tools available in Victorian England, made it impossible to build a working model. As a result the invention of the first practical computer would fall to an American.

As 1890 approached, the United States government faced a vexing problem. By law a census of the American population had to be taken every 10 years in order to reapportion congressional representation. It was written into the Constitution, so there was no getting around it. But the 1880 census had taken years to tabulate by hand, to the point the results were not available until it was almost time to take the next census. Worse, between natural increase and immigration the country's population had nearly doubled in the meantime. Clearly something had to be done to rectify the situation.

At the behest of John S. Billings, who had been a major official in the 1880 census, Herman Hollerith, a patent lawyer with an engineering background, began to investigate ways of mechanically tabulating the 1890 census. Because Hollerith left few records of the procedures by which he developed the tabulator, it often appears that it sprang fully-formed from his imagination, needing only the services of a skilled machinist to construct a working machine. There is evidence that his development path involved several false starts. For instance, he originally planned to encode the census information in the form of holes punched on a long roll of paper. He may have been inspired by the various methods used in automatic telegraphs, or the player pianos that were appearing on the market. The difficulties of such a system soon became obvious, and he looked for a method of storing data that would facilitate extracting any portion at need, without having to reel through an entire roll of paper tape.

He finally settled on punched cards, since stacks of cards could be subdivided or recombined to examine trends within subsets of data. However there is no evidence that he was inspired by Babbage's never-completed Analytical Engine, or even by the jacquard looms that inspired Babbage.

Nikola Tesla as a young man. He won the battle over the use of alternating current and developed the polyphase motor.

Instead Hollerith appears to have taken the idea of punched cards from the practice of certain train conductors of punching holes in certain locations on tickets to create a "punch portrait" of the ticketholder in order to combat fraud. Hollerith saw his cards as creating "punch portraits" of each person enumerated in the census.

The machine that would actually read the cards and tabulate the results was an electromechanical system, a notable jump from Babbage's purely mechanical system. The cards were read by a system of retractable pins that could pass through the card where holes had been punched, connecting with a corresponding cup of mercury, creating a circuit that advanced the hand on a dial in the back of the machine one notch. Although each card had to be fed into the reader manually, the Tabulator still enabled skilled operators to process census data far more rapidly than with hand tallies.

In 1886 Hollerith staged the first practical test of the Tabulator by processing vital statistics records for the Department of Health. This demonstration proved such an outstanding success that Hollerith was praised by the American Public Health Association. His concept proven, he produced several other Tabulators that were installed in other locations, including the New York City Department of Health. As a result of these successes, he was able to secure the contract for the 1890 census.

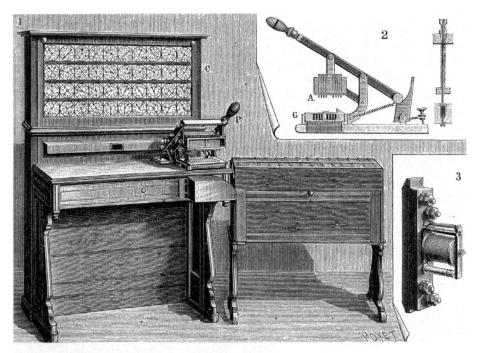

Herman Hollerith's punch card Tabulator was used for the 1890 census and leased for other purposes. IBM, Inc. is a direct descendant of his Tabulating Machine Company.

Dr. John Harvey Kellogg

The Gilded Age also marks the beginning of the modern science of diet and nutrition. Although diet reformers such as Sylvester Graham had preached better health through diet before the Civil War, their theories were based on ideas similar to the ancient Greeks' notion of the four humors. Hot and spicy foods were to be avoided because they aroused the animal passions, while plain foods were believed to foster virtue and self-restraint.

Dr. John Harvey Kellogg changed all that with the development of his sanitarium in Battle Creek, Michigan. Unlike his predecessors, he did not rely upon received wisdom about virtuous and vice-breeding foods. Instead he developed a system of laboratory kitchens in which to systematically test foods in search of the most healthful combinations.

Kellogg's theories were primitive, since he had only a hazy notion of the roles of carbohydrates, fats, and proteins in nutrition, and none at all of vitamins and minerals. But more important than the knowledge he possessed was the method by which he obtained and examined information. For the first time, dietary reform could progress on a rational basis rather than that of superstition and faddism.

Already Hollerith was thinking in the long-term. Rather than merely work for the census, he leased his machines. As a result, he was able to position himself and his company to take advantage of commercial possibilities for the data manipulation techniques his invention allowed. Unlike Babbage's Analytical Engine, the Tabulator was not a true general-purpose computer. However it had one enormous advantage over the latter: it was buildable with the technologies existing at the time. Hollerith was able to prosper even after short-sighted accountants at the Bureau of the Census decided to abandon his company for later censuses in favor of in-house tabulation. Shortly after the turn of the 20th century, the Tabulating Machine Company merged with two other companies to create International Business Machines (IBM), which would become one of the first pioneers in practical general-purpose computing technology.

THE CAMERA

Although photography was originally developed in the 1840s, for the next several decades it remained the province of the professional and the dedicated hobbyist. The collodion-based wet-plate process required immediate development, lest the emulsion dry and the image be lost. Thus only a person with darkroom skills and access to the necessary equipment could take photographs.

George Eastman developed a method of photography that depended not upon collodion, but upon a gelatin that could be stored for extended periods after exposure. However, it still had the limitations of a fragile glass plate. After numerous experiments, Eastman found a way to impregnate a roll of paper with two layers of photographic gelatin. This "American film" could be wound on a roll, which could be advanced by a mechanism that would expose each frame in turn.

In 1888 Eastman introduced the Kodak, the first point-and-shoot camera based upon his American film. It was a sealed product, which the user returned to Eastman's laboratories when the 100 frames were exposed. At the laboratories skilled darkroom technicians removed the film, developed it, and returned the photographs along with the camera, reloaded with fresh film. Armed with a user-friendly camera, the upper and middle classes took to amateur photography with striking enthusiasm, capturing a wide variety of images of ordinary life, which have since proved invaluable for historians.

DISSATISFACTION AND CHANGE

The wealth fostered by the industrial growth and technological innovation of the Gilded Age made it possible to look increasingly beyond the immediately necessary. People began to question whether workers should have to toil long

Inexpensive mass-produced "Brownie" box cameras from the early 20th century allowed amateurs to create their own good-quality photographs.

Improved optics assisted major advances in the medical field in the late 19th century. A microscope from 1880 (right) and a four-optor opthalmascope from 1874 (above).

hours in horrible conditions, or whether the wealthy and powerful should be free to run their corporations as they wished, even at the expense of the small and weak, or whether they should be reined in by rational legislation.

Technological advancements, including some of the foundations of life today, such as electricity, improved the lives of a few in the Gilded Age. However, former craftsmen who now toiled in factories and tenement-dwellers in increasingly polluted cities suffered the effects of rapid industrialization without enjoying many of its benefits. While electricity and improved sanitation would reach more people in the next few decades, similar disparities in access to technology's benefits would continue unabated.

LEIGH KIMMEL

Further Readings

Bray, John. *The Communications Miracle: The Telecommunication Pioneers from Morse to the Information Superhighway*. New York: Plenum Press, 1995.
Brooks, John. *Telephone: The First Hundred Years*. New York: Harper and Row, 1976.

Coe, Lewis. *The Telegraph: A History of Morse's Invention and Its Predecessors in the United States*. Jefferson, NC: McFarland & Company, 1993.

Davies, L.J. *Fleet Fire: Thomas Edison and the Pioneers of the Electric Revolution*. New York: Arcade Publishing, 2003.

Frizot, Michel, ed. *A New History of Photography*. Cologne: Könemann, 1998.

Gernsheim, Helmut. *The Origins of Photography*. New York: Thames and Hudson, 1982.

Haber, Barbara. *From Hardtack to Home Fries: An Uncommon History of American Cooks and Meals*. New York: The Free Pres, 2002.

Israel, Paul. *Edison: A Life of Invention*. New York: John Wiley & Sons, 1998.

Jonnes, Jill. *Empires of Light: Edison, Tesla, Westinghouse, and the Race to Electrify the World*. New York: Random House, 2003.

Lebow, Irwin. *Information Highways & Byways: From the Telegraph to the 21st Century*. New York: IEEE Press, 1995.

Lemagny, Jean-Claude and André Rouillé, *A History of Photography*. Trans. by Janet Lloyd. Cambridge: Cambridge University Press, 1986.

Misa, Thomas J. *A Nation of Steel: The Making of Modern America, 1865–1925*. Baltimore, MD: Johns Hopkins University Press, 1995.

Page, Arthur W. *The Bell Telephone System*. New York: Harper and Brothers, 1941.

Powell, Horace B. *The Original Has This Signature—W.K. Kellogg*. Englewood Cliffs, N. J. Prentice-Hall, Inc. 1956.

Prout, Henry G. *A Life of George Westinghouse*. New York: Arno, 1972.

Root, Waverly and Richard de Rochemont. *Eating in America: A History*. New York: Ecco Press, 1997.

Sandler, Martin W. *The Story of American Photography*. Boston, MA: Little, Brown, 1979.

Seifer, Marc J. *Wizard: The Life and Times of Nikola Tesla: Biography of a Genius*, Secaucus, NJ: Birch Lane Press, 1996.

Shearer, Stephen R. *Hoosier Connections: The History of the Indiana Telephone Industry and the Indiana Telephone Association*. Indianapolis, IN: Indiana Telephone Association, 1992.

Temin, P. *Iron and Steel in Nineteenth Century America: An Economic Enquiry*. Cambridge, MA: MIT Press, 1964.

Chapter 10

Entertainment and Sports

*"There must be more and better books, engravings,
and pictures, even in the humblest dwelling."*
— Andrew Carnegie

FOLLOWING THE CIVIL WAR the U.S. population increased dramatically, and the country began to industrialize at a rapid pace that forever changed life in America. Industrialization generated a great deal of wealth, some of which trickled down to expand the American middle class, and for the first time give disposable income to some in the working classes. Many individuals could suddenly afford to purchase products and services that had previously been beyond their reach. The middle class in particular drove the United States toward becoming an entrenched consumer culture. White-collar workers and their families had more money on hand, as did some in the working classes, and more time to spend what they had. In addition to purchasing products, many of those in the industrial economy who had disposable income chose to spend it on entertainment. The result was a revolution in the entertainment industry as well as the rise of spectator sports as a form of mass leisure activity.

PERFORMING ARTS

While theatrical performances were nothing new in Gilded Age America, the theater as a whole flourished during the period. Improvements in technology and transportation brought theater to a greater audience. English actors and producers routinely crossed the Atlantic and mixed with Americans to

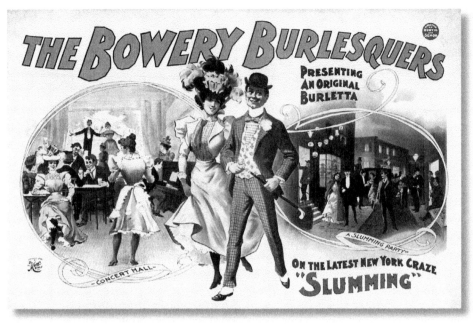

An 1898 burlesque show poster for a performance that played up class anxieties, with the characters apparently moving from a concert hall to lower Manhattan in "a slumming party."

help create a vibrant theatrical community in cities on the eastern seaboard, particularly New York. As railroads became more common in the United States, theater troupes were able to travel across the country, performing for the masses in large and small venues. Patrons of the arts in major cities helped sponsor the construction of grand theaters, and most towns of any size had some type of hall or building that could host theatrical performances. The coming of the electric light also allowed more complex performances to take place after dark. By the 1880s electric lighting brightened more than a mile of Broadway in New York, earning the theater district there the nickname "Great White Way," and helping the city become the center for theatrical activity in the United States. While still influenced by English theater, American productions of the Gilded Age took on a character of their own and included an increasing number of talented American-born performers. Among the most notable actors of the period in the

An 1897 Yiddish theater poster published in New York City.

United States were Edwin Booth, Joseph Jefferson, Clara Morris, and Richard Mansfield.

In the cities, many ethnic communities maintained their own smaller theaters in which performers acted out their experiences in the New World, as well as their hopes for the future. Theaters in Italian neighborhoods drew on the tradition of Italian opera to stage sentimental musical events, while Yiddish performers reflected the experiences of Jews in American cities. The musical comedy evolved into one of the most popular forms of theater in the United States, serving as a training ground for a host of musicians and playwrights, who in the 20th century would become leading figures in American entertainment. The business of

The "Great White Way" of Broadway in New York City, with crowds gathered for an outdoor projection of films in 1908.

theater also took on an American character of its own during the period. Just as prominent business magnates of the Gilded Age consolidated their holdings to form giant corporate monopolies, a handful of producers came together during the late 19th century to form the powerful Theatrical Syndicate that for some time held a virtual monopoly on major theatrical activity in the United States.

VAUDEVILLE
In addition to more traditional forms of theater, the era also saw the rise of vaudeville as a popular form of entertainment. With roots in the old fashion "medicine shows" that had been crisscrossing the country for decades, vaudeville shows offered their audiences an assortment of diverse performers. In an afternoon or evening an audience could watch singers, musicians, comedians, jugglers, short plays, and depending on the venue and character of the producer, risqué burlesque performances, all under one roof. Vaudeville shows were especially popular in the eastern cities where they were designed to appeal to a wide audience. Most vaudeville promoters hoped to draw paying customers of different ethnic persuasions, as well as mixed audiences of men, women, and children. Tony Pastor was an early vaudeville producer in New York City; some historians credit him with inventing the genre

The Barnum and Bailey Circus took advantage of public interest in the Spanish-American War for a naval-themed exhibition advertised in this atypical circus poster.

in the United States. As the 19th century closed, powerful producers such as Benjamin Franklin Keith and E.F. Albee owned lucrative theater chains and controlled most of the vaudeville business in the cities. While prominent touring performers sometimes visited smaller towns, local theaters in the hinterlands also sponsored vaudeville-style productions. Vaudeville declined in the years leading up to World War I, but as an entertainment form it had a great influence on future generations of radio and television performers.

As theater and variety productions continued to evolve, traveling entertainers crisscrossed the country as part of more traditional minstrel and medicine shows, both of which had been popular for decades. While their size and the complexity their performances varied, a medicine show bill could include musicians, singers, comedians, a "freak" show, and animal acts. As the name implies, the show was designed to draw a crowd that might be convinced to purchase various types of medicine. Usually the medicine appeared in bottle form, and was billed as a miracle drug that could cure almost any human malady.

Edwin Booth

Called by some the greatest American actor of the 19th century, Edwin Thomas Booth was born into a theatrical family near Bel Air, Maryland, in 1833 and began making regular appearances on stage as a teenager. During the early years of his career he toiled in the shadow of his famous father Junius Brutus Booth, appearing with him in numerous productions. After his father's death in 1852, Edwin Booth came into his own as an actor and drew critical praise and audiences throughout the United States and overseas. He later purchased the Walnut Street Theater in Philadelphia and also managed the Winter Garden Theater in New York, where he gained a reputation as one of the great Shakespearean actors of the period.

Booth's career was interrupted for a time after his younger brother, John Wilkes Booth, assassinated President Abraham Lincoln in 1865. The Booths had performed on stage together, and Edwin kept a low profile for months after the murder. He was also involved for several years in eventually successful negotiations to claim his brother's body for burial in the family plot. Overcoming the damage to his family name, Edwin Booth continued to perform, and in 1869 built his own venue, the Booth Theater, in New York. He assembled the finest repertory company in the city to perform there, and the troupe became well-known for their Shakespearean tragedies. When the U.S. economy took a serious downturn in the 1870s, the theater went bankrupt and Booth left America on a lucrative world tour. After returning home he founded The Players, a social club for actors and prominent patrons of the arts that met in his Manhattan mansion. The club quickly became an important center for creative activity in New York. In the last years of his life Booth continued to act, though he gradually reduced his schedule during the late 1880s. He died in New York on June 7, 1893.

Edwin Booth posing in his costume for Hamlet *in an 1870 photograph.*

Sitting Bull and Buffalo Bill against a painted backdrop of the outdoors in a studio photograph taken during the August 1885 Wild West Show.

With roots dating back to the 17th century in the United States, minstrel shows were usually performed in blackface by whites, and sometimes by African-American entertainers. Like the medicine show, they offered audiences a variety of entertainment, including music, dancing, and comedy skits as they created and reinforced a host of negative stereotypes of African Americans. Very popular before the Civil War, minstrel shows were in decline as the 19th century drew to a close in part because of competition from emerging forms of more sophisticated mass entertainment.

Music publishing began to emerge as big business during the last decades of the 19th century. As sales in the United States of musical instruments, especially pianos, increased during the Gilded Age, so did the demand for sheet music. The rise of musical theater and vaudeville performances that included music also encouraged more publishing. For most of the 19th century the music industry was little more than a disorganized collection of publishing houses scattered in major cities across the country, but this began to change during the 1880s. Just as the city became a major center for the theatrical arts, New York emerged as the center of the music publishing industry. The term "Tin Pan Alley" came to describe the concentration of music publishing houses in New York, and was later used to describe the music industry in general. Among the noted composers whose songs came out of Tin Pan Alley near the turn of the century were Charles K. Harris, Charles Coborn, and George M. Cohan.

THE CIRCUS

During the Gilded Age the circus was also a popular form of mass entertainment in both the cities and the countryside. As with the theater, circuses had toured America for decades, but after the Civil War, a handful of entrepreneurs created the circus industry as a profitable form of mass entertainment. In the latter half of the 19th century circuses could travel greater distances via the railroads, and as ticket sales increased, promoters began producing more lavish shows with exotic animals, death-defying trapeze acts, clowns, and side shows. Wisconsin businessman William Cameron Coup was one of the first to produce larger shows that offered entertainment in multiple rings. In 1871 Coup formed a partnership with famed promoter Phineas T. Barnum to create a circus that was billed as "The Greatest Show on Earth." This effort emerged as America's leading circus in an era when circuses were quickly becoming one of the country's leading forms of entertainment. Barnum eventually partnered with James Anthony Bailey to form the famous Barnum and Bailey circus, which was so large that it required three rings of entertainment. As Barnum and Bailey honed their operation during the last decades of the 19th century, another circus managed by the five Ringling brothers was also gaining popularity. The brothers had originally created a song and dance troupe in 1882, but soon added circus acts to their traveling show. They acquired their first elephant in 1888, and by the 1890s the Ringling brothers' circus was one of the most popular circuses in the United States. In 1907 the Ringlings purchased the Barnum and Bailey Circus, creating the Ringling Brothers, Barnum and Bailey Circus, the most famous circus in the history of American entertainment.

WESTERN THEMES

Reflecting the rise of mass entertainment, as well as easterners' fascination with anything western during the Gilded Age, William F. "Buffalo Bill" Cody in 1884 founded "Buffalo Bill's Wild West," a traveling show designed to bring the exotic trappings of the west to eastern audiences. Cody had a varied career as a soldier, guide, and bison hunter before creating the show that made him an American icon. Buffalo Bill's "Wild West" show toured annually for two decades, and was greeted at every stop by throngs of adoring fans eager to get a glimpse of the "true" west. Cody created a circus-like atmosphere for his shows, which included cowboy themes and dramatic recreations of events such as Custer's Last Stand, Native American attacks on wagon trains, shootouts between lawmen and outlaws, and the trials and travels of the pony express rider. Authentic western figures such as the famous Native American Chief Sitting Bull and trick-shot artist Annie Oakley toured periodically with the show, as did a host of cowboys, Native Americans, and military veterans. By the turn of the 20th century Cody was an authentic celebrity, and his shows had helped propagate a romanticized image of the west and western life that generations of Americans would take to heart.

Western themes were also used in dime novels, relatively short, melodramatic written works of fiction that were popular from the end of the Civil War until World War I. While some dime novels were based on the adventures of real characters, the stories were routinely embellished and over-dramatized. Typically the front cover would include equally embellished

This 1896 edition of Harper's featured a new story by Mark Twain—"Tom Sawyer, Detective."

artwork designed to grab the public's attention. In New York City the publishing house Beadle & Adams printed the first dime novels during the Civil War, and the books proved to be so popular that other firms quickly adopted the genre. Millions were printed and sold in the late 19th and early 20th centuries, captivating audiences across the country. In addition to stories about the west, other popular themes included life in the cities, crime stories, and romance.

MAINSTREAM LITERATURE

The Gilded Age also saw changes in mainstream American literature. Improvement in production, transportation, and mass distribution allowed more books to make their way into American homes, spreading the influence of a number of major American writers. While romanticism and idealism remained an important component of Gilded Age literature, many writers chose a more realistic approach, commenting with a critical eye on the positive and negative aspects of American life. Class struggles, feminism, corruption in city politics, and the darker side of American industrialization were common themes in the works of William Dean Howells, Stephen Crane, Henry James, and Kate Chopin. The most significant author of the period, and arguably the most famous writer in American history, is Samuel Langhorne Clemens, better known to his readers as Mark Twain. Twain produced fiction and non-fiction, and his social commentary was colored with humor and sometimes vicious satire. Among his notable works are *The Celebrated Jumping Frog of Calaveras County* (1865), *The Adventures of Tom Sawyer* (1876), *The Prince and the Pauper* (1881), and *The Adventures of Huckleberry Finn* (1885), which has been labeled by some as the first "Great American Novel."

BASEBALL

The Gilded Age also saw the rise of spectator sports as a very popular form of mass entertainment. Increased mobility, a developing mass media, and potential earnings made team and individual sports big business by the end

The Beadle Brothers

Brothers Erastus and Irwin Beadle helped found some of the most successful American publishing enterprises of the 19th century specializing in the cheaply-produced dime novel that brought thrills and adventure to the masses at an affordable price. The works that they produced were written in a sensational style, often depicting conflict between cowboys and Native Americans in the west, as well as the nefarious escapades of gangsters in big cities. They were designed to appeal to the masses through melodramatic stories and plot lines that tested the bounds of the reader's imagination.

Natives of New York, the Beadles ran a variety of printing businesses and magazine publishing concerns before their first novel series, "Beadle Dime Novels," began publication in 1860. The first book in this series, *Malaeska, the Indian Wife of the White Hunter,* was a great success, selling around 300,000 copies. Backwoods hunting tales, pirate adventures, and the Revolutionary War were early themes of the Beadle novels, which were promoted as "dollar books for a dime."

After the Civil War the subjects of the books changed with the times reflecting tales of the Wild West and "true crime" adventures set primarily in the cities. For easterners in the industrial age, a Beadle novel offered a great diversion from the day to day drudgeries of mundane lives, and the books routinely sold hundreds of thousands of copies.

During the 1860s Robert Adams, who at one time was an apprentice to Erastus Beadle, bought into the publishing firm, leading to a name change in 1870 from Beadle & Company to Beadle & Adams. The group also published titles under the subsidiary names Frank Starr and Company, Victor and Company, and Adams and Company, and organized an overseas venture, Beadle's American Library, that circulated their works in England.

Beadle and Adams continued publishing popular dime novels as well as magazines through the 1890s. In 1897, with all of the original principles in the firm dead, the enterprise was sold to other publishers and eventually discontinued.

A hunter battles a Native American on the cover of an 1860 Beadle's dime novel.

Cy Young

YOUNG, CLEVELAND

A Cy Young baseball card published by a tobacco company around 1909—the reverse features an ad for cigarettes.

Born into an Ohio farm family in 1867, Denton True "Cy" Young grew up to become a dominant pitcher, and one of the most legendary professional baseball players of all time. After a short stint in the minor leagues, Young began his major league career with the Cleveland Spiders in 1890. Pitching on a grueling schedule that saw him taking the mound every other day, he proved to be a workhorse and one of the hardest throwing pitchers in the game. On days that Young pitched, his catchers routinely added extra padding to their gloves to protect their hands from his fastball, and Young's nickname "Cy" was short for cyclone, a reference to the speed of his pitches.

In 1891 Young established himself as one of the era's great pitchers when he won 26 games. The following year he led the National League with 36 victories, including nine shutouts. It was the first of five seasons during which Young would win 30 games or more. In 1899 Young left the Spiders and signed with the St. Louis Perfectos for a then-hefty salary of $2,400. Two years later he went to the newly formed American League, winning 33 games for the Boston Americans (Red Sox). In 1903 he won two games for the Red Sox in the first World Series.

During a stellar major league career that lasted 26 years Young amassed statistics that will probably never be eclipsed. He ranks first all-time in number of wins for a professional baseball pitcher with 511 victories, and also ranks first all-time in starts, innings pitched, and complete games. Among his other notable achievements were three no hitters and the major league's first perfect game.

Young was elected to the Baseball Hall of Fame in 1937. Currently the best pitchers in the National and American Leagues are rewarded at the end of the season with the Cy Young award, which was named in his honor. Young lived long enough to enjoy the fruits of his success, and to accept innumerable accolades as one of professional baseball's true pioneers. He died in 1955 at the age of 88.

of the Gilded Age. By 1900 America's major cities in the east all had professional baseball teams, many colleges were fielding football teams, basketball had been invented, and boxers were fighting for the world heavyweight championship.

The history of baseball in America can be traced back to the early 19th century when the sport began to evolve as a version of an English game called "rounders." During the 1840s Alexander Cartwright, a member of a New York baseball club, devised many of the rules and regulations that would govern the modern game, and by the Civil War baseball was already referred to as "America's pastime." During the war baseball remained popular, and even occupied the idle hours of many federal troops in the field who played in clearings or pastures near their camps. In 1869 the Cincinnati Baseball Club, popularly known as the Cincinnati Red Stockings, became the first organized professional baseball team, barnstorming across the United States, taking on all challengers. The team captured the imagination of the American public and finished the year with an unblemished 57–0 record.

In 1871 the country's first major professional league, the short-lived National Association of Professional Baseball Players, was created with a loose collection of teams located in Boston, Chicago, Cleveland, Fort Wayne, New York, Philadelphia, Rockford, and Troy, New York. The association was poorly organized and plagued by internal squabbling over money, players who routinely jumped from one team to another at a moment's notice, and rumors of gambling. The association folded in 1875, but the following year a permanent organization, the National League of Professional Baseball Clubs (the current National League) formed with eight teams, the Boston Red Stockings, Chicago White Stockings, Cincinnati Red Legs, Hartford Dark Blues, Louisville Grays, Philadelphia Athletics, Brooklyn Mutuals, and St. Louis Browns. While the birth of the National League to many represents the genesis of modern professional baseball, the early game was primitive by modern

An 1869 print with portraits of members of the Cincinnati Red Stockings baseball club.

A panoramic photo of the field and packed stadium during the Harvard-Dartmouth football game held on November 14, 1903.

standards, and included a number of rules and practices that eventually disappeared, such as the need for nine balls to walk a batter, and the absence of fielding gloves, which were not used widely until the 1880s. Pitchers threw the ball underhanded and sometimes started as many as 70 games in a single season. Stolen bases and sacrifice flies were rare, as were home runs, in part because of the way that the balls were made. In 1876 George Hall of Philadelphia led the league with five home runs and Ross Barnes of Chicago won the hitting title, batting a now unheard of .429.

The National League flourished in the face of competition from the fledgling American Association, which began play in several major cities in 1882. Champions of the two leagues met seven times, with the National League winning most of the contests, in an early incarnation of the World Series, before the association folded in 1892. Through the 1890s baseball's popularity continued to swell as fans followed the careers of stars such as John McGraw, Willie Keeler, Ed Delahanty, and Cy Young. In 1895 the Philadelphia Phillies broke attendance records, reporting 474,971 total spectators for the season. By the turn of the century the National League included eight teams that would soon face a new and formidable rival group, the American League of Professional Baseball Clubs (the current American League), which formed in 1901. In 1903 the champions of each league played in the first modern World Series, with the Boston Red Sox defeating the Pittsburgh Pirates.

COLLEGE FOOTBALL

College football also became a popular spectator sport in the decades immediately prior to the turn of the 20th century. As with baseball, the development of football as a national pastime was an evolutionary process that began during the early 19th century out of a jumble of transplanted English games. Early football was something of a cross between rugby and soccer, a hybrid that would be unrecognizable to fans of the contemporary game. While the exact origins of modern college football are disputed, many recognize an 1869 contest between Rutgers and Princeton—which Princeton won by a score of six to four—as the first modern college football game. Others believe that the sport's origins date back to a meeting between Harvard and a Canadian team, McGill University, which took place in Cambridge, Massachusetts, in 1874. In this contest the schools used rules that were more closely associated with rugby than soccer, and as such the teams were allowed more latitude in handling the ball. Harvard won this contest by a score of three to zero. Still others recognize as the first intercollegiate game a contest between Tufts and Harvard that took place in Cambridge in 1875. Tufts emerged victorious in this contest by a scant margin of one to zero in an era when a touchdown was worth a single point.

Regardless of arguments over when and where the first game was played, college football quickly caught on in the northeastern United States. Rutgers, Columbia, Princeton, and Yale were charter members of the Intercollegiate Football Association, which loosely governed the sport until 1894 when the association disbanded. Walter Camp, who captained Yale's team during the late 1870s, was an early advocate of modernizing the game, and is generally recognized as the "father of college football." As a member of various committees dealing with the emerging sport, Camp helped establish many of the rules of the modern game, such as the play from scrimmage that replaced the

Female students playing basketball at Western High School in Washington, D.C., around 1899, after Senda Berenson of Smith College worked to popularize women's basketball in the 1890s.

This 1887 lithograph of Brighton Beach Race Course in New York presented horse racing as a glamorous spectacle.

rugby-style scrum, traditional offensive and defensive sets with 11 men on each side of the ball, the forward pass, and a system of downs by which the offense moved the ball. Camp also helped compile the first collegiate "All-American" team in 1889. By the 1890s the Ivy League schools, with Yale and Princeton leading the way, continued to dominate the sport, but college football had also spread to other parts of the country. In 1887 Notre Dame fielded the school's first team, and in 1896 the Big Ten became the first permanent major college football conference. Though they lagged behind the northeast and midwest, schools in the south were also fielding teams by 1900, as were some of the western schools.

BASKETBALL

The Gilded Age also saw the rise of basketball as a spectator sport in America. Canadian born James Naismith, a physical education instructor, created the game in 1891 at the Young Men's Christian Association (YMCA) Instructional Training School (later Springfield College) in Springfield, Massachusetts. Naismith was trying to come up with a sport that could occupy his students, and also be played indoors during the cold New England winters. At first basketball was played using a soccer ball, and players scored by throwing the ball into peach baskets that were attached to railings 10 feet off the ground. After a "basket," which counted as one point, players would have to stop the game and retrieve the ball using a ladder or a long stick. Unlike the modern game, as many as nine players per team might be on the court at any given time. Iron hoops with open-ended nets would not become standard equipment on basketball courts until just after the turn of the century. For some time basketball was popularized through the YMCA, but as more and more people took notice, crowds grew larger and sometimes rowdier, until the group took steps to disassociate itself with the game. By then many high schools and colleges were already fielding teams.

James J. Corbett, "Champion of the World," in 1893.

The first intercollegiate game was played on February 9, 1895, when Minnesota State School of Agriculture defeated Hamline College nine to three. On January 18, 1896, the University of Chicago defeated the University of Iowa 15–12 in the first game involving five players per team on the court during play. Senda Berenson, a physical education instructor at Smith College, was the key figure in popularizing women's basketball during the 1890s, writing a different set of rules for the women's game.

In addition to team games other spectator sports became popular in the United States during the last half of the 19th century. While horseracing had been an organized form of entertainment in America since the colonial period, it came into its own as a major spectator sport following the Civil War with the running of first Belmont Stakes in New York in 1867, the first Preakness Stakes in Baltimore in 1873, and the first Kentucky Derby at Churchill Downs in Louisville in 1875. Together these three races became horse racing's storied "triple crown."

In 1892 James J. Corbett knocked out John L. Sullivan at a highly publicized boxing match in New Orleans that many consider the first World Heavyweight Championship fight of the modern era. By 1900 newspapers were devoting more and more space to sports, and books and magazines about sports were becoming popular. Sports also had become big business during the Gilded Age, with teams and individual athletes generating large sums of money. As a result, be it team games or individual undertakings, sports during the era became an integral part of American culture as a popular form of entertainment, and as a successful form of commerce.

BEN WYNNE

Further Readings

Anderson, Ann. *Snake Oil, Hustlers and Hambones: The American Medicine Show*. Jefferson, NC: McFarland Publishing Company, 2004.

Brands, H.W. *The Reckless Decade: America in the 1890s*. Chicago, IL: University of Chicago Press, 2002.

Burns, Sarah. *Inventing the Modern Artist: Art and Culture in Gilded Age America*. New Haven, CT: Yale University Press, 1999.

Cashman, Sean D. *America in the Gilded Age: From the Death of Lincoln to the Rise of Theodore Roosevelt*. New York: New York University Press, 1993.

Giblin, James Cross. *Good Brother, Bad Brother: The Story of Edwin Booth and John Wilkes Booth*. New York: Clarion Books, 2005.

Henderson, Mary C. *Theater in America: 250 Years of Plays, Players, and Productions*. New York: HNA Books, 1996.

Honig, Donald. *Baseball: The Illustrated History of America's Game*. New York: Crown Publishers, 1990.

Jasen, David A. *Tin Pan Alley: An Encyclopedia of the Golden Age of American Song*. New York: Routledge, 2003.

Johannsen, Albert. *The House of Beadle and Adams and its Nickel and Dime Novels*. Norman, OK: University of Oklahoma Press, 1950.

Jones, John Bush. *Our Musicals, Ourselves: A Social History of the American Musical Theater*. Waltham, MA: Brandeis University Press, 2004.

Lewis, Robert M. *From Traveling Show to Vaudeville: Theatrical Spectacle in America, 1830–1910*. Baltimore, MD: The Johns Hopkins University Press, 2003.

Levine, Lawrence. *Highbrow/Lowbrow: The Emergence of Cultural Hierarchy in America*. Cambridge, MA: Harvard University Press, 1990.

Naismith, James. *Basketball: Its Origins and Development*. New York: Associated Press, 1941.

Ours, Robert. *College Football Encyclopedia: The Authoritative Guide to 124 Years of College Football*. Rocklin, CA: Prima Pub., 1994.

Powers, Ron. *Mark Twain: A Life*. New York: Free Press, 2006.

Schlereth, Thomas J. *Victorian America: Transformations in Everyday Life, 1876-1915*. New York: Harper Perennial, 1992.

Stevenson, Louise L. *The Victorian Homefront: American Thought and Culture, 1860*. Ithaca, NY: Cornell University Press, 2001.

Trachtenberg, Alan. *The Incorporation of America: Culture and Society in the Gilded Age*. New York: Hill and Wang, 1992.

Warren, Louis S. *Buffalo Bill's America: William Cody and the Wild West Show*. New York: Knopf, 2005.

Wolff, Rick, et al. *The Baseball Encyclopedia*. New York: Macmillan, 1993.

Chapter 11

Crime and Violence

"Chaos was the law of nature.
Order was the dream of man."
— Henry Adams

IN THE SUMMER OF 1869, an eyewitness in Abilene, Kansas, described a scene of lawlessness that could have come straight out of an old-fashioned cowboy movie. A cowboy rode his horse into a saloon and pointed a gun at the bartender, causing instant panic. Everyone in the bar went scrambling out. Then in San Francisco in 1881, a one-time resident of the mining town of Bodie, California, shot up the Mammoth saloon as well as the head of the bartender. The miner then promptly tried to stick a knife into a deputy who was escorting him to jail. While Abilene and the other cattle towns and mining towns in the west would eventually bring a fair degree of order and law to their communities, thus countering some of the myths about violence in the west, it was still a rough and sometimes dangerous place. But crime and violence were not limited to the frontier. Most of it happened in big cities through gangs. The mountains of Appalachia also saw conflict between the operators of whiskey stills and government "revenuers." And it took place—often very violently—in the south, where some whites took revenge for the extremes of Reconstruction and for the loss of the Civil War.

FRONTIER VIOLENCE AND CRIMINALS

While frontier towns between 1870 and 1900 gradually developed a system of law and order, they often started out with a high degree of crime and violence.

Some of the most well-known of these were the cattle towns of Kansas: Abilene, Ellsworth, Wichita, Dodge City, and Caldwell.

After the Civil War Texas ranchers wanted to reinvigorate their cattle businesses. They took advantage of the newly-built railroad lines just north in Kansas, and drove their cattle to these towns to be shipped to Chicago. They did this despite the fact that some of the cattle were infected with splenic fever, a contagious disease. The railroad and the cattle drive brought in a large influx of cowboys. Driving the herds through the countryside brought them into contact with the homesteads of local farmers, where the cowboys were often negligent in avoiding their fields. There are recorded instances of near violence, as in the example of the farm of S.L. Graham, who had his corn trampled. When he protested, the cowboys threatened to burn his farm and drew their guns on him, but in the end they left him alone.

Violence was prevalent in the towns, but not as much as movies and television shows have suggested. Dodge City is a good example. Founded in 1872, Dodge City drew its name from a nearby Army fort. It was about this time that the railroad ran a line near the town. At first the trains were used to transport buffalo hides, and between 1872 and 1874 850,000 buffalo hides were transported. Cattle drives began coming after the buffalo herds were decimated, and between 1875 and 1886 over five million cattle were brought to town. In 1876 the population was 1,200 and there were 19 saloons. Violence was often associated with three legal vices: gambling, prostitution, and drinking.

The first murder occurred in 1872 when a gambler shot another man. That first year there were a total of 15 murders. Eventually the town decided to bring law and order to Dodge. In 1873, after firing their first sheriff, the town created a "vigilance committee." At first it was effective, but soon the citizens realized the committee was worse than the criminals it had been charged to combat. The committee began to murder people. The town then hired a series of sheriffs, deputies, and marshals including Hamilton "Ham" Bell, William "Bat" Masterson, Ed Masterson, James Masterson, Wyatt Earp, and Bill Tilghman. They effectively cut down on the number of murders. Between 1877 and 1885 there were only 15 homicides recorded—as many as there were in the year the town was founded.

A more typical problem the town encountered is exemplified by a story that appeared in the September 29, 1877, edition of the *Dodge City Times*. The town had banned concealed weapons, but that didn't keep drunken cowboys from riding up and down the main street, shooting their pistols into the air. A cowboy by the name of A.C. Jackson was in the process of doing just that when town marshals Bat Masterson and Ed Masterson confronted him and ordered him to stop. When Jackson continued firing his pistol, they commenced to shoot at his horse. Jackson fled with Bat Masterson in pursuit. Masterson returned when he realized he was out of ammunition. Jackson's

The roughly built jailhouse for the former mining town of Bodie, California, which is now a ghost town and state park.

horse was found dead a couple of miles from town where Jackson was forced to walk to his camp.

Similar to Dodge City, Ellsworth, Kansas, had eight murders during its first year of existence, but only six between 1872 and 1875. The lawmen in Caldwell, Kansas, weren't always as lucky as those in Dodge. In 1881 the town marshal was killed during a shootout with five cowboys. In 1882 both the marshal and the assistant marshal were killed on the same day in two different incidents. Between 1879 and 1885 Caldwell had a total of 13 homicides.

MINING TOWNS

The cattle towns were not the only locations in the west where violence and crime occurred. The towns that grew up around the mining industry also experienced a high level of lawlessness. Whenever gold was struck in these towns, a boom would occur, and the towns would grow along with crime and violence. A well-studied example is the California town of Bodie.

When Bodie began to boom in February 1878, there was only a population of about 1,500. But there was also a steady stream of people coming in—about 10 per day. While there were only four boarding houses and about 200 private residences, the town at this time had 17 saloons and 15 brothels. By the end of 1878 the population was up to 4,000 along with over 40 saloons. The number of people and saloons contributed to the rowdiness and violence. Despite this, the town was in some ways safer than eastern towns and cities. The miners often said that they did not have to lock their doors at night, unlike in the east. There was little racial violence, and everyone was treated equally under the law. But in other ways, the town lived up to its violent reputation.

The history of Bodie is rife with anecdotes of drinking, gambling, and general mayhem. There are examples of card games during which men won $4,000 and $1,300, and one instance during which a miner gambled away his wife (the newspaper reported that she was more than happy with the transaction). The town also had a Chinatown with opium dens, and occasional tong wars. And while prostitution was not illegal, it sometimes led to violence, as in the case of Rosa Olague. Olague had a reputation for fighting with men and other prostitutes, and in 1879 she cut the face of a miner from his forehead to his chin. In this case she was acquitted on the grounds of self-defense.

Crime also occurred on the fringes of town. Since the stagecoach service from Bodie to Carson City carried an average of $250,000 in gold bullion per month, it soon became a target of thieves. The first stagecoach robbery occured in 1879. During the next year stagecoaches were robbed seven times. In 1881 they were robbed eight times.

Within the town itself robbery was rare. No banks were ever robbed in Bodie. Mugging (called "garroting" by the people of Bodie) was infrequent—only 10 during the boom years, and three other attempted muggings. Personal property theft usually involved the pilfering of items like blankets and firewood. Burglary of businesses was usually minor: a pawn shop had $700 worth of jewelry stolen, a store lost $75 worth of tea, coffee, and liquor, and a jewelry store lost $200 worth of merchandise. These were the only three instances when items stolen exceeded $50.

On the other hand, fistfights and gunfights were common, particularly on weekends. Most of these happened when someone thought that they were being disrespected. Between 1877 and 1883 there were 50 shootings, and guns were brandished often. In addition, there were 15 knife assaults, including one by a lawyer who knifed a stonecutter in the ribs after being punched in the eye.

WESTERN GANGS AND OUTLAWS

Outside of the towns, the west had its share of gangs and desperadoes. There were over 20 well-known gangs of the west during the Gilded Age; all were similar in nature, if not in degree. They committed train and stagecoach robberies, and took part in cattle rustling and horse thievery. One such gang was the Sam Bass Gang, which lasted from 1877 to 1878.

A one-time cowboy, Bass began his short criminal career by driving a herd of cattle from Texas to Kansas, and then stealing the money from the sales. His gang ended up eight men strong, including himself. They first robbed stagecoaches and banks. Then in 1878 they robbed two stagecoaches and four trains within a few months near Dallas, Texas. This provoked the Texas Rangers, who chased the gang across north Texas. As often happened, one of the gang members became an informant and told the Rangers that Bass planned to rob a bank in Round Rock, Texas. When Bass arrived there, the Rangers were waiting for him. A gun battle ensued and Bass was killed.

As crime in the Old West became romanticized, first through dime novels, and then later through films and television, the sites and locations of the encounters between sheriffs, marshals, and outlaws became famous. One such site is Tombstone, Arizona, with its cemetery, known as Boothill Cemetery, first laid out in 1878, where many of the famous victims of gunplay were buried. The location became so well-known that in the 1920s, souvenir hunters stripped away the last wooden burial markers.

Local residents interested in their history, and hoping to capitalize on the numerous curious visitors driving from nearby Tucson, attempted to restore the graveyard. Metal markers were provided by a local merchant, and the site cleaned up by Boy Scouts. Careful scouring of obituaries and other local records produced an historical record of those buried. Included were suicides, victims of shoot-outs, mining accident victims, and several killed in duels. Others buried in Boothill included victims of disease, failed medical operations,

The *Posse Comitatus* Act

Posse Comitatus is a law passed by Congress in 1878 that forbids—except in specially designated situations—the military from engaging in civil law enforcement. It was passed in direct reaction to the federal troop deployments during Reconstruction after the Civil War, when federal troops were often used for civil law enforcement. For example, in the Moonshine War they became members of a *posse comitatus* (that is, a posse) searching for illegal stills. They were also used to quell riots and to control elections.

The law has a long history in English law, particularly in the Magna Carta (1225) and the English Bill of Rights (1688). In the United States, the law can be circumvented by an act of Congress. For example, Congress has given the U.S. Coast Guard permission to enforce anti-drug laws. It does not apply to the National Guard as long as it is being directed by a state, rather than the federal government. The original law (with the recent addition of the Air Force) simply states: "Whoever, except in cases and under circumstances expressly authorized by the Constitution or Act of Congress, willfully uses any part of the Army or the Air Force as a posse comitatus or otherwise to execute the laws shall be fined under this title or imprisoned not more than two years, or both." The other branches of the military have been brought under the act by declarations from the Department of Defense.

Sam Bass's granite tombstone in Round Rock, Texas, which replaced an earlier marker damaged by souvenir hunters.

executions, conflicts with Native Americans, or animal bites. Apparently none of the approximately 300 interred died of old age. By far the most well-known of those buried at Boothill are all three of the fatalities incurred at the notorious gunfight at the O.K. Corral.

Although often depicted in fiction and film as classic struggles between the forces of law and order and those of crime, many of the famous gunfights of the old west reflected conflicts between rival political and familial groups. Sometimes the local marshals and sheriffs worked with friends and relatives to take advantage of their position, offering protection to their own gambling and prostitution establishments while harassing those of the competition.

Rumors persisted that the city marshal of Tombstone, Arizona, Virgil Earp, similarly exploited his position. The gunfight at the O.K. Corral on October 26, 1881, the subject of several movies and books, is usually remembered as one between law and order as embodied in Virgil Earp and his brothers Wyatt and Morgan, with their friend, "Doc" Holliday, on one side, and Frank McLaury, Tom McLaury, Billy Claiborne, Ike Clanton, and Billy Clanton on the other. The McLaury-Clanton group were known locally as "the Cowboys," and had a rowdy reputation, although they were hardly the hardened gang of criminals often depicted in film.

In a showdown in an empty lot near the O.K. Corral, the gunfight lasted less than half a minute, with at least 30 shots fired. Both the McLaurys were killed, as was Billy Clanton; all of the Earp faction except Wyatt Earp were wounded. Wyatt Earp and Holliday were brought up on murder charges (then cleared) and Virgil Earp was fired from his post.

URBAN VICE, GANGS, AND VIOLENCE

New York City teemed with new immigrants, excitement and—at the same time—crime. A large portion of this crime and violence was a result of the activities of organized gangs. While all of the large cities in America were infected with these problems to some degree, New York, being the largest, had more than its fair share of crime and violence. Gambling, though illegal, thrived in New York. There are estimates that in 1872 there were 200 gambling houses and hundreds of locations for playing illegal lotteries.

The *National Police Gazette*

The *National Police Gazette* was a highly popular 16-page newspaper—printed on pink paper—most popular during the 1880s and 1890s. It specialized in sensational crime stories, woodcut illustrations of scantily clad women (it even shocked people once with the picture of a bare breasted woman), sports stories, and gossip.

Some credit the paper with the invention of the sports pages and the gossip column. During its peak, its paid circulation averaged about 150,000 per week, and sometimes for special issues it reached 400,000. The reading circulation is considered much higher, as it was often passed onto others.

The *National Police Gazette* began in 1845, but at that time was much more conservative. It was obtained in 1887 by Richard Kyle Fox in lieu of money owed him by the previous owners. Fox has been judged as arrogant, bigoted, and vulgar—but he was a promotional genius who knew how to appeal to his public, primarily working-class men.

He never allowed any of his writers to have a byline with their own name—though he always signed his name when he wrote such columns as "Homicide Harvest" and "Murder Mania." The *National Police Gazette* kept the working class and lower class up to date on the latest lynchings, abortions, murders, and prize fights.

The cover of the March 13, 1847 edition of the National Police Gazette.

Like the frontier towns, New York City had its drinking establishments and bordellos. Just before the Gilded Age began, New York clergymen put the number of prostitutes in the city at 20,000. The police department's official tally was 3,300 prostitutes, 621 bordellos, and 99 hotels used for paid sex. One of the specialties of New York was the dance hall, such as the Haymarket, which remained a dance hall from 1878 until 1913. Aside from drinking and dancing with girls, the Haymarket specialized in private cubicles for can-can dances and peep shows. The area where the dance halls generally were located was known as the Satan's Circus District and included such establishments as the French Madam's, Egyptian Hall, Sailor's Hall, and the Star and Garter.

A favorite hangout of many gangsters was Armory Hall. It was run by Billy McGlory who had been a gang captain in the Five Points area during its heyday, leading such gangs as the Forty Thieves and the Chichesters. Armory Hall specialized in robbing drunks and, often, stripping them naked.

One of the creepiest gangs was known as the ghouls. They specialized in stealing bodies from cemeteries to sell to medical schools. The police generally looked the other way with the ghouls until one of the gangs stole the body of a prominent businessman, Alexander T. Stewart, and held it for ransom.

Prior to the Civil War, most of the gangs in New York were limited to the Five Points area, the Bowery, and the Fourth Ward. These were the areas where the slums were most prevalent. Poverty and discrimination against immigrants had a lot to do with the creation of these gangs. During the Gilded Age, the tenement slums began to expand to other parts of the city—and so did the gangs.

The Whyos were considered the top gang during most of this period. Their membership included a who's who of criminals for the time. They were not only known for their expertise at thievery, but also for their skills and ferocity at brawling. At one time they had dual leadership with Danny Driscoll and Danny Lyons, both of whom were eventually hung for committing murder. Other gangs of the period included the Hartley Mob known for transporting their stolen items in a hearse, the Molasses Gang, the Dutch Mob, the Hell's Kitchen Gang, the Gas House Gang, the Stable Gang, the Silver Gang, and many others.

Toward the end of the century the Eastman Gang, a famous Jewish-American gang led by Monk Eastman, would boast a crew of anywhere from 500 to 1,000. The same could be said of the Italian Five Points Gang, led by Paul Kelly (whose real name was Paolo Vaccarelli), an Italian American from Sicily. One of his later gang members would move to Chicago and be known there as Al Capone.

CROOKS AND HOODLUMS

One of the premier bank robbers in the country, upon whom many a Hollywood character has been modeled, lived and worked out of New York City: George Leonidas Leslie, also known as George Howard and Western George. Leslie was known for his meticulous planning, often getting the architectural plans for the banks he robbed (he had a degree in architecture from the University of Cincinnati).

He seldom took part in the actual robbery and was known to circulate in high society and to attend theatre openings and art exhibits. The New York Superintendent of Police, George Walling, conjectured that Leslie was responsible for 80 percent of the bank robberies in the country during his career. His take from these was estimated to be between seven million and 12 million dollars.

Many of the gang members were simply brutal enforcers and merciless hit men. A good example was Piker Ryan of the Whyos gang. During one of his arrests, police found a price list in his pocket for his "work": to blacken both eyes, he charged $4; to break a person's nose and jaw, $10; to bite off an ear, $15; to murder someone, a $100 minimum.

NEW ORLEANS

One of the largest cities in the south with a population of 191,148 in 1870, New Orleans had problems with crime and violence similar to New York. One difference may have been in the degree to which the under-world was directly connected to local government. Still, it had organized gangs, extortion, burglary, robbery, assaults, murders, pick-pocketing, and counterfeiting, just like in the city of New York.

Pinkerton's National Detective Agency, which introduced the use of mugshots, kept this criminal's photo in its files.

A number of the hoodlums in New Orleans at this time were on the city payroll and actually worked as henchmen for some of the politicians. One of the newspapers—the *Mascot*—noted in 1883 that a majority of the people arrested for being drunk and disorderly were, in fact, on the city payroll. In 1883 there was even a gun battle between rival politicians, including the criminal Sheriff and one of the tax collectors, in which three men were killed. A citizens' committee also noted that the police were mostly recruited from the criminal elements in the city.

The city was also a magnet for transient hoodlums. Criminals often traveled to other cities. New Orleans was one of their favorite spots to visit. Known criminals from New York, such as the pickpocket extraordinaire John Larney, nicknamed Mollie Matches, liked to spend time in New Orleans. Not only did robbers Little Dave Cummings and Billy Forrester visit there, but they also decided to rob a jewelry store and a bank while visiting.

Two of the most notorious of the homegrown gangs were the Yellow Henry Mob and the Spiders. The Spiders were often used by politicians to intimidate voters at polling booths. The Phil Oster gang was another successful gang. Oster, besides being an expert burglar, was also an exceptional counterfeiter who printed money for 45 years. Another stand-out thief was pickpocket Margaret Murphy, who specialized in lifting wallets at funerals. She was arrested at age 77 and boasted that she had been at her trade for over 60 years.

THE MAFIA IN NEW ORLEANS

Just before the Civil War, Sicilian immigrants began to appear in New Orleans, and some of them—the criminal elements in the group—set up gangs in the Second and Third Districts. They became known for robbery, assassination, extortion, and counterfeiting. They were identified as the Stoppagherra Society, a branch of the mafia. They were credited with 70 murders in a 20-year period, though the exact numbers are unknown.

Around 1881 the New Orleans mafia acquired a new boss, Charles Matranga. Matranga expanded his mob power to the docks, forcibly taking over from the Provenzano brothers, who supposedly had no connection to the mafia, but who were most likely part of a rival gang. A vendetta ensued and the Provenzano brothers were arrested in 1890 for attempting to kill Matranga.

The Provenzanos convinced Superintendent of Police David C. Hennessy that he should investigate further, since the mafia was involved. Hennessy had received a death threat from the mafia in 1881 when he had helped to deport a notorious Mafia leader named Giuseppe Esposito. As Hennessy began to investigate the Provenzano case, he received another death threat and was assassinated—just before he was to testify.

Nineteen people were indicted for his murder, including Charles Matranga, and a trial ensued for nine of them. Inexplicably all nine (one was a 14-year-old boy named Asperi Marchesi, who allegedly signaled to the killers when Hennessy was approaching) were found not guilty, despite overwhelming evidence, including eyewitnesses. The public was outraged and jury tampering was suspected. A mob then stormed the Orleans Parish Jail, killing all but nine of the 19. Ironically (or perhaps nefariously, as some argue) the survivors included Matranga, his lieutenant, Bastiano Incardona, Asperi Marchesi, and six others.

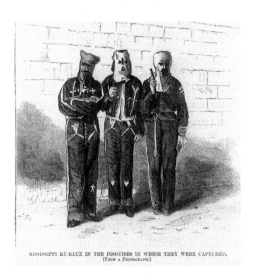

MISSISSIPPI KU-KLUX IN THE DISGUISES IN WHICH THEY WERE CAPTURED.
[FROM A PHOTOGRAPH.]

Mississippi Ku Klux Klan members in the disguises in which they were captured in 1872.

RACIAL VIOLENCE

With the withdrawal of Reconstruction troops in 1876, the southern states regained their power in state and local governments. They soon reinstituted many of the Black Codes that had earlier been deemed illegal, as well as new laws that instituted segregation. These codes worked to create de facto slavery, tying African Americans to labor on farms and chain gang labor, while segregation generally made African Americans second-class citizens.

At the beginning of the Gilded Age, the Ku Klux Klan also contributed to racial violence. The KKK was involved in beatings, torture, murder (approximately 400 between 1868 and 1872), and intimidation. It had begun in the late 1860s, but a series of laws passed 1870–71 brought its most blatant activities under control. But at the end of the Gilded Age, it was replaced with equally repugnant mob violence with frequent lynching.

THE REINCARNATION OF THE BLACK CODES

Black Codes had been implemented directly after the Civil War to varying degrees in all of the former Confederate states. Some of the codes made it a crime for African Americans to quit their jobs working on white-owned farms, and a crime to be unemployed if over the age of 18. These codes were declared illegal in 1877, but were partially resurrected. This was often done through what has been called a criminal-surety system. Under this system, if an African American committed a minor crime (such as being drunk in public), he was fined. If he was unable to pay the fine, a white employer could pay it and the African American would be obliged to work for him.

If a more serious crime was committed, the criminal could be assigned to a chain gang. At this time chain gangs were often leased out to private businesses for cheap labor. It wasn't uncommon for these private businesses to abuse their workers. An often cited example is the abuse of a chain gang

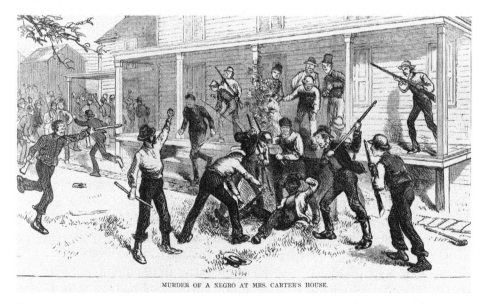

MURDER OF A NEGRO AT MRS. CARTER'S HOUSE.

This engraving of an armed lynch mob murdering an African-American man outside of a house in Pattenburg, New Jersey, in 1872 was published in Harper's Weekly *on October 12, 1872.*

This chain gang of convicts worked on the roads in Pitt County, North Carolina, in the fall of 1910. They slept in bunks in these wagons surrounded by armed guards and bloodhounds.

by the Greenwood and Augusta Railroad Company. Nearly 45 percent of the men on this chain gang died during service.

Segregation laws—especially those pertaining to railroads—also began to appear in the south almost immediately after the Civil War, but were temporarily rescinded during active Reconstruction. They began to appear again in the 1880s.

In 1896 the Supreme Court in *Plessy v. Ferguson* declared segregation legal. State laws that forbade African Americans to ride in the white section of railroad cars were declared valid. This would lead to many of the famous examples of segregation, such as white-only drinking fountains, and white-only schools. Collectively these became known as the Jim Crow laws. The 1890s also saw the effective disenfranchisement of many African Americans in the south through poll taxes and literacy tests.

Perhaps the worst of the violence was in the practice of lynching. Lynching was not limited to just African Americans, but they were the majority of victims. Lynching began to be documented in 1882 by the *Chicago Tribune*. Numbers were also tracked by the Tuskegee Institute and by the NAACP. The year with the most lynching was 1892, when 230 people were lynched in the country. Of these, 161 were African Americans and 69 were white.

Lynching took place in almost all of the states in the union, but approximately 90 percent took place in the south. Mississippi had the most lynchings, followed by Georgia and Texas. Lynching was mob rule and totally circumvented the justice system. According to the Tuskegee Institute, 11.5

percent of those lynched were killed for no specified crime, 41 percent were hung for felonious assault, 19.2 percent for rape, and 1.8 percent for insulting a white person.

APPALACHIA AND MOONSHINE

During the Civil War, the north instituted new taxes on liquor and other items to help pay for the war. When the southern states rejoined the Union, they too were made to pay the taxes. This federal tax on liquor ($.90 a gallon in the 1870s and then $1.10 in 1894) was resisted by many of the makers of whiskey, especially in Appalachia, though there were also illegal stills in Brooklyn, Utah, Alabama, Mississippi, Arkansas, Texas, and Missouri, among other places.

By 1891 the Appalachian region accounted for 77 percent of all of the moonshining in the country, with a large concentration in the mountainous regions of Georgia, Kentucky, North and South Carolina, and West Virginia. The Appalachian highlands of Georgia were a prime example of this concentration. In 1876 four-fifths of the federal prosecutions in that state were for illegal moonshining.

The making of spirits had been a traditional and respected activity all the way back to the 1700s. The practice had been brought to many of the colonies by Scots-Irish immigrants. It was often used by farmers for extra income. For them, this tax was a threat to their livelihood and an affront to their sense of independence and freedom. As a result, these citizens often refused to pay the taxes.

THE MOONSHINE WAR

But the government was not about to ignore this loss of taxation. It was estimated in 1877 that just in five southern states the federal government was losing between $2,000,000 and $2,500,000 annually. Using posses made of federal officials, federal marshals, citizens, and—at first—members of the army (until the Posse Comitatus Act was passed), the government acted with the help of informants to confiscate or destroy stills and make arrests.

Between 1875 and 1880 the government seized about 1,000 stills a year. The Internal Revenue Agency reported in 1880 that they had arrested 7,339 people during a four-year period. Twenty-six agents had been killed and 57 wounded. Casualties for the moonshiners were nearly impossible to gauge because they often carried away their dead and wounded.

After 1880 government casualty numbers began to decline. Moonshining continued, however. It is estimated that in 1896 there were between five and 10 million gallons of moonshine being produced. In the end, while they were able—to varying degrees over the years—to decrease the volume of moonshine produced, the government was never able to completely stop the practice.

CONCLUSION

While the Gilded Age is well known for its political corruption and for the excesses of Reconstruction, it was also a time of significant crime and vice. In most places and during most of the period, drugs and prostitution were totally legal. Still, historians are now in the midst of reassessing crime and violence on the western frontier, many claiming that earlier historians had exaggerated the mayhem. While movies and television have given the impression that death and destruction was nonstop—which is an untruth—the west was indeed often rough and violent. And many of the bandits and gangs—such as the Sam Bass Gang—have certainly been romanticized beyond what they really were: vicious and greedy.

Mob violence and legal segregation in the south, on the other hand, verged on the inhuman and was certainly as degrading as slavery itself, and arguably more vicious. And it must be asked if the collection of taxes or the sale of a gallon of moonshine was worth a single life during the Moonshine War. Finally, the urban areas in the country, with poverty, overcrowding, and often illiterate immigrants, were a breeding ground for gangs and criminals. The bigger the city, the bigger the problem.

WILLIAM TOTH

Further Readings

Asbury, Herbert. *The French Quarter. An Informal History of the New Orleans Underworld*. New York: Alfred A. Knopf, 1938.

Asbury, Herbert. *The Gangs of New York. An Informal History of the Underworld*. New York: Alfred A. Knopf, 1928.

Carr, Jess. *The Second Oldest Profession. An Informal History of Moonshining in America*. Englewood Cliffs, NJ: Prentice-Hall, 1972.

Courtwright, David T. *Forces of Habit. Drugs and the Making of the Modern World*. Cambridge, MA: Harvard University Press, 2001.

Dykstra, Robert R. *The Cattle Towns*. New York: Knopf, 1968.

Freidman, Lawrence M. *Crime and Punishment in American History*. New York: Harper Collins, 1993.

Guzman, Jessie P., ed. *1952 Negro Yearbook*. New York: William H. Wise, 1952.

Hunt, Thomas, and Martha Sheldon. *Deep Water: Joseph P. Macheca and the Birth of the American Mafia*. iUniverse, 2007.

Kansas Heritage Center. Available online, URL: http://ksheritagestore. org/research_tools.html. Accessed January 2008.

McGrath, Roger D. *Gunfighters, Highwaymen, and Vigilantes: Violence on the Frontier*. Berkeley, CA: University of California Press, 1984.

Miller, Wilbur R. *Revenuers and Moonshiners: Enforcing Federal Liquor Law in the Mountain South, 1865–1900*. Chapel Hill, NC: North Carolina Press, 1991.

Myrdal, Gunnar. *An American Dilemma*. New York: Harper Collins, 1962.

Rennert, Vincent Paul. *Western Outlaws*. New York: Crowell-Collier, 1967.

Reuter, Edward B. *The American Race Problem*. New York: Thomas Crowell, 1927.

Shrock, Joel. *The Gilded Age*. Westport, CT: Greenwood Press, 2004.

Smith, Gene. *The National Police Gazette*. New York: Simon and Schuster, 1972.

Chapter 12

Labor and Employment

"When men cannot assert their rights . . .
it is time . . . for the better protection of our labor."
— National Labor Tribune

TODAY, UNLIKE DURING the Gilded Age, we are accustomed to technological change. Even so, change can be disruptive to the job market and to the consumer. Consider the modern technological breakthroughs in telecommunications and the resulting shift of computer help desks from the United States to India. Even for a tech-savvy culture, change like this can be disconcerting. Change was even more disruptive during the Gilded Age. In 1860 over half of the labor force was agrarian and only 18 percent was involved in industry. Those not working on farms were generally skilled workers and apprentices who would work carefully on creating items like barrels, shoes, and furniture, handcrafting the products and totally involving themselves in the entire production.

But by 1870 mechanization and division of labor had begun in earnest, and life began to change significantly for workers in the United States. By 1900, for instance, only 40 percent of the population would still be involved in agriculture, this despite the fact that total farmland more than doubled from 408 million acres in 1870 to 838 million acres in 1900. Mining, manufacturing, and construction employment started the Gilded Age at 25.1 percent of the total workforce and ended at 30.5 percent. In 1870 transportation, trade, and finance employed 11.2 percent of the workforce and ended in 1900 with 16.8 percent. The service industry, including government work, began the period at 12.9 percent and ended at 14.7 percent of the total workforce.

AGRICULTURE

Ironically it was agriculture's success that diminished the number of people involved in agriculture in the United States. Through education, advancing technology, and science, farms began to overproduce and—as a result—to suffer a lower rate of return on crops. It became a matter of supply and demand, with more supply than demand, thus creating lower prices. While this was good for the consumer, it was often devastating for the farmer. Unfortunately between 1860 and 1890 there was a 50 percent decrease in the prices of wheat. Similarly the years between 1873 and 1894 saw the production of cotton double, while the price per pound fell from $.15 to $.06.

This trend toward increased yields partially began when the Department of Agriculture was created by President Lincoln in 1862. While certainly not a negative in itself, the Department of Agriculture did act as a catalyst for a more scientific approach to farming. Education was also provided by the Patrons of Husbandry starting in 1867. They became known as simply "the Grange." The Grange provided information on new planting techniques and equipment and acted as a social organization for farmers.

Other factors helped to increase production. One of the most important was the increasing mechanization of farm equipment. This trend began as early as 1820 with improvements and the mechanization through steam engines of such implements as harvesters, plows, cultivators, seed drills, hay rakes, and threshers. By 1892 gasoline engines were beginning to be used to power tractors, though on a limited basis.

State experimentation stations were also important in increasing farm yields. The first was established in 1875 in Connecticut. During the 1880s other states followed suit. Again, these stations helped to develop hardier, more productive crops. In addition to all of this, more land became available for the American farmer.

GOING WEST

The Homestead Act of 1862 allowed a homesteader a 160-acre parcel of free land in the west. By 1900 80 million acres of land had been parceled out through the Homestead Act. This, in conjunction with the Pacific Railway Act of 1862, opened up land in the west and provided a means of transporting crops to market. The railroads received 175 million acres of land, which they often sold or rented to the public.

A prime example of the potential productivity of farming in the west is exemplified by wheat farming in the Red River Valley of North Dakota and Minnesota. Here railroad officials contracted to have wheat grown on some of their land. In 1875 Oliver Dalyrymple was contracted to grow wheat and

These workers packed oranges in Florida for the national trade in the 1890s; the stacked orange crates in use in this period remained the standard style for decades.

produced 23 bushels per acre. In 1877 he managed to produce 25 bushels per acre. These production figures were outstanding. In 1915 the Department of Agriculture reported the average bushel of winter wheat per acre as 16.6 bushels and spring wheat 15.3 bushels per acre.

These production rates did not occur everywhere. After Dalyrymple's success, the Red River Valley had 82 farms of 1,000 acres or more growing wheat. But by 1883 drought and falling prices forced farmers there to scale down and diversify. Drought, low prices, and pestilence were the farmer's bane. It was even worse in the west at this time.

Economic failure was not entirely a matter of overproduction or the scourge of Mother Nature. There was the often high cost of shipping crops on the railroad. When the railroads had a monopoly on transportation in an area, they would often charge much more to carry freight than they charged in similar areas back east where multiple lines ran and competition kept the rates lower.

The government gave tax breaks to industries, but curiously not to farmers, as they had to pay the full tax. Interest rates from banks for the purchase of farming equipment were another added burden. In Kansas, for instance, interest rates could vary from 40 to 375 percent, and farmers sometimes had to pay burdensome special fees. And in the south tenant farming and sharecropping

The President's Diary

President Rutherford B. Hayes retired from the White House in 1881 after serving just one term, and worked on humanitarian causes the remainder of his life. As president, Hayes lost the support of the Republican Party with his less than flattering view toward trusts and his concern over the concentration of wealth in a few hands. Excerpted below are passages from his diary written in 1886 and 1887 where he voices his concerns regarding trusts.

January 22, 1886. Friday. How to distribute more equally the property of our country is a question we (Theodore Clapp and I) considered yesterday. We ought not to allow a permanent aristocracy of inherited wealth to grow up in our country. How would it answer to limit the amount that could be left to any one person by will or otherwise? What should be the limit? Let no one receive from another more than the law gives to the chief justice, to the general of the Army, or to the president of the Senate. Let the income of the property transmitted equal this, say $10,000 to $20,000. If after distributing on this principle there remains undistributed part of the estate, let it go to the public.

March 19. Friday. No man, however benevolent, liberal, and wise, can use a large fortune so that it will do half as much good in the world as it would if it were divided into moderate sums and in the hands of workmen who had earned it by industry and frugality. The piling up of estates often does great and conspicuous good. Such men as Benjamin Franklin and Peter Cooper knew how to use wealth. But no man does with accumulated wealth so much good as the same amount would do in many hands.

December 4, 1887. Sunday. In church it occurred to me that it is time for the public to hear that the giant evil and danger in this country, the danger which transcends all others, is the vast wealth owned or controlled by a few persons. Money is power. In Congress, in state legislatures, in city councils, in the courts, in the political conventions, in the press, in the pulpit, in the circles of the educated and the talented its influence is growing greater and greater. Excessive wealth in the hands of the few means extreme poverty, ignorance, vice, and wretchedness as the lot of the many. The previous question is as to the danger of the evil.

often led farmers to diminished incomes and increased debt because farmers paid rent and endured excessive credit rates.

In addition to the adversity from overproduction, weather, taxes, and fees, the American farmer during the Gilded Age was forced to compete internationally while most manufacturers were not. The government artificially kept the prices of many American manufactured goods, such as farm equipment, high by taxing imported goods with tariffs. But there were no tariffs on

These volunteer interpreters at the Florida State Fair Grounds in Tampa demonstrate shingle making and other carpentry skills used more than a century ago.

imported foods. As a result, the wheat farmer for example had to compete with wheat from Canada and Australia, thus driving American prices—and American profits—down.

All of this combined to take America from a primarily agrarian society to a primarily industrial society. Fewer and fewer people were employed on farms, and more and more were employed in factories, foundries, steel mills, and mines.

MINING AND RAW MATERIALS

One of the most important raw materials for industry in the Gilded Age was coal. The census of 1870 rated coal the most profitable natural resource in the country, valuing coal production at $73,524,992. The next closest raw material to coal was petroleum, valued at $19,304,224. By 1900 the United States would produce 31.9 percent of all the coal in the world.

The workers who produced all of this coal were primarily new immigrants. Between 1877 and 1890 there were six million immigrants to the United States. These immigrants were mainly from northern and western Europe. While a good many of the coal mines were located in the Appalachian area, a good example of the immigrant mixture in the mines is Braidwood, Illinois, in 1873. At the Vermillion Coal Company in Braidwood, about 50 percent of the miners were Irish; 25 percent were English,

Scottish and Welsh. There were also miners from Sweden, Italy, Germany, France, Belgium, Poland, and Russia, as well as some native born miners. There were no child labor laws at this time so mines, in general, also included boys as young as nine years old. The younger ones worked as door boys, driver boys, and breaker boys.

THE DEPRESSION YEARS

Both 1873 and 1893 are important years for labor in the United States, as they were economic depression years. For coal miners, this meant that the production of coal—and thus work—would have to decrease. In human terms it meant that there would be layoffs and potential wage losses. In 1874, 25 percent of the miners were laid off and the wages for digging coal went from $1.25 a ton to $1.10 a ton. But even before the 1873 depression, demand had begun to slacken.

The Civil War had created a huge demand—9.5 million tons near the end of the war. This production, despite a lower demand after the war, continued building, reaching 16.1 million tons by 1870. Early on a small portion of the overproduction problems could perhaps be attributed to technology—new explosives and steam powered drills. Later in the century, the effect of mechanization would increase. In 1891 the average tonnage per man per day was 2.57; by 1899 it was 3.05 due to technology. But the primary source

Blacksmiths using traditional tools as shown in this display continued to play a major role as general mechanics through the last decades of the 19th century.

of overproduction in the 1870s came from the way the business was structured. Many of the coal companies leased their land and their contracts stipulated a minimum tonnage—regardless of market demand. And because of the seasonal nature of the business (coal was, among other things, used for home heating), it was difficult for owners to gauge the correct amount to produce.

In large part because of the depression of 1873, labor leaders began to press hard (though it had been suggested as early as 1836) for eight-hour work days—and not just in the coal industry. The major reason for this was to reduce overproduction and periods of idleness for the worker. An 1884 report from the state of Pennsylvania showed that coal miners were idle 186 days of the year. But success in this area during the 19th century was restricted to a limited number of localities and industries and to federal workers, who gained the eight-hour work day in 1868.

By 1900 petroleum use had gone beyond such forms as lamp kerosene.

Coal mining, like all underground mining, was—and is—difficult and dangerous labor. During the Gilded Age the average work day was 10 hours, and the average daily wage over a 30-year period was about $1.60. Young boys in the mine made between $.65 and $.75 per day. Statistics show that from 1872 until 1902, 10,000 men and boys were killed in the mines and 25,000 injured. In addition a portion of miners' wages went back to the mining company through the company store where they bought or leased their equipment and often rented their housing.

Other metals and raw materials that helped to create labor and employment included copper, iron ore, lead, nickel, lumber, petroleum, marble, slate, zinc, gold, and silver. Lumber, of course, was important in the building trades and for the creation of the railroads. For most of the 19th century petroleum was used for kerosene and lubricants, but toward the end of the century (with the beginning use of the combustible engine) it began to be used for gasoline. Iron ore had a huge impact upon industry in the United States as it was used in the creation of household implements (such as stoves), agricultural implements, and steel.

INDUSTRY

The Gilded Age was the boom period for American industry. Between 1865 and 1900 industrial production in the United States increased by 700 percent.

It is in industry that division of labor, mechanization, and technology had its most profound effect on worker productivity. Between 1860 and 1890—a mere thirty years—the U.S. government issued 440,000 patents for new inventions. From 1776 to 1860, there had only been 36,000 patents. Clearly it was a time for many firsts and many industry milestones. Skyscrapers were first built during the Gilded Age; the sleeping car was invented, as well as the telephone, the light bulb, the air brake, and even Coca-Cola and the zipper—among many other things. These changes created more jobs, cheaper and—in most cases—better products, but at the cost of dehumanizing the work experience.

A good example of the effect of division of labor and technology is in the shoemaking industry. This industry went from the individual shoemaker to the wholesale manufacture of shoes. Prior to about 1850 shoes were made with hand tools, most of which had been used for centuries. In 1846 the sewing machine was invented and gradually filtered its way into the shoemaking business. There were other machines added as well: beating out machines, power sole-molders, and foot die machines. Lynn, Massachusetts, had been one of the centers of shoe making in America since 1635. In 1795 they made 300,000 pairs of shoes. In 1877 after division of labor and technological innovations, they made 14 million pairs of shoes.

Another example of division of labor through new machinery was in the cigar industry. Prior to 1869 a single cigar maker would create each cigar, rolling it by hand. In 1869 a simple machine, the mould, was introduced. While this did not create the intricate division of labor of the shoemaking industry or the garment industry, it did bring up one of the primary labor issues of the day: the loss of jobs through the use of non-skilled workers, especially women and children. It is said that a person could be taught to use a mould, which was used to shape the filler tobacco, in two weeks time, while it took three years to properly teach someone to hand roll a cigar. And because women and children could be hired for less than a master cigar roller, it was a financial bonus for

The "Rawleigh Man" was a travelling peddler, bringing manufactured products to rural districts aboard his specially-designed horse-drawn wagon.

African-American women and a few men sorting tobacco at the T.B. Williams Tobacco Company in Richmond, Virginia, around 1899.

the employer and it sped up the process. Many workers were against this. Nevertheless the cigar industry thrived during the Gilded Age. The city of Tampa, Florida, for instance, had around 200 cigar factories employing 12,000 workers from diverse ethnic backgrounds and an annual payroll of nearly $2 million.

The cigarette industry experienced similar innovation that increased productivity. Prior to 1881 tobacco companies sold pouches of tobacco and consumers had to roll their own cigarettes. But in 1881 James Buchanan Duke invented a cigarette machine that made 200 cigarettes a minute. Eight years later Duke was selling 800 million cigarettes a year.

CITIES OF INDUSTRY

The steel industry is another example of a great American industry. The Carnegie Steel Company was the premier example. In Homestead, near Pittsburgh, the steel worker worked 13.5 hours a day, six days a week. Fifty percent of the workers made less than $12 a week, and the average was less than $15 a week. Even for its time this was considered minimum subsistence pay. The

The Pinkerton National Detective Agency

Allan Pinkerton (left) standing with President Lincoln and Major General McClernand at the Battle of Antietam, October 3, 1862.

Allan Pinkerton was a classic example of the new American. Born near Glasgow, Scotland, on August 25, 1819, Pinkerton was forced to flee Scotland the day after his wedding due to his involvement in a radical group, the Chartists, who were agitating for a more personal say in the government. He started his own barrelmaking company in Chicago (an ardent abolitionist, his shop also functioned as a stop in the Underground Railroad) but after successfully helping the police to break up a counterfeiting ring, he began working as a detective for the City of Chicago.

In 1850 he and his brother Robert began the Pinkerton Detective Agency. His company logo, an unblinking eye with the words, "We never sleep," was the source for the phrase "private eye." The Federal Bureau of Investigation was also modeled after its organization. The company soon became famous for its detective work, especially in railroad robberies. During one of their railroad investigations, they uncovered a plot to assassinate President Lincoln before his inauguration. Lincoln then used Pinkerton to do spy work during the Civil War and Allan Pinkerton uncovered and arrested a southern spy, Rose O'Neal Greenhow. After the war, the company solved train and bank robberies and pursued wanted men, including the James-Younger Gang and Butch Cassidy and the Sundance Kid, who fled to South America.

The company grew unpopular with portions of the public for its protection of private businesses and the lives of strike breakers. The most famous example was during the Homestead Strike in 1892 at the steel mill owned by Andrew Carnegie. The plant manager, Henry C. Frick, hired the Pinkerton Agency to protect the plant and the strike breakers against the approximately 3,000 strikers. Three hundred Pinkerton men, armed with rifles, came by barges down the river and were told by the strikers not to land. They did and gunfire broke out (no one knows who fired first). The Pinkertons retreated to their barges and a gun battle raged for 14 hours. The strikers tried to sink the barges with a flaming railcar, dynamite, and oil. In the end three Pinkerton men were killed and nine workers were dead, and the Pinkertons surrendered. Many sympathized with the strikers, not the Pinkerton men.

workforce, like those in the mines, was often made up of immigrants. In fact there were 161 different ethnic groups working in the Homestead mill. Out of all this, the steel industry in the United States by 1900 was producing 36.7 percent of all the steel in the world.

Within cities, sweat shops had also sprung up. These were primarily related to the garment industry. They, too, used many immigrants—most often women—and had developed from the craft of tailors (who would create a piece of clothing from beginning to end) to the division of labor and piece work of mass-produced clothing. Some of the most famous examples were those found in the slums of Manhattan, particularly in the tenements of the Lower East Side. Here manufacturers would contract a sweat shop to assemble clothing. These shops were most often located in immigrants' apartments, typically only three rooms large. Yet the shop itself might employ anywhere from four to 30 workers.

Division of labor broke down into such jobs as sewing machine operator, button sewer, baster, presser, finisher, and helper. The workers could work from 15 to 18 hours a day. The manufacturer would supply the contractor with cut material and then pay by the bundle of clothes made. An example supplied by the East Side Tenement Museum for 1900 demonstrates a typical pay scale for 300 coats assembled: $9.00 for the button sewer, $15 for the sewing machine operator, and $13.30 for the baster.

Women sewing clothes at a small table in a sweatshop on Suffolk Street in New York City's Lower East Side in 1908.

Women labeling cans of "Veribest" brand products in Armour's Packing Plant in Chicago in 1909.

New York and Pittsburgh were not the only cities to have a particular industry associated with them. For Chicago, it was the meat packing industry. Perhaps the first technological breakthrough in this industry was the invention in 1872 of ice-cooled units to store meat. This enabled them to process meat during warm weather. Then in 1882 Gustavus Swift invented the refrigerated railroad car. But most importantly, perhaps, the meat industry created the assembly line method, which would later be extremely important to the Ford Motor Company and other modern factories.

The cyclical nature of much of this industrial work led some workers to join unions. This especially happened during the two depressions, in 1873 and 1893, when many layoffs and wage cuts occurred. Unfortunately the friction at these times between management and workers often led to violence.

UNIONS

The Gilded Age can be seen as the beginning of the labor movement in the United States. Labor unions were not as popular as they are today. This was due in part because people enjoyed the new consumer goods made at lower prices and, in general, people held more conservative, pro-capitalist beliefs, including the belief in private property. In fact in 1900 union workers made up less than three percent of the total labor force.

In general, labor unions argued for limited immigration, an eight-hour work day, and limits on the employment of women and children. Their reasons for supporting these issues were not always the same as today. Their main goal was to keep as many people employed in a regular fashion at the highest wages possible. Many of the unions focused only on skilled workers. As division of labor and new technologies emerged, companies found ways to use unskilled laborers to do many of the jobs of skilled workers. This sometimes led the unions to fight to keep the employment of women, immigrants, and children to a minimum because all of these groups—usually unskilled—would work for lower wages. There was little other recourse for the unions, as unionization was not universal nor was it compulsory.

Samuel Gompers

A one-time apprentice shoemaker and a cigar maker, Samuel Gompers—another example of the classic new American—became one of the most important of America's labor leaders. He was one of the founders of the American Federation of Labor (AFL) and served as its president until his death. He took the AFL from a membership in 1886 of 50,000 workers to almost three million by 1924.

Born in England on January 26, 1850, he quit school at age 10 and for nearly three years worked first as a shoemaker's apprentice, and then as a cigar maker's apprentice with his father. Then in 1863 he immigrated to the United States with his family. Like many Jewish immigrants, they first lived in a tenement in Manhattan's Lower East Side. He went to school at night and continued to work making cigars. He became a naturalized citizen in 1872.

His first leadership role in the unions was in 1875 when he was elected president of Local 144 of the Cigar Makers' International Union (CMIU). While holding the post of vice president in the national CMIU during the 1880s and 1890s, he also became instrumental in the creation of the Federation of Organized Trades and Labor Unions in 1881. This organization then became the AFL in 1886. When the union started, its treasury held the sum total of $160 and Gompers's office was described as an 8-by-10 room in a shed.

Gompers's philosophy during the Gilded Age was to focus only on skilled workers—but not any one particular skill. He brought skilled workers from many trades into one umbrella organization. He tried to steer the AFL away from socialism and violence. His goals included the eight-hour work day, better working conditions, and, of course, higher wages. He was also a patriot and supported America's involvement in World War I. After the war President Woodrow Wilson appointed him to the Commission on International Labor Legislation at the Versailles Peace Conference.

Gompers died on December 13, 1924.

Samuel Gompers at his desk in 1908. His innovations at the AFL increased its membership and included an emphasis on nonviolence.

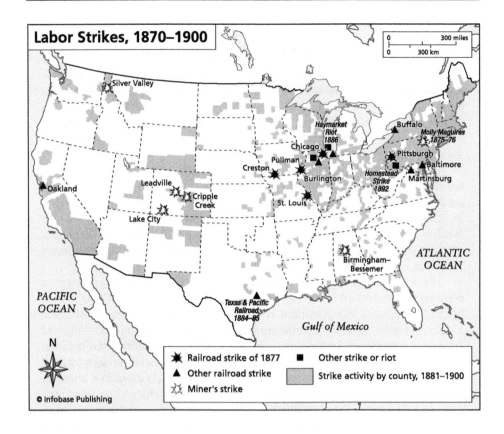

Some of the larger unions included the Knights of Labor, founded in 1869; the American Railway Union (1893); the Amalgamated Association of Iron and Steel Workers (1876); the American Federation of Labor (1886); the United Mine Workers (1890); and the Cigar Makers' Union (1864). There were also other, smaller unions, including the Knights of St. Crispin (1867), which represented shoe workers, the Iron Molders Union (1859), the Colored National Labor Union (1869), and the International Ladies Garment Workers (1900).

Between 1881 and 1894 there were about 14,000 labor conflicts, though the majority were nonviolent. Nevertheless state militias were sometimes brought in to quell disturbances, and federal troops were sometimes used in the 1870s during railroad strikes. There were also several examples of extreme violence during the Gilded Age.

The Pennsylvania coal mines in the 1870s are a prime example. Though the facts are controversial, many people blamed the brutal Irish secret society, the Molly Maguires, for the violence. Regardless who actually was behind it, labor strife in the coal fields led to the murder of about 50 people, including a number of the mine managers.

Chicago in 1886 is another example. This was the location of The Haymarket Square bombing. It was preceded by violent demonstrations in other cities including Milwaukee, Wisconsin, where seven protestors were killed by the National Guard. Several unions were present in Chicago, including both the nonviolent Knights of Labor and the socialist group the International Working People's Association, led by anarchist Albert Parsons. When strike breakers attempted to cross the picket line, violence broke out, four people were killed, and the Chicago police intervened. Parsons then planned a rally for the next day at the Haymarket Square. There a bomb was thrown and seven police officers were killed as well as four workers. Finally there was the 1892 Homestead Strike where strikers and Pinkerton employees, sent to protect the strike breakers, had a 14-hour gun battle, leaving three Pinkerton men and nine strikers dead.

The Grange also worked as a type of union at times. They attempted to unite farmers together in cooperatives that set up stores and processing plants. At their peak, the Granges had 1.5 million members and 20,000 chapters. But they began to decline as an economic force during the 1880s. Related to the Granges was the Farmers' Alliances, a more political force that came into power—and went out of power—in the 1890s. They connected with the dissatisfied farmers in the north and south and became attached to the Populist Party.

CONCLUSION

While some industrialization and division of labor had begun in the first part of the 19th century, the Gilded Age was arguably the time of the most dramatic changes in labor, employment, and the economy in the history of the country.

On the positive side, the United States became one of the most dominant countries in the world during the years between 1870 and 1900. Huge waves of immigrants came into the country, and America truly became a melting pot. They generally found jobs, though employment could be irregular. This was not because industry and agriculture were not producing—there was a huge boom in productivity and technological improvements. Generally it was because supply and demand—for many complicated reasons—were often not balanced.

On the negative side, wealth was not yet distributed in an equitable way. In 1890, there were 12 million families in the United States, but 11 million of those families had a yearly income of less than $1,200, with the average at only $380 a year. As a result, the Gilded Age also saw the beginning of American labor unions that attempted—sometimes violently—to create economic equality.

WILLIAM TOTH

Further Reading

Bolles, Albert. *Industrial History of the United States*. Norwich, CT: The Henry Bill Publishing Company, 1881.

Davis, Lance E., Jonathan R.T. Hughes, and Duncan M. McDougall. *American Economic History: The Development of a National Economy*. Homewood, IL: Richard D. Irwin, 1969.

eHistory at OSU. "Coal Mining in the Gilded Age and Progressive Era." Available online, URL: http://ehistory.osu.edu/osu/mmh/gildedage/default.cfm. Accessed January 2008.

Gutman, Herbert G. "The Workers' Search for Power." In *The Gilded Age*. Ed. by H. Wayne Morgan. Syracuse, NY: Syracuse University Press, 1970.

Hakim, Joy. *An Age of Extremes*. New York: Oxford University Press, 1994.

Klein, Herbert S. *A Population History of the United States*. New York: Cambridge University Press, 2004.

Mintz, Steven and Susan Kellogg. *Domestic Revolutions: A Social History of American Family Life*. New York: The Free Press, 1988.

Morgan, H. Wayne. "Populism and the Decline of Agriculture." In *The Gilded Age*. Ed. by H. Wayne Morgan. Syracuse, NY: Syracuse University Press, 1970.

Rasmussen, Wayne D. *Readings in the History of American Agriculture*. Urbana, IL: University of Illinois Press, 1960.

Sinclair, Andrew. *A Concise History of the United States*. Stroud, UK: Sutton Publishing, 1999.

Yellowitz, Irwin. *Industrialization and the American Labor Movement 1850–1900*. Port Washington, NY: Kennikat Press, 1977.

Chapter 13

Military and Wars

"From where the sun now stands,
I will fight no more forever."
— Nez Perce Indian Chief Joseph

FOLLOWING THE CIVIL WAR the U.S. Army found itself in the unfamiliar role of overseeing military reconstruction of the former Confederate states. In addition, as Reconstruction drew to a close the Army was drawn increasingly into intervention in urban labor disputes. Although to some extent this task was an extension of the work the Army had performed in putting down wartime draft riots or the racial riots of Reconstruction, at the same time Army commanders were often unsure how to act when called upon to do so. Only the president could authorize the use of military force in domestic disputes when requested to do so by the governor or legislature of a state or territory, but the Army lacked clear guidelines regarding how exactly to perform once the orders had been issued.

In general, the Army's mission was to act as an armed and organized police force to make sure that federal, state, or territorial laws were obeyed during a strike. In the event, however, the efforts of strike breakers to interfere with an employer's efforts to conduct business as usual by hiring other workers sometimes spilled over into confrontations and even violence.

The post–Civil War era also saw a long-needed reform of the militia system. There was no national uniformity to the reform, which pursued different paths in the individual states, but after 1875 developments increasingly followed similar courses. Most but not all of the states referred to their reformed militias as the National Guard. There were both white and African-American guard units, although in the south the latter gradually disappeared as the Jim Crow system of racial segregation took root. Like the Army, National Guard units were used frequently during outbreaks of labor unrest.

Technological and tactical innovations were other notable hallmarks of the post-bellum era. Improvements in weaponry for both land and naval forces revolutionized warfare in the late 19th century, exemplified by the rapid victories of Prussia in the Austro-Prussian War of 1866 and the Franco-Prussian War of 1870–71, and by the growing ability of European nations to project their power overseas and build new colonial empires in Africa and Asia. Improvements in steam technology made sail-powered warships obsolete and the replacement of ironclad boats with vessels protected by steel made naval ships more formidable. Advocates of military modernization in the United States stressed the necessity of keeping up with European rivals for national security and for improving the nation's economic power abroad. Officers also fully recognized the positive effect that a more active and updated military would hold for their own careers. Accompanying the technological modernization of the armed forces was an evolution in strategic and tactical doctrine. In the Army, military reformer Emory Upton attempted to internalize the lessons learned from the Civil War and adapt tactics to fit the world of the breech-loading rifle. Naval theorist Alfred Thayer Mahan was a vigorous proponent not only of a modernized Navy, but also of an America able to use naval power to protect its overseas interests and expand the nation's power through control of the oceans.

These changes were interrelated to the nation's political and military policies and the cultural mood. Manifest Destiny, the old idea that the United States was destined to stretch from coast to coast, became linked to Social Darwinism and Western views of white racial and cultural superiority and the consequent "need" to spread Western civilization through domination and conquest, while dominating foreign markets. The latter meant that the nation would have to compete increasingly with rival imperialist powers from western Europe and, eventually, Japan. For the United States, this meant completing the subjugation of Native Americans at home, and the spread of American influence in the Caribbean and Pacific.

NATIVE AMERICAN CONFLICTS

The outbreak of the Civil War in April 1861 did not bring an end to ongoing conflict between the U.S. government and the Native American peoples of the west. This was despite the fact that most regular Army units were sent eastward to participate in the war. Instead, the place of the regulars was taken by volunteer units raised for from six to 12 months' service or for the duration of the conflict.

The source of the ongoing troubles was the continuing pressures that white settlement placed on the Native Americans west of the Mississippi, a process that went unabated despite the struggle that threatened the nation. The organization of the region into territories and states also continued. The gold and silver mines of the west were crucial to the federal war effort, and their protection had to be ensured. In addition the secession of the southern states and the Civil War forced some tribes to take sides or split. In the Indian Territory (modern Oklahoma), close to the military operations of the Mississippi Valley and the guerrilla violence that wracked Missouri and Kansas, the tribes that had been forced westward during the administration of Andrew Jackson found themselves directly caught up in the Civil War.

The Creeks, Seminoles, and Cherokees divided into pro-Union and pro-Confederate factions, while the Chickasaws and Choctaws sided with the Confederacy. Federal incursions into the Indian Territory culminated in the battle of Honey Springs in July 1863, in which the pro-Confederate

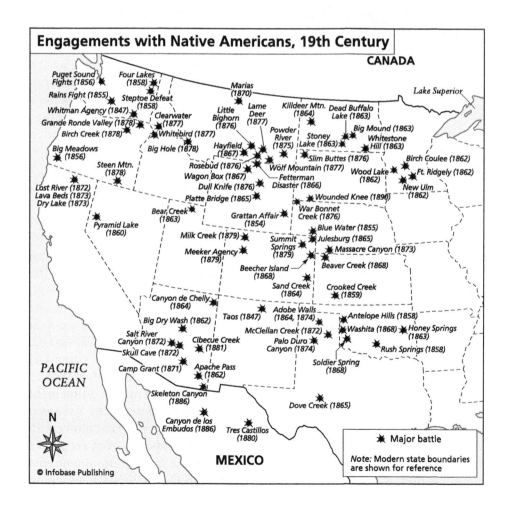

Engagements with Native Americans, 19th Century

Colonel Christopher "Kit" Carson, whose harsh tactics helped the U.S. Army in the Indian Wars.

Native Americans were decisively defeated. Many fled the area, although some remained active; the last Confederate force to surrender in 1865 was that of Brigadier General Stand Watie, a Cherokee.

Other violence was unrelated to the war. In the southwest fighting broke out between the U.S. Army and the Mimbres and Chiricahua Apaches in February 1861 after federal officers accused Cochise, leader of the latter people, of responsibility for a raid in fact committed by another Apache tribe. The conflict subsided briefly when Confederate forces occupied part of the Arizona Territory, as the newcomers prudently decided not to antagonize the Native Americans. When the Confederate effort to seize the region collapsed in early 1862, volunteer forces loyal to the United States led by Brigadier General James H. Carleton moved into the area, and fighting soon resumed.

By early 1863 the violence had claimed the life of Mangas Colorado, leader of the Mimbres Apaches. By that time the conflict had spread to the Mescalero Apaches and the Navajos. Troops under Carleton and Colonel Christopher "Kit" Carson, the former "mountain man," defeated the Mescaleros by 1863 and the Navajos by 1864, campaigns in which Carson's ruthless tactics against the Native Americans' means of sustenance proved crucial to U.S. victory. The Navajos and Mescaleros were exiled from their homes to Bosque Redondo on the Pecos River. Many died due to the harsh conditions of reservation life. The Mescaleros escaped and returned home in 1865, while the Navajos were allowed to go home in 1868. In the meantime, Carson went after the Comanches and Kiowas, who had been troubling the Santa Fe Trail. Carson's command and the Kiowas fought to a draw at Adobe Walls, Texas, in November 1864.

In the western plains, the Fort Wise Treaty of 1861 led to the confinement of some Cheyenne and Arapahoe into a reservation south of the Arkansas River in exchange for their traditional lands. Not all chiefs went along with the treaty, however, and resentment grew as land pressures from settlers in the Colorado Territory mounted. As tensions arose over an imminent vote for statehood, it was the whites who struck first. Colonel John Chivington launched attacks against the Native Americans, either out of fear of a possible attack or seeking a pretext for war; both Chivington and Governor John Evans harbored political ambitions. Retaliatory raids from the Native Americans followed. Although peace terms were arranged in September 1864 between Black Kettle, a prominent Cheyenne chief, and Major Edward W. Wynkoop, who was friendly toward the Native Americans, public pressure and Chivington's own aggressiveness led to a more fatal outcome. Chivington launched a surprise attack on Black Kettle's camp at Sand Creek on November 29, 1864, slaughtering nearly 200 Native Americans.

In Minnesota violence broke out in 1862 between starving Sioux living on a reservation and white settlers. In August 1862 nearly 400 settlers were killed. Colonel Henry H. Sibley of the Minnesota militia led forces that retaliated, defeating the Native Americans in September. The surviving Sioux fled westward, many joining other Sioux tribes. U.S. Major General John Pope had already arrived by that point to take command of the Military Department of the Northwest. Under Pope's authority, Sibley moved into the Dakota Territory against the Sioux in 1863.

By the end of 1864 Pope had been granted control of much of the Trans-Mississippi West, embodied in the Department of the Missouri. Most of the major Native American tribes were by then restless as a result of the Sand Creek Massacre. Pope launched a major campaign against the Plains tribes in the spring of 1865, but it ended inconclusively, with the federal forces unable to bring the

This 1868 engraving shows Native Americans from the camp of Black Kettle, who were captured by General Custer in a later incident, being marched through the snow.

Emory Upton and Army Reform

Military reform became an important issue after the Civil War. The heavy casualties inflicted on both sides due to the use of infantry lines several ranks deep, or large columns of troops advancing in the face of rifle and artillery fire, which only improved in accuracy as the war progressed, led to calls for change among Army commanders. Active and former officers either calling for change or forecasting its necessity ranged from William Tecumseh Sherman and Philip H. Sheridan to George B. McClellan. Sherman in particular took an active role, especially after he became general of the army under the presidential administration of Ulysses S. Grant. Sherman especially emphasized the importance of a better educational curriculum for aspiring officers, not only including West Point, but also a specialized school for cavalry and infantry instruction at Fort Leavenworth, Kansas.

Among the key figures advocating military reform in the post-bellum era was Emory Upton, a protégé of both Grant and Sherman. A native of New York, Upton was a West Point graduate who rose rapidly through the officer ranks during the Civil War. On two occasions he was allowed to experiment with the use of looser attack formations of infantry than was the norm. Upton's ideas were shaped directly by his disgust at the loss of life in Civil War combat.

In 1867 he summarized his ideas in the book *A New System of Infantry Tactics, Double and Single*, which the U.S. War Department adopted for both the Army and the National Guard. Upton's system advocated loose formations of troops, organized around four-man squads for flexibility. Infantrymen would fight more often in single-rank lines rather than mass formations, to minimize casualties when advancing or defending against opponents armed with the latest breech-loading rifles and repeater rifles.

In addition to his efforts at tactical reform, Upton advocated changes in organization and policy. He was critical of the army's staff system, and advocated the creation of a general staff inspired by that of Prussia, which had emerged as the greatest European military power in the years immediately following the Civil War. In addition, Upton was critical of the army's subordination to civilian officials who often lacked any experience in military affairs. In this matter he also followed the example of the Prussian general staff, which had few checks from civilian political leaders.

Upton also believed that the continuing reliance of the United States on a small peacetime army, supplemented during wartime by raising temporary regiments of volunteers, was a major weakness. He advocated instead a larger peacetime army that would be increased by the mobilization of well-trained reservists, another hallmark of the Prussian system. Upton's views met resistance, and it would not be until after World War I when American military leaders would fully institute infantry tactics adapted to the realities of modern firepower.

This painting by Amos Bad Heart Bull, an Oglala Lakota Sioux artist, narrates the Battle of Little Bighorn from a Native American perspective.

Native Americans into a major battle. War weariness among the public and the volunteer forces alike made another effort impossible for the moment.

For the next several years American policy toward the Native Americans was divided, with the War Department favoring aggressive military action to subdue the tribes, while the Interior Department espoused a more peaceful approach. Fighting continued nevertheless, as tribes continued to resist further white encroachment. A particular source of friction was the Bozeman Trail, a route running from Fort Laramie in Colorado into the buffalo-hunting grounds of modern-day Montana. Ongoing tensions with the Sioux, the Cheyennes, and the Arapahoes over the Bozeman Trail culminated in December, 1866, when a small band of U.S. cavalrymen under Captain William J. Fetterman were ambushed and wiped out near Fort Phil Kearny by a group of Native Americans under the leadership of the Oglala Sioux warrior Red Cloud. The resulting squabbling over future actions illustrated the conflicts within U.S. policy, as Lieutenant General William T. Sherman called for harsh action and even the possible extermination of the Native Americans, a view shared by other key figures including future president Ulysses S. Grant. At the same time, a committee under Senator James R. Doolittle of Wisconsin blamed white settlement for much of the policy and called for greater oversight of Native American affairs by the government. An expedition in 1867 against the Native Americans under Major General Winfield Scott Hancock, who had replaced Pope, came to nothing.

Minor actions continued in the following years, with the U.S. forces gradually gaining advantage. Peace treaties were signed with various tribes in an

This depiction of a line of U.S. soldiers at the opening of the Battle of Wounded Knee is based on a description provided by the 7th Cavalry.

effort to get the Native Americans to stay on well-defined reservations; these efforts met with mixed results, as not all chiefs would agree to come to terms, while many of the younger warriors, angry at the cessions of land which resulted, refused to submit. By 1868 Hancock had been replaced by the aggressive Major General Philip H. Sheridan, a protégé of Grant and Sherman who favored an aggressive policy. During the winter of 1868 Sheridan launched a campaign spearheaded by Lieutenant Colonel George Armstrong Custer and the 7th Cavalry. Trailing Cheyenne raiders, in November Custer came upon the camp of Black Kettle, who had not participated in the attacks. Once again, Black Kettle's camp was ambushed. Unlike the occurrence at Sand Creek, the chief did not escape this time.

Under the Grant administration, affairs related to Native Americans became more centralized, with the Indian Bureau becoming a part of the War Department. Grant's former wartime aide, Ely S. Parker, an Iroquois Native American, was appointed to head the bureau. Grant espoused a peaceful policy toward Native Americans that still called for their submission to the United States and resettlement onto reservations. Some progress was made toward ending longstanding conflicts, such as the negotiation of a peace with Cochise in 1872. Other conflicts continued and new ones erupted, as the needs of Native Americans were often not met by government officials as promised and as encroachments on their lands continued. Toward the middle of the 1870s, three major conflicts erupted on the Great Plains: the Red River War of 1874–75, the Great Sioux

War of 1876–77, and the Nez Perce War of 1877. Although the Army received some setbacks, most famously at the Battle of the Little Bighorn in June 1876, it was increasingly successful in suppressing the tribes and confining them to reservations. In the southwest, new fighting arose with the Mimbres and Chiricahuas Apaches in 1879 due to the harsh conditions of reservation life. The war continued until 1886, when the Chiricahua leader Geronimo surrendered. By this time, major tribal resistance had ended. There would be one more significant clash between the Army and Native Americans in December 1890, when an attempt to disarm some Miniconjou Sioux at Wounded Knee, South Dakota, led to fighting and the virtual annihilation of the band.

MANIFEST DESTINY GOES ABROAD

While the Indian Wars were fought within the borders of the United States, the nation was also concerned with foreign affairs. During the Civil War the government was concerned with encroachment from European powers in Mexico. Archduke Maximilian, brother of the Austrian emperor, had been set up by the French emperor Napoleon III as puppet ruler of Mexico, violating the Monroe Doctrine in the process. Distracted by the sectional conflict, the United States could do nothing until the Civil War was over, at which point diplomacy and an American military buildup on the Mexican border contributed to the French decision to leave.

By the time the French left Mexico in 1867 the Army and Navy were well into a reduction in strength typical of earlier post-bellum demobilizations and decommissions. Most of what remained of the Army was concentrated in the south or in the west. Although the strength of the Army continued to drop throughout the Reconstruction era, the reduction of the Navy, although initially severe, proved to be short-lived following the *Virginius* crisis with Spain in 1873. The *Virginius* was a former Confederate blockade runner engaged in carrying arms and rebel troops involved in a revolution in Cuba, a Spanish colonial possession. Stopped by a Spanish warship in international waters, the *Virginius* was boarded and many of its passengers and crew executed. Although the *Virginius* was acting in violation of U.S. neutrality policy, it was still an American vessel, and thus war with Spain threatened.

This group of African-American soldiers in 1899 fought in the Spanish-American War.

This mortar, captured in the Spanish-American War, is on display at Fort San Marcos, in Saint Augustine, Florida.

Although diplomacy averted the threat of a conflict, the panic revealed the weakness of the U.S. Navy. When the available fleet assembled off Florida for possible action in early 1874, it was small in size and strength. Proponents of the navy began pushing for expansion and reform. Rebuilding and modernization did not begin until the 1880s, including the introduction of battleships by the end of the decade. The naval expansion marked the beginning of what some have called the military-industrial complex, as rearmament and modernization was made possible by government contract bids to such growing firms as Carnegie Steel and Bethlehem Steel.

THE SPANISH-AMERICAN WAR

As the 19th century drew to a close, tensions were on the rise again between the United States and Spain over Cuba. In 1895 another revolution broke out on the island. The guerrilla war grew increasingly nasty. The United States remained neutral, despite hope from the guerrillas that it would intervene. Pressures mounted on U.S. President William McKinley to act, however, both out of humanitarian concern for the victims of Spain's harsh reprisal policies

Alfred Thayer Mahan and Navalism

The army was not the only branch of the U.S. military after the Civil War to have advocates for reform. Rear Admiral Stephen B. Luce played a role comparable to that of William Tecumseh Sherman in advocating educational reform, embodied by the U.S. Naval Institute and the Naval War College, established in 1873 and 1884 respectively. One of his protégés emerged as an influential figure in naval circles at home and abroad. Alfred Thayer Mahan was the son of Dennis Hart Mahan, a long-time instructor at West Point. The younger Mahan entered the Naval Academy and served during the Civil War, where he first met Luce. Mahan was invited by Luce to teach at the Naval War College in 1885. While there he published two books that caught the attention of advocates of a modernized, expanded Navy and political figures with imperialist ambitions: *The Influence of Sea Power Upon History, 1660–1763* (1890) and *The Influence of Sea Power Upon the French Revolution and Empire, 1793–1812* (1892).

Mahan's book examined the role of naval power in the successes of the British empire. His work aspired to be a grand synthesis of naval thought and action, attempting to find the immutable principles of naval success as illustrated through the British model. The ideas that Mahan advocated were the necessity of naval power for national protection, isolating and defeating a nation's enemies, and projecting military power abroad by protecting trade and dominating foreign markets. For the United States, this meant not only protecting America's shores and being able to defeat the navies of European rivals, but dominating the Caribbean and ensuring access to, and domination of, lucrative Asian markets. To achieve these goals, the U.S. Navy needed to modernize and create a large battleship fleet. Colonies needed to be acquired, including Hawaii as a stepping-stone to Asia, and a canal linking the Atlantic and Pacific in Central America needed to be built under American control.

Mahan's ideas were embraced with enthusiasm by proponents of naval reform. This was also a time when the old idea of Manifest Destiny was evolving into a call for imperialism beyond the nation's continental boundaries. European nations with imperialist ambitions, as well as the rising Asian power of Japan, found much in his work to justify their foreign policies. Yet Mahan's work remains subject to criticism. Besides its lack of originality, his efforts to use historical examples to provide a timeless framework were weak. He did not take into account the fact that England's success as an imperial naval power was due to a particular set of circumstances, as much as it was due to superior naval strategy or national policy. Despite this, Mahan achieved status as an unquestionable prophet among U.S. naval circles, while his ideas provided a baneful influence on not only the foreign and military policies of his own nation, but also those of other major powers. His legacy would be an acceleration of the imperialist and colonial ambitions already in play in his era, as well as a growing international naval rivalry that would contribute years later to the outbreak of a world war.

Teddy Roosevelt and his "Rough Riders" at the top of the hill they captured in the Battle of San Juan.

and imperialist ambitions of bringing the island into the U.S. sphere of influence. U.S. naval strategists were already planning for the contingency of a war.

In early 1898 a crisis erupted between the two nations. On February 15, the battleship U.S.S. *Maine* blew up in Havana harbor, losing over half its officers and crew. While the event was almost certainly an accident, an official naval investigation concluded that the ship had struck an underwater mine. This interpretation fanned suspicions among many American people that Spain was responsible. War fever swept the United States; both countries formally declared war in late April. The U.S. strategy would be to strike out at the Spanish colonies, in accordance with the pre-war naval strategy. Cuba would be the main effort, although secondary targets such as the Philippines were also included. As in earlier wars, the Army had to be expanded, and thus volunteer regiments were recruited, such as Colonel Leonard Wood's 1st U.S. Volunteer Cavalry Regiment (the "Rough Riders"), which would soon achieve fame under the leadership of Wood's second-in-command, Lieutenant Colonel Theodore Roosevelt, until recently assistant secretary of the Navy. Former Civil War officers (including some ex-Confederates) would lead units in combat for the last time.

The United States struck the first major blow of the war, although it occurred not in Cuba, but in the Philippines. Admiral George Dewey's squadron destroyed its Spanish counterpart at the battle of Manila Bay on May 1. Dewey lacked troops to make all of the Spanish forces in the islands surrender, however. Two other American squadrons blockaded a small Spanish squadron in Santiago Harbor in Cuba. After much prodding from McKinley, a U.S. invasion fleet was launched in mid-June, made up primarily of regular forces (including the army's four African-American regiments), and a few volunteer units such as the Rough Riders. The force was dispatched with uncertain goals, as the Navy only wanted troops ashore to capture the forts guarding Santiago Harbor, while the Army commander, Major General William R. Shafter, reserved the option of moving on the town of Santiago itself. Following initial landings in late June, Shafter decided on the latter option without consulting his naval colleague. Minor skirmishing was succeeded on July 1 by the pyrrhic American victories at El Caney and San Juan Heights, where larger American forces advanced under heavy fire against outposts held by badly outnumbered but determined Spanish troops. The attacks illustrated vividly the perils posed to foot soldiers advancing against prepared positions defended by troops armed with the latest firepower, a scenario that had only worsened since the days of the Civil War. Nevertheless the battles stirred the patriotic imagination of many Americans back home, thanks to newspaper coverage which emphasized the heroism of the regulars and volunteers.

Fearful that Santiago would fall, the Spanish governor of Cuba ordered the blockaded squadron to break out of the harbor, resulting only in its destruction by the larger American fleet. The result gave the Americans the option of dispatching one of its Atlantic squadrons to the Pacific, where Dewey was threatened by a large approaching Spanish fleet; realizing this, Spain ordered its recall, allowing the United States to secure its victory in the Philippines. Meanwhile, although the Army considered a withdrawal from the Santiago front, it achieved the surrender of the Spanish forces in Cuba instead. A new American expedition was launched against Puerto Rico, while land forces were sent on to the Philippines. Spain agreed to terms in August. Cuba received independence, while Puerto Rico and Guam were ceded to the United States. A subsequent conference granted the Philippines to the United States in December 1898.

AN INTERNATIONAL POWER

The Spanish-American War made the United States an international power. Dewey's victory at Manila Bay seemed a vindication of Mahan's theories. The outcome had a price, however. Even before the fighting ended in Cuba, relations had broken down between the U.S. forces and the Cuban revolutionaries, due to arrogant behavior on the part of Shafter (including a denial of any role for them in the Spanish surrender ceremony). The United States would not formally recognize Cuba as an independent nation until 1902, and American economic interests were firmly protected in the Cuban constitution. A worse situation brewed in the Philippines. Filipino revolutionaries formed their own republic before the American infantry requested by Dewey arrived, and the former were not happy with the subsequent American occupation of Manila. They were even less pleased by the cession of the islands to the United States. In 1899 a rebellion broke out, leading to a guerrilla war, which lasted until 1902.

Other troubles awaited in Asia, as the United States was soon embroiled alongside other imperialist powers in suppressing a major nationalist uprising in China. As the 19th century gave way to the 20th century, the U.S. armed forces would grapple with these and other conflicts associated with the nation's imperialist goals, as the western powers inched closer to a disastrous world-wide conflict.

MICHAEL W. COFFEY

Further Readings

Coffman, Edward M. *The Old Army: A Portrait of the American Army in Peacetime, 1794–1898*. New York: Oxford University Press, 1986.

Cooling, Benjamin Franklin. *Gray Steel and Blue Water Navy: The Formative Years of America's Military-Industrial Complex, 1881–1917*. Hamden, CT: Archon Books, 1979.

Cooper, Jerry M. "The Army and Industrial Workers: Strikebreaking in the Late 19th Century." In *Soldiers and Civilians: The U.S. Army and the American People*. Ed. by Garry D. Ryan and Timothy K. Nanninger. Washington, D.C.: National Archives and Records Administration, 1987.

———. *The Rise of the National Guard: The Evolution of the American Militia, 1865–1920*. Lincoln, NE: University of Nebraska Press, 1997.

Crowl, Philip A. "Alfred Thayer Mahan: The Naval Historian." In *Makers of Modern Strategy: From Machiavelli to the Nuclear Age*. Ed. by Peter Paret. Princeton, NJ: Princeton University Press, 1986.

Hutton, Paul Andrew. *Phil Sheridan and His Army*. Lincoln, NE: University of Nebraska Press, 1985.

Jamieson, Perry D. *Crossing the Deadly Ground: United States Army Tactics, 1865–1899*. Tuscaloosa, AL: The University of Alabama Press, 1994.

LaFeber, Walter. *The New Empire: An Interpretation of American Expansion, 1860–1898*. Ithaca, NY: Cornell University Press, 1967.

Millet, Allan R. and Peter Maslowski. *For the Common Defense: A Military History of the United States of America*. New York: The Free Press, 1994.

O'Toole, G.J.A. *The Spanish War: An American Epic—1898*. New York: W.W. Norton and Company, 1984.

Steward, T.G. *Buffalo Soldiers: the Colored Regulars in the United States Army*. New York: Humanity Books, 2003.

Utley, Robert M. *The Indian Frontier of the American West 1846–1890*. Albuquerque, NM: University of New Mexico Press, 1984.

Chapter 14

Population Trends
and Migration

"Give me your tired, your poor . . .
Send these, the homeless, tempest-tost to me."
— Statue of Liberty (Emma Lazarus's "The New Colossus")

THE TWO MAIN population trends of the Gilded Age were the boom in immigration—especially "new immigration," as Americans called the growing waves of immigration from countries without existing ties to the United States—and the redistribution of the native-born American population, as acquired territory was populated. While the rural population of the country doubled over the 30-year period, the urban population tripled, and the ongoing deruralization of America was underway. The increase in American agriculture was due principally to the overall expansion of the country, and all things industrial outpaced all things agrarian.

Much of that agricultural expansion goes hand in hand with the opening of the Great Plains, the last major agricultural frontier. While the total number of American farms only doubled, the number of farms in Kansas, Nebraska, and the Dakotas increased 800 percent. The Homestead Act and the Desert Land Act were passed to encourage settlers to move to those previously sparsely populated areas, by giving parcels of 160 acres to anyone who promised to build a home there, with additional acreage for those willing to plant trees or irrigate, depending on local needs. The building of the railroads and the adoption of open-range cattle ranching did much to encourage settlement of the plains, while the Oklahoma land runs helped to settle that territory virtually overnight.

CHINESE SETTLEMENT

In 1850 there were 758 Chinese living in the United States. By 1900 there were more than 100,000, most of them having arrived between the Civil War and 1880. The Chinese came to work cheaply as manual laborers, employed largely by the railroads, and settled in small communities and Chinatowns all along the transcontinental railroad tracks. Even more than most immigrant groups, they were discriminated against from the beginning, with labor unions petitioning for strict immigration quotas; not until halfway through the 20th century were Chinese immigrants allowed to become American citizens.

Under the Qing Dynasty, it was illegal for natives to leave China—but in the 19th century, the power of the dynastic rulers was failing, and in practical terms the law was rarely enforceable. Those leaving the country would first depart for a European colony in Asia—Portuguese-controlled Macau, for instance, or British Hong Kong—and from there embark for the United States. Merchants could bring their wives and children with them, but laborers had to travel alone—many of them had families they intended to return to, and to whom they sent money once employed in America. Some villages sent their entire young male population abroad, providing an influx of foreign cash.

The Chinese were different in ways, and to degrees, that European immigrants were not. Few Chinese converted to Christianity, and Confucianism, Taoism, Buddhism, and ancestor worship were foreign belief systems with strange alien practices to most Americans. As late as 1950 only a minority of Chinese immigrants could speak English beyond a handful of phrases. Most Chinese immigrants—because they continued to visit China to see their families—continued to follow the Qing Dynasty law,

A man wearing a queue working as the first telephone operator in San Francisco's Chinatown.

This 1900 caricature entitled "As the Heathen See Us" imagines the Chinese viewpoint on events in America, such as lynchings and anti-Chinese riots.

which required men to shave the front of their heads and braid the remaining hair. Chinese men without their braids would often be barred from re-entering the country, but in America it made them appear not only strange, but unwilling to assimilate. The United States has long considered itself a melting pot, but it has repeatedly demonstrated intolerance for those bits which refuse to melt.

The difficulty of assimilating and the rapid pace of immigration led to the creation not only of the various Chinatowns, but also of various Chinese organizations that acted as a support network both for practical purposes and social reasons. At the same time, in many Chinese immigrant communities, the sex trade grew rapidly and lucratively. Very few Chinese women immigrated to the United States—even if there had been jobs for them, they were held responsible for caring for their extended family in China. Chinese men were at liberty to work in the United States—however illegally in the eyes of the Qing Dynasty—precisely because it was the women in their families who tended to the children and the elderly, and kept the household running.

The absence of women from Chinese immigrant communities—and the discovery in the 1870 census that nearly two-thirds of the Chinese women in California (where San Francisco had had a growing Chinatown since the Gold Rush) worked as prostitutes—was yet another log on the fire of anti-Chinese discrimination. The Page Act, passed five years later, put a staggering amount of control over Asian immigration (most of which was Chinese) in the hands

This team of Chinese firefighters in Deadwood, South Dakota, had just won a race through town on the Fourth of July, 1888.

Rural Chinese Settlement

A number of rural Chinese settlements were established in the last half of the 19th century, in addition to the Chinatowns in the bustling cities. Quite often these settlements were populated by Chinese who faced legal or social pressures in white cities. The Gold Rush town of Weaverville, outside of San Francisco, had a large population of Chinese fleeing the racism of the city, and the nearby town of Locke was established for the same reasons. Chinese Camp, California—sometimes called "Chinee"—was once a prosperous Gold Rush town and continued to thrive on mining until the end of the century.

Other small Chinatowns were settled throughout California and Nevada, and like other frontier towns they were often little more than small settlements with only two or three public buildings—a post office might double as the bank; a general store might also serve as the meeting hall and provide English translation services for a small fee. Many frontier Chinese communities had joss houses, multi-faith temples encompassing the major Chinese religious practices of Confucianism, Taoism, Buddhism, and ancestor worship. Self-governed Chinese communities also set up near rough-and-tumble frontier towns like Deadwood, where white sensibilities were less delicate than in the more established cities. Like many small frontier towns that have since dwindled, many of these rural Chinatowns are now preserved as museums and tourist attractions.

of the American officials processing would-be immigrants at their port of departure. The act allowed these officials to deny departure rights—to prevent the immigrant from coming to America—to any Asian immigrant that the official considered "obnoxious," and probably a prostitute or felony convict.

THE CHINESE EXCLUSION ACT

The growing number of Chinese inflamed anti-Chinese sentiments, which had started early in California with a state supreme court ruling that Chinese—like African Americans and Native Americans—were barred from testifying against whites in court. The economic troubles following the Civil War and Reconstruction brought with them the usual resentment of cheap labor, which in the areas where the Chinese had settled meant Chinese labor. Never mind the fact that the Chinese had been actively sought out by white business owners looking to profit from men who had families back home motivating them to work hard, but who because of that distance were available to work long hours for low wages. Those business owners, when confronted by labor interests and white workers unable to keep their jobs, blamed the Chinese for making it economically unfeasible to hire white men. Local and state laws were passed to restrict the rights of Chinese, and pressures were exerted on people in power in order to bring about the 1882 Chinese Exclusion Act, a federal law and the first major restriction enacted on U.S. immigration.

The Exclusion Act first and foremost banned from entrance into the country all Chinese laborers, skilled or unskilled, for the next 10 years, and required restrictively difficult paperwork from non-laborers (such as professionals, students, and merchants) seeking to immigrate, as well as the approval of the Chinese government. Furthermore, though U.S. citizenship had been redefined and broadened following the Civil War, Chinese were explicitly banned from citizenship (unless they were born in the United States).

When the act's 10-year term expired in 1892, it was immediately renewed by the Geary Act, which increased the punishment for violating any of the above and required all resident Chinese to carry a resident permit demonstrating that they had not entered the country illegally. Failure to have the permit in one's possession, even if it was simply at home, was punishable by deportation or a year of hard labor. The Exclusion Act had proven unpopular with many people, and when the Geary Act upped the ante, it was challenged in court—but the Supreme Court upheld it in an 1893 decision, with three justices dissenting. The act was also refined to extend its effect to all Chinese immigrants, not just laborers. Chinese immigration stopped in its tracks.

FORCED NATIVE AMERICAN MIGRATION

In the century that followed the 1776 Declaration of Independence, the new United States quickly moved to allow settlement of the west, despite earlier treaties with Native American tribal groups. By the 1820s and 1830s, the federal government, the states, and pioneer pressure had forcibly removed entire groups to areas west of the Mississippi. The United States established a pattern of removing native peoples to land considered worthless, then forcibly uprooting these groups once again when white settlers sought to expand into the territory.

Red Cloud Speaks

Red Cloud, chief of a tribe of the Teton Sioux Nation, toured the east in 1870. On July 16 he gave a speech at Cooper Union in New York City where he outlined the history of relations between the U.S. government and the Native Americans, and called for honest government agents and native maintenance of their own lands. Parts of that speech are excerpted below.

My brethren and my friends who are here before me this day, God Almighty has made us all, and He is here to bless what I have to say to you today. The Good Spirit made us both. He gave you lands and He gave us lands; He gave us these lands; you came in here, and we respected you as brothers. God Almighty made you but made you all white and clothed you; when He made us He made us with red skins and poor; now you have come.

When you first came we were very many, and you were few; now you are many, and we are getting very few, and we are poor. You do not know who appears before you today to speak. I am a representative of the original American race, the first people of this continent. We are good and not bad. The reports that you hear concerning us are all on one side. We are always well disposed to them. You are here told that we are traders and thieves, and it is not so. We have given you nearly all our lands, and if we had any more land to give we would be very glad to give it. We have nothing more. We are driven into a very little land, and we want you now, as our dear friends, to help us with the government of the United States.

And I am going to leave you today, and I am going back to my home. I want to tell the people that we cannot trust his agents and superintendents. I don't want strange people that we know nothing about. I am very glad that you belong to us. I am very glad that we have come here and found you and that we can understand one another. I don't want any more such men sent out there, who are so poor that when they come out there their first thoughts are how they can fill their own pockets.

We want preserves in our reserves. We want honest men, and we want you to help to keep us in the lands that belong to us so that we may not be a prey to those who are viciously disposed. I am going back home. I am very glad that you have listened to me, and I wish you good-bye and give you an affectionate farewell.

In the second half of the 19th century, the U.S. Army fought more than 1,000 battles in an effort to place remaining Native American tribes on reservations throughout the west. These reservations removed native peoples from land that white settlers desired. The federal government also attempted, with various policies during the 19th and 20th centuries, to weaken tribal loyalties and to turn natives into "Americans," that is, Christian, English-speaking farmers. An 1887 law sought to break up the reservations by allotting farms of up to 60 acres to Native American households. This left Native Americans even less living space, as any leftover land was given to white settlers. The process was also rife with corruption. Economic failure, sickness, and despair were too often part of life on the reservations.

EUROPEAN IMMIGRATION, NEW IMMIGRATION, AND ELLIS ISLAND

European immigration into the United States during the Gilded Age was primarily to the north and midwest. As economically depressed as the country was as a whole for part of this period, the south was especially poverty-stricken, and its native white and African-American sharecroppers had trouble enough making ends meet. There were no significant opportunities for new arrivals with neither land nor family ties, nor did the usual advantage of being willing to work cheaply work in immigrants' favor in this case, when many sharecroppers worked for little more than the ability to pay down their debt to their employer.

The European-born population nearly doubled between 1870 and 1900, much of it the result of trends already in motion before the start of the period. The Irish continued to steadily populate the areas where Irish and especially Irish Catholic neighborhoods had been established. German Lutherans dissatisfied with the reforms enacted on their church by the King of Prussia continued to set out for the United States where they could pursue their faith on their own terms. As part of the wave of "old immigration," as it would be called by the end of the period, these immigrants shared the American traditional concern with religious freedom and self-determination. Somewhat fitting with that were the hundreds of thousands of Jews who immigrated to the United States, many of whom were fleeing persecution across Europe, and pogroms in Russia.

But while the "old immigration" had come primarily from northern and western Europe—Great Britain and Ireland, France, and the Scandinavian countries, the countries which had along with Spain been involved with the original colonization of North America—the "new immigration" of the late 19th century originated in southern and eastern Europe, Russia, and Asia, parts of the world where few native-born Americans had family ties. Most of the old immigrants had been Protestants; few of the new immigrants were, and the dividing line between Protestants and Catholics was much sharper in that century than it is today.

Ellis Island Name Changes

An immigration officer examining documents and newcomers at the Ellis Island immigration station around 1907.

It is popularly believed that many immigrants had their names changed—simplified, usually—by officials at Ellis Island. Versions of this story vary from the immigrant who has his name "translated" into English, so that Arnold Zimmermann becomes Arnold Carpenter; the immigrant whose name is mangled by the English-speaking official who misspells it, simplifies the spelling, or just makes something up; and of course, in *The Godfather II*, Vito Corleone, who bears the name of his birthplace. But there is no evidence any of this ever occurred.

Ellis Island provided only one half of the processing involved in immigration—a similar process, after all, was involved in getting on the ships to begin with, and that process involved at least as much paperwork as at Ellis Island. Not only did the Bureau of Immigration employ translators for dozens of languages, the paperwork in the immigrant's point of origin would have been filled out by literate native speakers with no likelihood of misspelling or otherwise garbling a countryman's name. The ship's passenger manifest was also prepared long before arrival.

However the stories are not entirely wrong; they simply have the burden of responsibility on the wrong body of people. Many immigrants changed their names as they moved to the United States—as, indeed, many immigrants had changed their names upon moving to other countries then or in the past. A foreign name would be strange, and could mark one for generations. Many immigrants wanted to assimilate, and while changing their own name from Zimmermann to Carpenter would not rid them of a German accent or their Old Country ways, it would provide their future children—who would be born in America—with an "American identity." It could also be useful to adopt an American name to avoid prejudices against specific groups—as many Jews have adopted gentile-sounding names to avoid anti-Semitism, even if they were overt about their Judaism—and to avoid the hassle of bearing a name other people would have difficulty spelling or pronouncing.

Americans began to talk about that distinction, and about perceived differences in the values and worth of the different waves of immigration. The response to Chinese immigration is well-known, and there were strong anti-immigrant sentiments in general throughout the country. Anti-immigration and anti-Catholic platforms became instrumental in politics. While the old immigrants were seen as cousins, metaphorically—country cousins sometimes, or strange in their ways—the new immigrants were complete outsiders, and there were many who questioned whether there was any room for them. Unlike previous eras, there was not enough money or labor to go around, and so these immigrants were often forced into poverty—and thus thought of as poor and dirty—or worked cheaply in order to survive, and were blamed for taking jobs away from "real" Americans.

Young immigrants: A girl and a boy standing with their possessions in a room full of trunks inside the Ellis Island immigration processing station.

Nativist and anti-Catholic groups often blended together. As anti-immigrant feelings surged in the 1880s, they were strongly supported by Protestant Irish immigrants who cared not about keeping immigrants out of the United States, but about preserving the country as a Protestant nation. Catholics were suspect for their allegiance to the Pope (and the longstanding association between the Vatican and the monarchies of Catholic nations, though Lutherans had been just as involved in German and Scandinavian politics), their different rituals and ceremonies, and their reverence of the Virgin Mary to a degree not held by Protestants. Urban legends spread about everything from strange indoctrination ceremonies for priests, to sexual abuse of nuns, to cannibalism, none of it with any basis in fact.

SIX-SECOND EXAM

In 1892, in response to the growing wave of immigration and particularly the growing number of poor immigrants, Ellis Island was established as an immigration processing station. Located in New York Harbor in sight of the Statue of Liberty, Ellis Island was the largest of 30 processing stations opened by the federal government, and was used to process the majority of immigrants who arrived by third-class passage or steerage. The distinction is illustrative of the times: immigrants who could afford first or second class (which few could) were admitted to the United States without question. Everyone else had to be processed by officials of the Bureau of Immigration.

Each would-be immigrant was first given a six-second physical examination, their clothes marked with chalk if further checking was needed. According to the following key, the exam was designed to check these areas:

B: Back
E: Eyes
F: Face
FT: Feet
H: Heart
M: Vagina
N: Neck
P: Lungs, or conduct a general physical

An inspector examines a woman's eyes during a physical examination at Ellis Island.

Waiting at Ellis Island: a large crowd of European immigrants sit outdoors waiting for processing. The "new immigration" of the Gilded Age meant arrivals to the United States were increasingly from southern and eastern Europe, Russia, and Asia.

Sc: Scalp
C: Conjunctivitis (pink-eye)
CT: Chlamydia trachomatis (infectious eye disease that causes blindness)
G: Goiter
K: Hernia
Pg: Pregnant
S: Senility
SI: Special Inquiry
X: Possibility of mental illness
Circled X: Strong suspicion of mental illness

The six-second exam took place primarily as the would-be immigrants climbed the stairs from the baggage area, in part because this was a good opportunity to see if they had any difficulties exerting themselves. People with obvious health problems were either sent home or held in the medical facility, depending on the specific condition and the current state of affairs at the station. Thousands died over the course of Ellis Island's operation, many of them of treatable conditions. The rest were asked 29 questions of practical concern and bookkeeping. A few were rejected at this stage, if they were believed to be too unskilled to find work, but even accounting for the contagious, the mentally ill, and the criminal, 98 percent of immigrants were admitted to the

United States within a few hours, or after a couple days, in the case of the temporarily ill.

THE END OF THE FRONTIER

The Eleventh U.S. Census was taken in 1890, the first to be compiled on a tabulating machine—which should have been newsworthy enough, but with the release of the census figures, the Census Bureau announced that henceforth they would no longer track westward migration. The frontier had closed up, the bureau explained: while for all of American history, even before nationhood, there had been a general staggering westward movement as the line of American civilization advanced steadily toward the Pacific, there was now no significantly-sized area of sparse population. There were no more empty spaces, in other words—not of a significant size defined by the Census Bureau. There remained wilderness and unused land and large areas of low population density like in the southwestern deserts. However there was no longer a clearly defined "frontier." As the popular mind heard it, there was no more Wild West left.

A young historian, Frederick Jackson Turner, took this as an opportunity to study the effect of the frontier on American history. Few countries were settled the way the United States had been, with colonists transforming the land into a nation, and then expanding it into empty spaces. Turner presented his findings, his "frontier thesis," three years later at the 1893 convention of the American Historical Association at the World's Columbian Exposition in Chicago.

HISTORICAL PERSPECTIVE

Having studied evolution with a geologist, Turner adopted some of those ideas to discuss the changing character of the American nation and American identity. Rejecting the popular notion of "germ theory," which said that American institutions had all been carried over from Europe in "germ form" and simply adapted to local conditions, Turner proposed that the existence of the frontier had been the defining American characteristic.

Americans kept only those European trappings for which they had a use, Turner said, and as each generation moved further west, it became more American, less European. Westward expansion caused the nation to become more democratic, more disdainful of aristocracy and intellectual elites, more rowdy, more individualistic. The frontier had been a safety valve where society's restless elements could escape from the eastern United States to live life on their own terms, an opportunity that didn't exist in European countries without leaving the country itself (as many did to settle the New World).

That the frontier had now closed raised the question, then, of what would happen to an America that was no longer defined by this characteristic—a question which, with the coming of the new 20th century, seized the imagination of many Americans. Turner remains one of the most significant figures in the study of American history.

BILL KTE'PI

Further Readings

Brownstone, David. *The Chinese-American Heritage*. New York: Facts On File, 1988.

Chang, Iris. *The Chinese in America*. New York: Penguin Books, 2004.

Cohen, Lucy. *Chinese in the Post–Civil War South*. Baton Rouge, LA: Louisiana State University Press, 1984.

Lai, H. *Becoming Chinese American*. Walnut Creek, CA: AltaMira, 2004.

Lee, Erika. *At America's Gates*. Chapel Hill, NC: University of North Carolina Press, 2003.

Pfaelzer, Jean. *Driven Out*. New York: Random House, 2007.

Turner, Frederick Jackson. *The Significance of Sections in American History*. New York: Henry Holt and Company, 1932.

Yung, Judy. *Unbound Feet*. Berkeley, CA: University of California Press, 1995.

Chapter 15

Transportation

"A railroad is like a lie, you have to
keep building it to make it stand."
— Mark Twain

TRANSPORTATION HAS ALWAYS reflected national trends in American life. In the previous period of American history, the need to expand westward beyond the Appalachians had spurred both road-building and canal-building during the age of internal improvements in antebellum America. In a similar manner, railway building, which became the dominant mode of transportation in the Gilded Age, benefited from the need to settle the vast territory west of the Mississippi. Similarly a need for convenient access in the burgeoning urban areas led to a boon in railway building, which mirrored Gilded Age values of bigness and external grandeur. Quite often railroads epitomized the underlying concept of glitter on the outside, but internal dross in terms of the effects on political culture and equity in American life. Although some historians often date this period well into the 20th century, others date this period to 1893 when the Panic of 1893, actually a very severe depression, caused great hardship with effects lingering until 1897. The excesses, which had partially been caused by policies with respect to railroads on the part of local, state, and federal governments, led to a swing in policies.

Railroads were an integral part of American expansion. The country saw its population grow to 75 million by 1900. A large part of this increase was due to immigration—both permanent and temporary. Many immigrants were looking for the proverbial streets paved with gold, which is an apt

Horace Greeley (1811–72)

Horace Greeley, a journalist, crusader, and politician, is famous for his phrase "Go west, young man," and is credited with inspiring tens of thousands of young settlers to travel westward to the territories beyond the Mississippi River. Westward migration was so common in the Gilded Age that by 1890 the continental United States no longer had a discernable frontier. Greeley's role in this movement is commemorated today by the town of Greeley, Colorado.

Greeley was a latter-day version of Benjamin Franklin, who achieved prominence in so many careers that he wielded a great deal of influence. Starting as a printer, he helped found the first version of the *New Yorker*, the first literary magazine in America. Greeley was a founder of the *Tribune*, which later became the *Herald-Tribune* and still, along with the *New York Times*, publishes as the *International Herald Tribune*.

Horace Greeley also became prominent for his crusades. He was an early advocate of the temperance movement, but it was in his advocacy of the antislavery movement that he was most famous. He is credited with converting many people in the north to the abolitionist cause that helped in the election of Abraham Lincoln in 1860.

After the Civil War he spoke out against the rampant corruption of the Ulysses S. Grant administration. He was so well-respected that in 1872 a coalition of liberal Republicans and Democrats nominated him for president. However he lost the election to Grant, and a few weeks later died, exhausted by the rigors of the campaign and worn out by the strain of attending to his dying wife. Although he never achieved the highest office, his influence continued long after his death, especially in inspiring western migration and indirectly contributing to the impetus for transportation links to the west that served to bind the nation.

metaphor for the Gilded Age. Population growth in turn reflected two of the salient features of the age, the rise of the cities and the opening of the American west. In the latter instance, the older group of immigrants, Germans, Scandinavians, Czechs, and Slovaks, immigrated to the upper middle west, the plains states and parts of the mountain west and Pacific Coast. They were attracted by the easy land terms of the Homestead Act of 1862 and land offered by railroads.

New York City especially was a byproduct of this movement, with a majority of its four million inhabitants immigrants or the offspring of immigrants by 1900. It was also a period of internal migration as the triumph of Jim Crow laws in the south climaxed with *Plessy v. Ferguson* in 1896, and the institution of tenant farming and sharecropping drove both African Americans and poor whites to the cities of the midwest, and to a lesser extent the northeast. There was an influx from rural areas to the cities, which came to depend upon rail transportation to transport people from residence to job and back again.

Ongoing industrialization led to the appearance of machine-made goods, a situation that saw trained craftsmen replaced with unskilled labor in centralized locations. These masses were compatible with speedy mechanized transport. The educational system was revamped so as to serve the emerging urban working class. The expanding "common school," which had focused on K-8 education before 1870, was now extended so that secondary schools were transformed into high schools. Toward the end of the 19th century, many localities and states made school attendance mandatory and began to set up three tracks—vocational, agricultural, and academic—that supported the emerging railroad network and the industrial society that grew along with the rails. While the commercial track honed bookkeeping and secretarial skills, the vocational track of woodworking, metal, and later electronic training helped prepare people for factory employment while also offering a "hidden curriculum" that trained future workers in regard to punctuality, reliability, and persistence on task. The railways were interested in the most malleable of these employees as career ladder prospects for jobs as foremen and conductors—the original blue collar jobs. Others might take training courses and night school or correspondence courses to become mid-level

In this 1868 Currier and Ives print entitled "Across the Continent—Westward the Course of Empire Takes Its Way," a symbolic train heads into open land, leaving settlement in its wake.

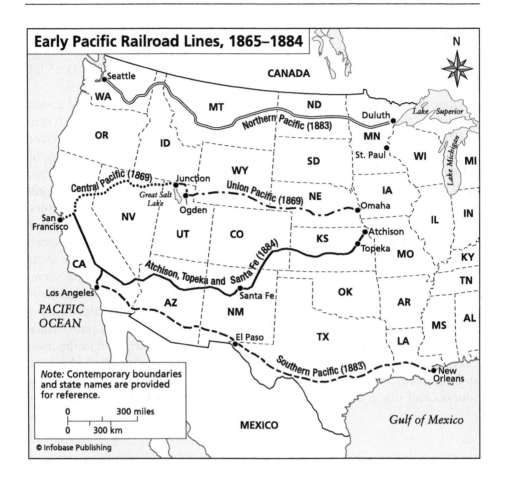

Early Pacific Railroad Lines, 1865–1884

Note: Contemporary boundaries and state names are provided for reference.

0   300 miles
0   300 km

© Infobase Publishing

managers with the blessing of the railway employers in the emerging white collar bureaucracy.

The changing transportation system affected life in many ways beyond education, of course. More profound and basic was the impact on the commercial life of the nation. Since rails could carry the produce of farms far from the growing regions to markets in distant states, one consequence was the growth of specialized agriculture. Instead of farms producing mixed produce of grains, meat, vegetables, and fruit, whole regions began to specialize in wheat production, corn production, orchards, or cattle raising, on land and in climates most suited to those specialties. Partly as a result of this efficient specialization, prices on most commodities entered a long-term decline in the period from the Civil War through the 1890s. With falling prices, those who controlled capital benefited, while those who paid fixed mortgages or depended on wage rates that could be dropped along with prices suffered. Much of the social protest of the era came from farmers who felt victimized by bankers and the railroads, and from rail, factory and mining workers, who felt exploited by large employers.

The Gilded Age was a time of great invention. More than 500,000 patents were registered, many of which were related to work including railroad operations. Thomas Edison developed many new devices, including the phonograph and light bulb, which later became the property of General Electric. Alexander Graham Bell developed the telephone, which ultimately evolved into American Telephone and Telegraph (AT&T) or Bell telephone. Oil began its march to dominance in fossil fuels with the Standard Oil Trust, which controlled 90 percent of refineries.

The U.S. Steel Corporation controlled a similar percentage of steel production by 1900. Railroads also consolidated and their size ultimately contributed to the reforms associated with the Progressive Era. As mileage increased fourfold during the period, there was plenty of opportunity for growth, especially in the 1880s when 72,000 miles of rail were laid. Cities became dependent on rail-related transportation, such as trolleys, street cars, and cable cars. More directly, the use of refrigerated cars and the development of the air brake, which promoted both speed and safety, made the railway as dominant in transcontinental travel as it had been in the cities.

Railroads became symbolic of many trends of the age, both positive and negative. On the negative side were political scandals such as Credit Mobilier and sweetheart deals with the government whereby railway companies received land virtually for free, in return for a 50 percent discount to the government. These deals ultimately victimized small farmers and immigrants and led to the monopolization of railways at the hands of new "robber barons" such as J.P. Morgan, Jay Gould, Cornelius Vanderbilt, John D. Rockefeller, and Edward Harriman. Exploitation on the grounds that bigness led to greater efficiency was eventually challenged in the next decade.

On the positive side, railroads acted as an engine for the economy. The railroads encouraged commercial farming by assisting settlers west of the Mississippi to acquire cheap land and grow produce, which could be transported to distant markets. The construction of railroads proved a boon for the industrializing economy by providing a market for iron and steel products in the building of trains, and the coal industry by providing a market for energy. Water transportation via canals, coastal traffic, river boats, and steamships continued especially for goods in bulk, but the railroads soon became the dominant mode of transport, especially as road construction remained dormant.

RAILROAD DOMINANCE

By 1870 railroads were becoming the dominant form of transportation for both passengers and freight. In 1869 the Union Pacific coming west met the Central Pacific coming east at Promontory Point, Utah. This development capped the evolution of rail building, which had increased the mileage of railroads over 20 times between 1840 and 1870 and was to almost quadruple again from about 54,000 mi. in 1870 to 193,000 mi. in 1900. In part, this reflected the development of long-range railroads across the continent in a basically east-west direction, as the west gradually opened up to both settlement and economic exploitation. In this respect, by the early 1880s, four more transcontinental railroads had been constructed—the Northern Pacific, the Great Northern, the Southern Pacific, and the Atchison, Topeka, and Santa Fe.

The government had come to see the railroads as a primary tool of national development. To forward this purpose, the government gave more than 1.5 million acres to the railroads, which the railroads were then free to sell to western settlers. It was to be a mutually beneficial relationship. Miners would send their silver, gold, copper, and lead from the mountain west. Loggers would send their lumber from the northwest. Cattle and livestock would be sent from the plains extending from Texas to eastern Montana, and agricultural produce from throughout the west would be sent east to feed a growing nation, thereby providing the railroads with steady business. By 1890, also assisted by the Homestead Act, the railroads had brought more than five million people into the west.

"GO WEST, YOUNG MAN"

In pursuit of this goal, the first national advertising campaign was begun, especially in the newspapers and mass magazines of the time, to persuade people to settle in the west. Prominent people such as editor Horace Greeley, who became famous for his exhortation to "go west, young man," were solicited to give endorsements. The Northern Pacific Railroad went so far as to claim that most illnesses could be cured by migrating to the west. The main audience for this campaign were farmers who were informed that crops could be grown almost anywhere because climate and soil conditions were so favorable. The small farmers who heeded the call westward felt deceived when periodical droughts, locust attacks, flooding, and drought brought hardships. The climax of the hardships was the Great Blizzard of 1888, which did great damage to the cattle industry as well as to farmers. A large portion of the lands that had been settled at the urging of the agents of the railroads was in fact marginal for farming, as they consisted of the "badlands" of the western Dakotas, as well as dry areas in western Kansas, Nebraska, and Oklahoma and eastern Colorado, Wyoming, and Montana. The Oklahoma land rush of 1889 concentrated on eastern Oklahoma, while the drier and presumably less valuable western part (until oil was discovered) remained Native American territory.

Other segments of the population, such as factory workers living in urban areas and immigrants from Europe both peasant and proletarian, were attracted to the campaign by the quintessential attraction of American life—the promise of having land of one's own. The dispossessed from the east and overseas viewed this prospect as the greatest attraction. For all comers, the railroad

Many towns were developed along America's spreading railroad lines. This railroad depot in Orlando, Florida, was built in the 1880s.

companies promised the land available to them either directly or through the Homestead Act, which gave up to 640 acres as long as the land was farmed for five years and improvements were made. As farmers faced declining prices for their products and heavy railroad rates to carry the goods, they turned to states to pass rate regulation, the so-called Granger Laws, of the 1870s. When those laws were declared unconstitutional by the Supreme Court, settlers and farmers founds some relief in the establishment of the Interstate Commerce Commission in 1887, empowered to federally regulate railroads.

Railroads were vital in the development of new towns between 1870 and 1900 between the Mississippi and the Pacific Ocean along the line of rail. They served as the lifeline, which broke the isolation through bringing goods in and out, as well as exporting the products of the region. They helped to form a new directional bias as, unlike the Mississippi that flowed from north to south, they placed the routes east to west. On the negative side, the railroads could indulge in stock "watering," whereby cattle could be charged by the pound, including the water weight. This increased the weight and drove up costs. Railroads colluded with large cattle operations to raise the overall price by weighing the cattle after watering. The consumer, along with the small farmer and shipper, were to join the list of people with grievances against the railroads in the next era.

Railroads affected local urban ecology, as well as the country's place in the world economy. Towns would spread out on both sides of railway tracks.

Practical Bicycles

Originally introduced in the late 18th and early 19th centuries, the bicycle did not become popular until around the time of the Civil War. The typical modern design—two equally sized wheels with a chain drive on the rear wheel—was called the "safety bicycle," and was invented in 1885 and popularized shortly thereafter. The safety bicycle was significantly more popular, especially in the United States, than the "penny farthing" design or "ordinary bicycle," characterized by a significantly larger front wheel. The new bicycle was more comfortable, easier to control, faster, and much more stable, which in turn made it easier to turn corners without fear of toppling over. Long a novelty or a device only for the experienced rider, the bicycle quickly became a practical mode of transportation, especially in rural areas without public transportation or hired carriages.

In 1890 pneumatic tires were introduced for bicycles, making them more reliable and less prone to flats, and therefore more reliable for trips into or through town. A bicycle—even a 19th-century bicycle ridden by the average man on the street—carried its rider about four times faster than walking, and could have a basket attached for groceries or other small goods. It was not as fast or as strong as a horse, and it took more out of its rider, but it was cheaper and did not need food or extraordinary care, except to keep it out of the rain and occasionally replace a tire. Just as the railroads had made the Great Plains accessible, the bicycle made small rural towns closer together, and made the center of town closer for the people living on its outskirts—particularly the children and teenagers.

This crank-pedal bicycle design, with only a slightly larger front wheel, dates to the 1880s.

There would literally be a "right" and a "wrong" side of the tracks, which depended on the prevailing winds and the direction of smoke discharge. Thereafter, factories were established on the wrong side of the tracks as well as "mom and pop" stores, stores for immigrants, and relatively cheap business establishments. The good or right side was the site for higher end businesses as well as residences. The produce from the west carried from the prairies by the railways were shipped overseas, as well as to urban centers within the country. New markets for American agriculture, including new variants of grain and cereal, made America the new granary of the world by 1900. Along with riverboats and ocean liners, the railroads also exported iron and steel products as America came to dominate the global machine-tool industry. The advent of refrigeration also served to make American fruits, vegetables, and meat available nationally and globally.

The railroads had become so central to life in America that they both changed and mirrored economic and technological trends. By the 1880s railroad networks were so powerful that cattle drives were no longer necessary. After the blizzard of 1888, winter feeding lots were opened and spur lines could go to the vicinity of cattle and other livestock growing areas and transport them directly to the slaughterhouse. Earlier the cattle drives had used the Chisholm Trail and other routes from Texas to Montana to drive cattle to rail centers at Dodge City, Abilene, and Elliot, Kansas; and Sedalia, Missouri. As a result although cattle-raising continued as a major industry, the legendary cowboy became less crucial.

As the use of the lister, thresher, reaper, and multi-seed mechanical planter were perfected and became more widespread, thereby increasing the yield per acre, the railroads increased their trunk lines to bring even more people to new areas of settlement and bring out the increased produce also made possible by refrigeration. The telegraph was used as a way of giving advance information to passengers and shippers, as well as alerting conductors and brakemen of possible accidents and other hazards ahead. By the early 1880s

A crowd watches the first train on the Gilbert Elevated Railroad passing through Sixth Avenue, near the Jefferson Market Police Court, in New York City on April 29, 1878.

These trolley cars, decorated with electric lights and carrying a band for an excursion on a summer night around 1900, represented a new form of entertainment based on transportation.

trains were using the electronic locomotive headlights that provided night lights for trains, which were now going 70 miles per hour. At the other end of the spectrum, railroads initiated economic and technological change as well as mirroring it. It was their concern about making the trains run on time that led to the adoption of global and national time zones in 1884.

URBAN TRANSPORT

Along with western settlement, the other major development in American life during this period was the spread of industrialization and urbanization, which produced new population concentrations. The incidence of equine epidemics led to a search for more reliable, as well as speedier, forms of transportation. Hygiene and efficiency mandated this change. The growth of steel metallurgy also spurred the use of electric and steam-powered transportation, which could run on steel girders. Elevated electric railroads were constructed as early as 1868 and became common in the 1880s. In New York, the EL or "elevated" was operating daily in New York, and other cities began to emulate it.

Related forms of urban transport began to appear. They often were adaptations of the local environment. One innovation was the cable car. Utilizing a steam engine at a central location, a cable was installed on rollers in an underground location. A handle was then attached to the cable car that reached the underground cable. It thus allowed the car to stop or start at a predictable speed. The cable car, as was the case of the elevated, gradually replaced the horse. It was especially good at navigating hilly terrains at 10 miles per hour. But it operated not only in hilly San Francisco, but also in cities such as New York, Chicago, Philadelphia, and Washington, D.C. By the mid-1880s these vehicles carried millions of people each year.

If there was one form of urban transport that characterized the Gilded Age, it was the trolley. By 1880 generators had been developed that would produce a large amount of electricity. By the end of that decade, Frank Sprague had perfected a system in which electrical current was supplied directly to an electric motor car through overhead wires. The cars were connected to the wires by a pole placed on the roof of each car. A grooved wheel was placed at the top of the car, which transferred the electricity to the car. This wheel was called a "trotter," which is how a trolley was named. The trolley originated in Richmond, Virginia, and by 1900 virtually every town or city had a trolley system. Unlike the elevated or cable car, however, the trolley soon came to be seen as a vehicle of leisure as well as transportation. Trolley lanes were constructed to go to amusement parks. In fact, many owners of these parks were trolley operators, so that riders could get reduced rates on trips to amusement parks and the park fees might even be waived. The movie *Meet Me in St. Louis,* which centers around the 1904 World's Fair, prominently features the role of the trolley in taking people to and from the fair. These were not the only purposes served by this dominant form of urban transportation.

In the early days, the trolley or its variant, the street car, would have mail boxes in which passengers could drop a letter. The conductor would then drop it off at a post office that was on its regular route. Some of the larger trolleys even had postal workers on the cars. Other tasks occasionally performed included hauling garbage, cleaning streets, carrying water, and serving as a fire engine.

The trolley, before it began to be replaced by the automobile,

Trolleys, carts, and carriages share the street on Broadway in New York City in 1892.

Steamships, Schooners, and Barges

Between 1870 and 1920 the advent of steam engines in naval transportation coincided with the immigration from Europe of almost 20 million people. As people sought a new and better life, the steamship offered the cheapest and safest route to America.

For as little as $30 immigrants could travel below deck or in "steerage." The ocean voyage could take anywhere from two weeks to a little over a month. Although relatively inexpensive, steerage could be overcrowded as steamships sought to maximize their profits by packing as many as 2,000 to 3,000 people per voyage. People were often sick, and in grave danger if the ship capsized or flooded.

The majority of immigrants, as many as 12 million, would land at New York Harbor at Castle Garden and Ellis Island. They would see the Statue of Liberty, completed in the 1880s as a gift from France. Upon landing, the immigrant would have to take various tests that measured mental and physical fitness. If a passenger failed a test, they could be sent back to their home country, often on the same ship that brought them. In contrast to the steamship ocean liners, most of which were foreign-owned, the schooners that plied intercoastal trade were both sail- and steam-powered, and were domestically owned. Operating on both coasts, they specialized in bulk traffic.

On the east coast, fishing ships centered at Gloucester, Massachusetts, sailed to waters off Cape Cod on the Georges Bank or to Newfoundland. These ships could be of great size, ranging from 100-foot two-mast ships, to 600-foot three-mast ships, and were capable of transporting cod, mackerel, and halibut.

Barges and schooners transported tobacco from Virginia, as well as building materials such as bricks, lime, sand, and stone. Fuel such as coal was carried by these schooners, as well as the larger barges. In the northwest, ships were used to transport timber and lumber. These vessels dominated coastal trade well into the early 1900s.

The schooner Moshulu was used for grain transport in the late 19th century.

Late 19th-century technology, reflected in this modern Amish four-seat buggy, remained a practical and traditional means of transport well into the 20th century and beyond.

also played a role in the evolving urban landscape. Over a period of time, it served as a conduit between where people lived and where people worked. Operators realized by the 1890s that people who might go to the countryside during the weekends and holidays could go in the other direction and visit the city for recreation and other purposes. In conjunction with real estate developers, trolley companies would extend trolley lines into the country-side. Cities that often had jurisdiction over the surrounding areas agreed to install utilities such as sewer and water connections and locate local school systems so that people felt free to move to the countryside to find a refuge from congestion, pollution, noise, and the general dirt of the city. The suburb was born as people with some degree of means felt that with transportation they could enjoy suburban amenities in the countryside, while traveling to the city for shopping and recreation.

WATER TRANSPORTATION

Although various types of rail transportation dominated American life dur-ing the period, water and road transportation remained important. Schoo-ners, steamships, and barges continued to dominate coastal and transoce-anic trade. The dominant forms of transportation of the previous period, the canal and riverboat, continued to play an important role in American life.

Although overtaken by rail before 1870, the largest of the canals, the Erie Canal, remained important and continued to do substantial business in this period. As the connecting link between New York City and Lake Erie and the Great Lakes via the Hudson River at Buffalo, it was a conduit for immigrants disembarking first at Castle Garden and then at Ellis Island during this period. It also was a more inexpensive carrier of bulk produce, although slower than the rail. The freight shipped by the Erie Canal did not peak until 1880. As the canals including the Erie were at least partially state-owned, they did not charge the exorbitant fees often associated with rail at this time. In fact, during the next era, the Erie Canal was expanded. Nonetheless with the advent of the automobile and truck and the continued dominance of rail transportation, canals were rapidly becoming a tourist curiosity by 1900.

Somewhat more lasting if also declining, in part because steam had replaced sail by 1860, were the riverboats. They continued to carry bulk goods, especially on the major rivers to the west—the Ohio, Mississippi, and Missouri. By 1890 their economic importance had diminished, but the steamboat had found a new rationale, in addition to some barge traffic. The larger surviving steamboats came to be associated with showboats, which had attracted musicians, dancers, singers, actors, and other entertainers who routinely staged plays at various stops and onboard. Gambling also continued on these ships. People began to take scenic tours in the summer, when most of the rivers were navigable.

ROAD TRANSPORTATION

During the Gilded Age some forms of transportation that had been considered necessities in previous times enjoyed a comeback as the cult of wellness took hold. Exercise in the form of walking and running became prominent. This was due to more hygienic roads as concrete and brick were used, and feces on cow paths and horse trails gradually disappeared. The cumulative effect of macadamized roads, which had been part of the road building phase in the National Improvement era of 1790 to 1840, was applied to both city and some rural areas. The newer roads were generally free of human debris and of the dust and mud associated with dirt roads. Roads were broadened, sidewalks were introduced, and trees were planted on the side. This was especially true in residences on the "right" side of the tracks as well as in the leafy new suburbs. Walking to go on errands became more of a pleasure and less of a hazard. Starting with Central Park just before the Civil War, parks made their appearance in many cities. It became quite fashionable to promenade in the parks, especially on Sundays, for recreation as well as exercise.

This trend was also evident in the new sport of biking, which was no longer a hobby of the rich. By 1890 pneumatic rubber had replaced wooden

wheels so that bicycles were now safer. A few of these even became gas powered or steam powered, as the transition to motorcycles had begun.

Some residuals remained from the past. Stagecoaches drawn by horses
continued to be used in the west, while in the cities it was still common to
see the horse car refurbished with cast iron and glass windows, which could
carry up to 40 passengers. As late as 1881 some 100,000 horses were used
to pull 18,000 cars of various types. On farms, of course, horses continued
to pull wagons internally and to market (as well as some freight in the cities
such as building materials and fuel), and there were horse-drawn plows before
the complete triumph of the tractor. Horse-drawn vehicles were also used in
municipalities for various purposes, such as carrying firemen and garbage before urban services took hold in the next period. There was also a cavalry for
soldiers, as illustrated by the "Rough Riders" of the Spanish-American War
and San Juan Hill.

NORMAN C. ROTHMAN

Further Readings

Barnes, Demas. *From the Atlantic to the Pacific, Overland*. New York: Arno
     Press, 1973.
Boulton, W.H. *The Pageant of Transport through the Ages*. New York:
     Gordon Press, 1976.
Bourne, Russell. *Americans on the Move*. Golden, CO: Fulcrum, 1995.
———. *Floating West: The Erie and Other American Canals*. New York: W.W.
     Norton,1979.
Chapelle, Howard. *The Search for Speed*. New York: W.W. Norton, 1984.
Gardiner, Robert and Greenway, Abel. *The Golden Age of Shipping: The
     Classic Merchant Ship, 1900–1960*. New York: Book Sales, 2001.
McLuhan, T.C. *Dream Tracks: The Railroad and the American Indian*. New
     York: Harry N. Abrams, 1985.
Sandler, Martin W. *Galloping Across the USA: Horses in American Life*. New
     York: Oxford University Press, 2003.
———. *Straphanging in the USA: Trolleys and Subways in American Life*.
     New York: Oxford University Press, 2003.
———. *On the Waters: Ships and Boats in American Life*. New York: Oxford
     University Press, 2003.
———. *Riding the Rails in the USA: Trains in American Life*. New York:
     Oxford University Press, 2003.
Tunis, Edwin. *Frontier Living*. New York: World Publishing Company, 1961.
Whitman, Sylvia, *Get Up and Go: The History of American Road Travel*.
     Minneapolis, MN: Lerman Publications Company, 1996.

Chapter 16

Public Health, Medicine, and Nutrition

"There are houses, well known to sanitary boards and the police, where fever has taken a perennial lease."
—Charles Loring Brace

DURING THE GILDED AGE there were a significant number of advances in the knowledge and practice of public health, medicine, and nutrition. The Industrial Revolution had changed life in the United States in unprecedented ways, and the needs of working-class America received a good deal of attention. These fields made great strides in curing and controlling communicable diseases. Until 1878 states continued to hold some responsibility for identifying and quarantining individuals and ships suspected of harboring passengers and crew with various diseases. At that time Congress passed the national Quarantine Act, giving the Marine Hospital Service oversight and implementation of quarantines and allotting funds for investigation, control, and prevention of diseases such as yellow fever and cholera. By the final years of the Gilded Age all states had created their own boards of health, as had hundreds of cities and counties. In response to the new emphasis on health, sanitation, and nutrition, and due to major medical advances, the death rate dropped to 19 per 1,000/population in 1900.

The wealth that defined the Gilded Age was accompanied by a surge of reforms in which governments, social reformers, and philanthropists initiated programs and practices based on the new understanding of the importance

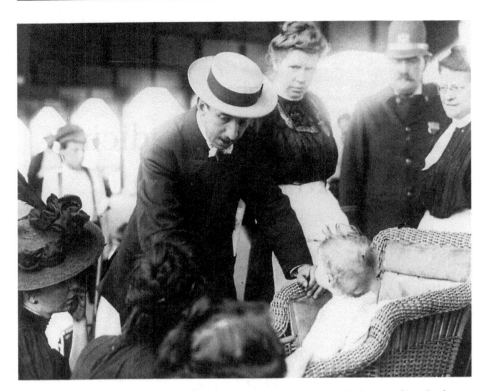

A doctor for the New York Health Board supervising the care of babies in hot weather, checks on a very young patient on a hot day in New York City around 1900.

of cleanliness and the belief that social services were an essential element in maintaining an adequate standard of living. By the 1890s municipal governments had grown more sophisticated than at any time in American history, and their regulatory functions had vastly increased. Most cities established police and fire departments to protect residents and provided public sewer and water systems. Streets were paved and regularly cleaned. Electricity was readily available in many areas, and improved transportation provided unprecedented opportunities for both business and pleasure.

GENERAL PUBLIC HEALTH

Between 1789 and 1889 American life expectancy rose from 34.5 to 41.7 years. However improvements were less noticeable among African Americans, for whom mean life expectancy during the Gilded Age was 33.7 years. Heart disease, influenza and pneumonia, tuberculosis, and infections of the gastrointestinal tract were the leading causes of death in the United States at the turn of the century in 1900. Typhoid fever and malaria continued to take a toll, and children were particularly susceptible to diphtheria, measles, whooping cough, scarlet fever, rheumatic fever, meningococcal infections, and syphilis. Periodic outbreaks of diarrhea, dysentery, and smallpox also occurred. Most hospital admissions for children were a result of diarrhea or Vitamin D deficiency. Children were particularly susceptible to diseases in the summer months, and conditions were worsened by poverty, parental ignorance, and inadequate physician training. However the Gilded Age ushered in a period when children's health issues were given more attention; and over the following decades, great strides were made in decreasing infant and child mortality and in protecting children from diseases caused by poor living conditions and improper care.

During the Gilded Age research established a strong link between infant mortality and the health status of American mothers. Many reformers believed that the ill health of women was associated with restrictive clothing. Corsets that were tightly laced tended to push breasts up, cinch waists, and compress reproductive organs. As a result many women had difficulty with menstrual periods, and the bodies of some women became deformed, leaving them unable to bear children in an era when fertility was highly prized. Efforts to avoid such conditions led to the use of devices known as pessaries, made of rubber, ivory, wood, or steel, which were placed in the vagina to support the uterus. Frequent infections were associated with the use of these devices, which were also used for birth control. Dress reformers insisted that shorter shirts worn without corsets would improve both health and fertility.

Tuberculosis continued to be a major threat to American health. Because most physicians believed that there was no cure for the disease, treatment centered on providing fresh air, rest, and abundant food. However the establishment of sanitariums such as the one opened by Dr. Edward Trudeau (1848–1915) in 1884 in the Adirondack Mountains of New York provided a measure of hope. Similar sanitariums were subsequently established by health departments, churches, and voluntary health organizations and by companies who viewed them as money-making opportunities. Canadian physician William Osler (1849–1919) became convinced that both tuberculosis and typhoid could be cured. He insisted that improved sanitation was the key to wiping out both diseases. In 1898 Osler supplemented an anonymous anti-tuberculosis donation with his own money, and created an experimental laboratory. Two years later Osler's "Home Treatment of Tuberculosis" and Adelaide Dutcher's "Where the Danger Lies in Tuberculosis" revolutionized the medical approach to treatment and offered support for the theory that tuberculosis was often correlated with a patient's occupation.

Epidemics of yellow fever also continued into the Gilded Age, with outbreaks occurring on an almost annual basis. New Orleans, Louisiana, was hit the hardest of all American cities. During an outbreak of yellow fever in 1853, 40 percent of the population contracted the disease, and 10 percent of the victims died. In July 1878 another major yellow fever epidemic hit New Orleans. After four people died, the officials of upriver towns began placing all ships sailing from New Orleans under quarantine. Despite these efforts, the disease spread along the Mississippi River. Some 100,000 Americans became ill and approximately 20,000 died. Many people who fled the affected area carried the disease with them, spreading the disease as far away as Ohio before it ran its course. Although plague never threatened Americans as it did Europeans, in the latter 19th century, outbreaks of plague followed trading routes. In 1895, for instance, traders traveling from India to the New World introduced the plague to San Francisco.

The reform movements of the Gilded Age led to increased concern over worker safety, particularly that of miners. An essential activity of the Industrial Revolution, mining originally centered in Kentucky and Virginia, but later

Granola and Corn Flakes

After graduating from Bellevue Medical College in New York City, physician and health reformer John Harvey Kellogg set out to improve the eating habits of the American consumer. Kellogg was heavily influenced by Sylvester Graham (1794–1851), a noted vegetarian health reformer and the inventor of the Graham cracker. When Kellogg took over the Western Health Reform Institute of Battle Creek, Michigan, in 1876, he re-christened the facility the Battle Creek Institute, and called it a health university. Kellogg introduced a diet plan made up of natural foods with only small amounts of protein. He advocated the avoidance of meats, fish, and poultry and advised that eggs and sugar should be consumed only in small quantities. Butter, coffee, tea, and cocoa were entirely banned from Kellogg's suggested diet plan. Bran, on the other hand, was considered an essential element to good nutrition.

In 1877 Kellogg introduced the first cold breakfast cereal, which he called Granola because it was composed of multiple grains. Kellogg subsequently became a dedicated vegetarian. By 1893 he had added Granose Flakes (now Corn Flakes) to his offerings and insisted that his new cereal would replace the need for meat at the breakfast table. His claim was somewhat justified by the revolution that occurred in American homes. In addition to the health value of Kellogg cereals, Americans were quick to see the advantage of breakfast products that could be prepared in a matter of minutes. Over the following decades Kellogg was responsible for developing 30 food products, including peanut butter. Despite his success in the food industry, Kellogg continued to practice medicine, performing 22,000 surgeries in his lifetime, specializing in abdominal surgeries. He also invented exercise, diagnostic, and therapeutic devices. Today, in addition to offering a wide range of breakfast cereals, the Kellogg Company, which nets $11 billion annually, has expanded its products to include cookies, crackers, toaster pastries, fruit snacks, and frozen waffles.

spread to 20 other states as the demand for fuel increased. By 1879 the United States was producing more than 40 million tons of anthracite and bituminous coal annually. By 1900 production had multiplied six fold, and the workforce had grown fivefold, elevating the United States to the leading producer of coal in the world. Mines of the Gilded Age tended to be poorly ventilated, and few safety precautions were taken. As a result significant amounts of dust were regularly inhaled by miners, and the introduction of undercutting machines created even greater health hazards. In response to demands for reform, by the 1880s mines and factories were regularly inspected. Some companies hired physicians to oversee the health of their workers. Some railroads opened their own hospitals; and in the west, labor unions often provided basic medical care. At the turn of the century, company physicians were often the only basic health providers in isolated areas.

CHILDREN'S HEALTH
Between 1870 and 1885 infant mortality in the United States dropped from 170 to 123 deaths per 1,000 live births. Despite this significant drop, urban infants were twice as likely to die as rural infants. African-American infants faced an even greater risk, with a mortality rate of 278 deaths per 1,000 live births for males, and 237 per 1,000 for females. Gastrointestinal diseases

This man sat outdoors in the snow at a tuberculosis "camp" in Ottawa, Illinois, in 1908 in the belief that fresh air alleviated the disease.

were responsible for one fourth of all deaths of infants under one year of age, chiefly because of the consumption of contaminated milk. Because cow's milk was stored in unsanitary containers, it often soured even before it reached the market. Some grocers disguised the sour smell by adding chemicals to the containers.

Infants from poor families often suffered from malnutrition because milk was diluted with water to save money. Some formulas were inadvertently diluted with water from contaminated wells. Some mothers hired wet nurses from infant asylums or lying-in hospitals that served unwed mothers to breast feed their children. The wet nurses were forced to leave their own infants behind to be fed by bottle. In 1893 New York philanthropist Nathan Strauss (1848–1931) established the first milk station in the United States, offering nursing bottles of pasteurized milk that had been formulated for infants. Rochester, New York, subsequently established a public milk station, and other cities followed suit. These nursing stations became a place for young mothers to learn how to care for their infants and keep them healthy. As a result the practice of using wet nurses was relegated to history.

Scurvy, a disease caused by Vitamin C deficiency, was common among infants in industrialized nations from the 1860s until the outbreak of World War I. In the latter years of the 19th century, researchers came to believe that infant scurvy was caused by microorganisms rather than diet. It was not until the turn of the century that researchers realized the rise in infant scurvy was caused by the practice of replacing breast feeding with the use of evaporated

Milk bottles were made out of clear glass starting in 1886 so that consumers could inspect the milk. The photo at right shows bottles being sterilized with heat at a dairy around 1910.

milk and infant formulas, which contained no Vitamin C. Studies conducted by Norwegian researcher and pediatrician Axel Holt (1860–1931) in the latter years of the 20th century led to the discovery that Vitamin B-1 deficiency (thiamine) could cause beriberi in infants.

One of the major reasons for improvements in children's health and nutrition during the Gilded Age was the rise in the number of physicians devoted to caring for children. In 1880 the American Medical Association created a special pediatric section. Eight years later the American Pediatric Society was established in response to the increased emphasis on children's well-being. At the time there were only about 50 physicians in the United States who cared for children exclusively. By the early 20th century, there were more than 500 physicians who spent at least half of their time providing pediatric services. At the same time the number of child welfare workers involved in teaching parents about proper nutrition and sanitation, rehydration for children with diarrhea, and disease prevention also expanded significantly.

MEDICINE

The public dispensaries that had served the poor and working class in the past virtually disappeared in the Gilded Age. Between 1870 and 1900 the number of hospitals in the United States grew from 100 to 6,000. These hospitals were financed by cities, groups of physicians, and philanthropic and humanitarian groups. Specialty institutions such as the Mayo Clinic in Rochester, Minnesota, and the Menninger Clinic in Houston, Texas, gained world-wide renown. Mental hospitals were established to serve as custodians for the mentally ill, and almshouses were converted into hospitals for the poor. By the turn of the 20th century psychoanalysis was catching on in the United States. The nursing profession also underwent major reforms, and by 1900 more than 400 nursing schools had been established.

By the last quarter of the 19th century, advances in scientific knowledge had led to a greater understanding of the causes of diseases that had devastated Americans during previous centuries, and new methods of controlling diseases were formulated. The greatest changes of the Gilded Age were in the new emphasis on the practice of social medicine after 1885 in response to the demands of the Industrial Revolution and the need for adequately trained physicians. Johns Hopkins Hospital opened in 1889, followed four years later by the opening of the Johns Hopkins Medical School, revolutionizing the practice of medicine in the United States. Admission standards for physicians were tightened, and a more rigorous curriculum was instituted, emphasizing the scientific method in conjunction with clinical and laboratory training.

Along with William Henry Welch (1850–1934), who served as the first dean of the new Johns Hopkins Medical School, the course of American medical history was transformed by the work of others who came to Johns Hopkins. Canadian William Osler (1849–1919), the head of the Department of Medicine,

William Henry Welch (1850–1934)

No single individual was more influential in the medical revolutions of the Gilded Age than William Henry Welch, the first dean of the Johns Hopkins Medical School, which transformed the practice of medicine in the United States in the late 19th century. Welch began attending medical classes in New York in 1872. After graduating from the College of Physicians and Surgeons in 1875, he served an internship at Bellevue Hospital where he chose pathological anatomy as his field of specialization. During subsequent studies in Europe, Welch was taught by some of the best minds in European medicine. Upon returning to New York in 1878, Welch began teaching pathological anatomy and general pathology at Bellevue. In 1885 he agreed to set up a pathology laboratory at Johns Hopkins and returned to Europe where he studied laboratories set up by such eminent medical researchers as Louis Pasteur (1822–95) and Robert Koch (1843–95).

Welch taught pathology at Johns Hopkins University until he became the first dean of the Medical School in 1893. In that capacity he recruited faculty and designed a curriculum that completely reshaped the course of American medicine. In 1896 Welch accepted a position as the first director of the Johns Hopkins University School of Hygiene and Public Health and became the first director of the Institute of the History of Medicine at Johns Hopkins in 1929. Welch believed that government initiatives coupled with medical knowledge could end poverty and abolish major threats to public health. Throughout his adult life Welch served on boards and commissions designed to improve global health through the advancement and application of medicine. His contributions to both American and global health were so significant that a ceremony honoring him on his 80th birthday in 1930 was broadcast around the world. During the broadcast, President Herbert Hoover (1874–1964) recognized Welch's contributions in the fields of pathology, public health, the history of medicine, and medical education.

became a leading advocate of public health and social justice. William S. Halsted (1852–1922), the chief of the Department of Surgery, earned the title of the "father of American surgery." Professor of Gynecology Howard A. Kelly (1858–1943) brought attention to issues surrounding women's health and rights. At Massachusetts General, which also played an essential role in the transformation of American medicine in the Gilded Age, Richard Cabot (1868–1939), the chief of out-patient clinics, was so convinced that there was a strong connection between social conditions and illness that he was willing to fund the establishment of a social-medicine department at his own expense.

Women also played significant roles in the medical revolution of the period. William Halsted's wife Caroline (1861–1922) was a pioneer in surgical nursing

This mask for delivering anesthetic ether and chloroform was invented in 1890 by Carl Schimmelbusch of Berlin, and remained in use into the 1940s in the United States.

and introduced rubber gloves into the operating room in order to protect medical personnel from the strong disinfectants needed to kill germs. Edith Holt Bloodgood and her sister Winifred Holt Mather founded the New York Association for the Blind, established the Lighthouse movement to help the blind learn to lead normal lives, and organized the American Association for the Prevention of Blindness. Edith Houghton Hooker (1879-1948), a Johns Hopkins graduate, established the St. George's Guild shelter for unwed mothers and babies and campaigned for sex education, birth control, and social hygiene.

Medical researchers of the Gilded Age continued the work of earlier researchers who had discovered germ theory and began isolating the bacteria that caused specific diseases. In 1884 the bacillus of diphtheria and typhus were discovered. In 1900 Dr. Joseph Lister (1827–1912), the leading pioneer in the field of antiseptic medicine, came to the United States, paving the way for a transformation in the way surgeries were performed. New methods of alleviating pain were developed. Treatment of hospital patients was further improved through enhanced knowledge of the importance of diet and by improvements in lighting, medication, and medical instruments. By

1890 many hospitals had begun conducting their own research. At the turn of the century, American medicine was further advanced by the initiation of X-rays as a diagnostic tool, and by the availability of large medical libraries. After Herman Biggs (1859–1923) and J. Mitchell Purden founded the first bacteriology laboratory in 1892, diagnostic laboratories funded by physicians, universities, government agencies, and philanthropists were established throughout America, vastly improving the ability of physicians to diagnose and treat illnesses.

PUBLIC HEALTH AND SANITATION

The issue of public health received a good deal of attention throughout the Gilded Age. In 1872 the American Public Health Association (APHA) was formed, bringing together a coalition of health professionals from various trade organizations to facilitate the exchange of medical information. Illnesses caused by spoiled and contaminated foods were common. Children were particularly vulnerable to such diseases, frequently contracting what became known as "milk sickness." Home delivery of milk products was instituted to cut down on the time milk was in transit or in stores. By 1886 milk was placed in glass bottles so that consumers could inspect it before purchase. The pasteurization of milk introduced in 1895 was capable of solving all problems with contaminated milk; but many easterners were fearful of purchasing it.

American families of the early Gilded Age obtained water for home use in a variety of ways. Nearby waterways, cisterns, and rain barrels were common water sources, and clean water was carried in and dirty water removed in buckets and pails. Farm families often had kitchen pumps located over wells or connected to tanks operated by windmills. Water for tenement families was obtained from water hauling carts, street hydrants, and water taps in central hallways. The most fortunate families had home plumbing connected to city water

This style of wooden wheelchair carried patients in the mid-1880s.

mains. By 1876 most cities with populations over 10,000 offered water supplies in more affluent neighborhoods. It was not until 1915 that public water was available in smaller communities. In small rural towns, public wells provided clean water. Residents could also choose to have water delivered directly to their homes in barrels. Some small cities built systems of reservoirs that piped water into homes. These large water towers, which are still common sights in small town America, became common landmarks and were often decorated with the name of the city and its current population.

Until the 1880s sewage systems were uncommon in most American cities. In areas where sanitation rules did not exist or where they were not strictly enforced, waste removal was frequently a personal affair. "Scavengers" were sometimes hired to collect and remove wastes from privies. Many

This ceramic inhalator from the mid 1870s was used for breathing camphor, eucalyptus oil, and other aromatics to clear the lungs.

families simply dumped waste in back yards or on public streets and vacant lots. The first sewer systems were built in Pennsylvania and Massachusetts in the late 19th century. As other cities began constructing sewage systems, local governing bodies passed ordinances banning the dumping of wastes in sewers.

During the Gilded Age, the emergence of sanitarians intent on improving public health in the United States paved the way for substantial changes in American homes, particularly in the homes of the urban poor who lived in tenements that were overcrowded, unsanitary, and poorly ventilated. Sanitarians excoriated plumbers, insisting that they perpetrated disease through a combination of ignorance and incompetence. Unlike upper and middle class Americans, few members of the urban poor had regular access to private bathtubs, which cost around $15 in the 1890s. One New York study revealed that 90 percent of tenement residents had no private bathing facilities. Instead bathing took place at courtyard hydrants, in hall sinks, or in shared tubs. Many residents were justifiably afraid of shared tubs because of the risk of

Ninety percent of New York City tenement residents had no private bathing facilities. These girls are using a public bathhouse in New York City after the turn of the century.

contracting diseases. Consequently a typical tenement dweller might bathe only six times a year. To combat this problem, some cities began offering "floating baths" in the summer months. Members of the public used these facilities to cool off, as well as for bathing. By 1889 New York had 15 "floating baths" serving thousands of residents.

Reformers and sanitarians alerted the public to a number of health threats in and around the home, including sewer gas, damp cellars, poor ventilation, and dirty carpets. In response Americans began opening their windows at night, boiling water before it was used, and using disinfectants to clean their homes. The more dedicated members of the public regularly tested the air and water in their homes for pollutants, drank bottled water, and instituted healthier lifestyles. States and cities created their own boards of health, charging them with monitoring public health and enforcing sanitation laws. Of all major American cities, New York had the most effective Board of Health. In 1887 officials enhanced the city's ability to fend off disease by establishing laboratories on Staten Island, an arrival point for immigrants, in an effort to identify cases of cholera and typhus before they could spread. These labs paved the way for the Hygiene Labs of the 1930s.

THE FOOD INDUSTRY

Food availability and trends in the Gilded Age reflected the expansion of agriculture, the growth of the cattle industry, and improved manufacturing processes. With the increase in the number of farms in the Great Plains, wheat flour production climbed, increasing from around 83 million barrels in 1890 to almost 120 million barrels by 1917. Meat, particularly beef, was regularly consumed by Americans of all classes.

During the Civil War American meat packing activities had centered on the Union Stockyard in Chicago, which provided fresh meat for Union soldiers. Cattle had roamed freely down the streets as they were transported between the eastern and western rail lines. This situation led to disaster when the Rust Street drawbridge collapsed, plunging pedestrians and cattle to their deaths. In response, a single stockyard was erected. By 1890 the Chicago stockyards were selling billions of pounds of meat products each year, including 2.7 billion pounds of fresh beef, 1.1 billion pounds of fresh pork, 529 million pounds of ham, and 666 million pounds of bacon.

While coffee continued to be the most popular non-alcoholic beverage, milk consumption rose significantly, increasing from two billion pounds in 1870 to 18 billion in 1900. Dairy production moved from New York and Pennsylvania to Iowa and Wisconsin during the Gilded Age. The introduction of refrigerated rail cars in the 1880s transformed the American food industry, providing a means of shipping fresh meat, milk, fruit, and vegetables. Ice consumption was heavy in the hot climates of the south, and by 1880 there were 20 ice plants in the area. By the turn of the century, 600 mechanically cooled storage warehouses were located throughout the country.

New technologies in food processing and preservation coupled with the transportation revolution to increase food options. Canned foods continued to be popular, and manufacturers were constantly improving the canning process. By the last quarter of the 19th century, most large canning companies were operating on the assembly line, drastically increasing consumption. In 1880 John Mason revolutionized home canning by creating the "Mason jar" with its tightly sealed lid. New stoves and increased access to refrigeration changed home cooking. By 1870 iron cooking ranges were available for home use. During the next few years, 43 varieties of heating and cooking stoves reached the market. By the turn of the century, most kitchen stoves were equipped to burn coal, rather than wood.

HEALTH, NUTRITION, AND FAMILY

Between 1850 and 1900 American eating habits changed drastically. Most Americans continued to eat three meals a day, but working families began eating the heaviest meal in the late afternoon or early evening because some family members were at work or school during the day. Lunch for factory workers generally consisted of food brought from home or items purchased

Dining Out in the Gilded Age

The excesses of the Gilded Age were very much in evidence whenever Americans entertained. Special occasion dinner menus were particularly elaborate. In 1880, for instance, a dinner at New York's Delmonico's honoring General Winfield Scott Hancock (1824–86), the Democratic presidential candidate, included the following courses:

Raw oysters
Choice of soups
Hors d'oeuvres
Fish
Saddle of lamb and filet of beef
Entrée of chicken wings with green peas
Lamb chops garnished with beans and mushrooms
Stuffed artichokes
Terrapin en casserole à la Maryland
Sorbet
Canvas-back duck and quail
Ice creams, jellied dishes, banana mouse, and French pastries
Fruit and petit fours
Coffee and liquors

Breakfasts at large hotels during this period consisted of beefsteak, kidneys, lamb chops, tripe, clams, omelets, cold cuts, various potato dishes, beans, and breads. Even in dining rooms set aside for children and nurses, menus included rolls, breads, hot cereals, beefsteak, mutton, chops, ham, fish, liver, bacon, codfish cakes, boiled or scrambled eggs, kidney, corned beef hash, tripe, clams, and potato dishes.

Restaurants of the American west were not as elaborate as those in the east, often consisting of dirty shacks where menus included only fried meat, rancid bacon, and stale eggs. Biscuits were so hard they were referred to as "sinkers." However dining out in the western United States was transformed in the 1880s when Frederick Henry Harvey (1835–1901) established a chain of restaurants at railroad depots that specialized in generous portions and outstanding service. For $.75, the Harvey restaurants offered a dinner menu that included bluepoint oysters on the shell, fillets of whitefish with Madeira sauce, and lobster salads. For the entrée, customers could choose capon with Hollandaise sauce, roast sirloin of beef au jus, sugar-cured ham, duck, or stuffed turkey with cranberry sauce. Side dishes included boiled sweet potatoes, Elgin sugar corn, asparagus, and peas. Served with hot coffee, desserts consisted of apple pie, mince pie, cake, New York ice cream, oranges, grapes, or cheeses. In 1882, with the full cooperation of the railroad industry, Harvey erected a four-story hotel near Las Vegas.

from street vendors. Lunch counters were also available in some areas. Before the advent of hot school lunches, most children carried lunches from home.

The consumption of alcohol was heavily tied to social classes. Members of the upper and lower classes continued to consume large amounts of alcohol, but there was an increasing trend toward nonalcoholic beverages among the middle class in the northeast and midwest. Family meals of the Gilded Age generally included soup, meat, and vegetables. Salads, coleslaw, and desserts were occasionally added to the menu. The meat course generally consisted of lamb prepared with a mint or pickled sauce, boiled meats such as pork or corned beef, turkey stuffed with bread, butter, cream, oysters, and egg yolk, organ meats such as liver, kidney, sweetbreads, or fish. Vegetables were commonly accompanied by a potato dish of some sort. Pies, puddings, cakes, and ice cream were the most popular family deserts.

During the Gilded Age, attention was also focused on promoting healthy sleeping habits and hospitality. Some physicians advised against double beds for married couples because of wiggling, cover hogging, and bad breath. For some doctors, sex more than once a month was viewed as unhealthy. Reformers of the period were adamant about ending the practice of infants and small children sharing beds with adults. However working-class families did not always have the means to comply with these suggestions, and many continued to share beds and bedrooms well into the 20th century.

Americans were justifiably afraid of tuberculosis in the Gilded Age. The fear of contracting the disease led some people to stop kissing others, even family members. Reformers advocated the use of paper tissues rather than cloth handkerchiefs. As part of the new emphasis on fresh air as a means of preventing tuberculosis, sleeping porches and fresh-air modifications to existing bedrooms became common. Many families slept on screened porches, even in the cold winter months. They remained reasonably warm by using sleeping bags designed for the purpose. Other sleepers opted for a window bed that placed the head outside the window under an awning, with the body in a bed inside the bedroom. A typical sleeping porch was 12 ft. sq. and could hold two adults in a double bed and three children on cots. Some families opted to build separate outside sleeping sheds with flaps that opened on the southern and western sides, and wire screens to protect sleepers from mosquito bites.

Some of the social reforms instituted to stop the spread of tuberculosis, such as proscriptions against public spitting and the practice of turning down sheets on hotel beds, are still with us today. Another invention of the era, Kellogg's Corn Flakes, is ubiquitous. Other facets of Gilded Age health and nutrition have faded away, but the attention paid to public health by the medical profession and reformers of that era has had a lasting impact on such areas as children's health, infectious diseases, sanitation, and our daily habits.

Elizabeth R. Purdy

Further Readings

Bennett, James T. and Thomas J. DiLorenzo. *From Pathology to Politics: Public Health in America.* New Brunswick, NJ: Transaction Publishers, 2000.

Cassedy, James H. *Medicine in America: A Short History.* Baltimore, MD: Johns Hopkins University Press, 1991.

Chase, Allan. *Magic Shots: A Human and Scientific Account of the Long and Continuing Struggle to Eradicate Infectious Disease by Vaccination.* New York: William Morrow, 1982.

Derickson, Alan. *Black Lung: Anatomy of a Public Health Disaster.* Ithaca, NY: Cornell University Press, 1998.

Gregory, Alexis. *The Gilded Age: The Super-Rich of the Edwardian Era.* London: Cassell, 1993.

Grob, Gerald N. *The Deadly Truth: A History of Disease in America.* Cambridge, MA: Harvard University Press, 2002.

Grover, Kathryn, ed. *Dining in America 1850–1900.* Rochester, NY: University of Massachusetts Press and the Margaret Woodbury Strong Museum, 1987.

Haber, Barbara. *From Hardtack to Home Fries: An Uncommon History of American Cooks and Meals.* New York: Free Press, 2002.

Husband, Julie and Jim O'Laughlin. *Daily Life in the Industrial United States, 1870–1900.* Westport, CT: Greenwood, 2004.

Kiple, Kenneth F. *Plague, Pox, and Pestilence.* London: Weidenfeld and Nicolson, 1997.

Kyvig, David E. *Daily Life in the United States, 1920–1939: Decades of Promise and Pain.* Westport, CT: Greenwood, 2002.

Levenstein, Harvey A. *Revolution at the Table: The Transformation of the American Diet.* New York: Oxford, 1988.

Market, Howard. "For the Welfare of Children: The Origins of the Relationship between US Public Health Workers and Pediatricians." *The American Journal of Public Health* (v.90/6, 2000).

Ogle, Maureen. *All the Modern Conveniences: American Household Plumbing, 1840–1890.* Baltimore, MD: Johns Hopkins University Press, 1996.

Pillsbury, Richard. *No Foreign Food: The American Diet in Time and Place.* Boulder, CO: Westview, 1998.

Stacey, Michelle. *Consumed: Why Americans Love, Hate, and Fear Food.* New York: Simon and Schuster, 1994.

Taylor, Lloyd C., Jr. *The Medical Profession and Social Reform, 1885–1945.* New York: St. Martin's, 1974.

Williams, Susan. *Savory Suppers and Fashionable Feasts: Dining in Victorian America.* New York: Pantheon Books, 1985.

Index note: page references in *italics* indicate a figure or illustration; page references in **bold** indicate main discussion.

Produced by GOLSON MEDIA

President and Editor	J. Geoffrey Golson
Layout Editors	Oona Patrick, Mary Jo Scibetta
Managing Editor	Susan Moskowitz
Copyeditor	Ben Johnson
Proofreader	Mary Le Rouge
Indexer	J S Editorial